Godzilla Takes the Bronx

Godzilla Takes the Bronx

The Inside Story of Hideki Matsui

Jerry Beach

TAYLOR TRADE PUBLISHING
Lanham • New York • Dallas • Boulder • Toronto • Oxford

Published by Taylor Trade Publishing
An imprint of The Rowman & Littlefield Publishing Group, Inc.
4501 Forbes Boulevard, Suite 200
Lanham, Maryland 20706

Distributed by National Book Network

Library of Congress Cataloging-in-Publication Data

Beach, Jerry, 1973–
    Godzilla takes the Bronx : the inside story of Hideki Matsui /
Jerry Beach.— 1st Taylor Trade Pub. ed.
        p. cm.
    ISBN 1-58979-113-4 (hardcover : alk. paper)
    1. Matsui, Hideki. 2. Baseball players—Japan—Biography. 3. New York
Yankees (Baseball team)—History. I. Title.
GV865.M372B43 2004
796.357'092—dc22   2003025951

∞™ The paper used in this publication meets the minimum requirements of American National Standard for Information Sciences—Permanence of Paper for Printed Library Materials, ANSI/NISO Z39.48–1992.
Manufactured in the United States of America.

To my precious Michelle
Who always warned me I might have to get a real job,
but always believed it wouldn't come to that.

To Dad
Who always left me the sports section to read in
the morning, never said no to a trip to the bookstore,
and learned, a la Matsui, to bat left-handed in order to
level the playing field in our wiffle ball games.
But who, more importantly,
was my first fan and is my best friend.

Contents

Acknowledgments

A guy who started the 2003 season writing an email newsletter about Major League Baseball and ended it authoring a book about Hideki Matsui could not have done it without a lot of love, support, constructive criticism, and occasional kicks in the pants from a lot of people.

First, to my agents, Frank R. Scatoni and Greg Dinkin of Venture Literary: I have no idea why you decided to pitch this idea to an Internet scribe who kept badgering you with Met-related book ideas. I'm just eternally grateful that you did. Thank you for helping a dream come true.

To my editor at Taylor Trade Publishing, Jill Langford: Thank you for believing in the project and for your patience and good humor throughout the process. I could not have finished this book as quickly or efficiently without your guidance. Maybe this is the year for your Cubbies . . .

To Rob Cuni, who was the first photographer I thought of when this book was in the planning stages and the best man for the job: The book wouldn't be the same without your outstanding photo work. Thanks for your professionalism and for the rides to and from Toronto.

The game stories, features, and columns filed by New York's baseball writers were an invaluable resource in the research and writing of this book. Thank you to the staffs of *Newsday*, the *New*

York Daily News, the *New York Post*, the *New York Times*, the *Record* of Bergen County, the *Newark Star-Ledger*, the *Journal News*, the *Hartford Courant*, the *Times Herald-Record*, yankees.com, and mlb.com. An additional thank you to Denis Gorman for his research assistance.

The *Newark Star-Ledger*'s Lawrence Rocca, the Bergen *Record*'s Bob Klapisch, and the *Journal News*' Kit Stier were also kind enough to forward me their Matsui-related stories and columns at the very beginning of my research process. Thank you also to Robert Cassidy of newsday.com, who shared with me video footage of New York ballplayers talking about Matsui.

Dozens of Major League Baseball players and executives were kind enough to share their thoughts on and memories of Matsui and the history of American-Japanese baseball relations. Thank you to Aaron Boone, John Flaherty, Mike Mussina, Jeff Nelson, Jorge Posada, Robin Ventura, and Bernie Williams of the New York Yankees; Bret Boone, Mark McLemore, John Olerud, Dan Wilson, and Hide Sueyoshi of the Seattle Mariners; Omar Minaya, Todd Zeile, and Joe Vitiello of the Montreal Expos; Roberto Alomar and Mark Buehrle of the Chicago White Sox; Jason Anderson of the New York Mets; Julio Franco of the Atlanta Braves; Dan Gladden of the Minnesota Twins; Derrek Lee of the Florida Marlins, and Darrell May of the Kansas City Royals.

Especially appreciative tips of the cap go to May (who spoke to me for half an hour before and after a matinee game at Yankee Stadium) and Zeile (who gave me his typically thoughtful answers mere minutes after he mediated a draining meeting in the Expos' clubhouse regarding the team's destination for 2004).

Special thanks also to Warren Cromartie, whose recollections of Matsui and of life and baseball in Japan bolstered the book's first chapter. Thank you to Dan Leberfeld for helping set up the interview between Cromartie and me. Cromartie's autobiography, *Slugging It Out In Japan*, and Robert Whiting's *You Gotta Have Wa* were also invaluable in my researching and writing, as were the periodicals *Sports Illustrated*, *Time*, *Playboy*, and *USA Today*

Baseball Weekly, the *Yomiuri Shimbun* newspaper and the websites baseballlibrary.com and baseball-reference.com as well as ESPN.com and SI.com.

Thank you to the Bay Shore-Brightwaters Public Library and the North Babylon Public Library on Long Island and the Parsippany-Troy Hills Free Public Library in New Jersey for the use of their materials and resources.

Interviews with media members who covered Matsui also provided valuable information and "color" for the book. Thank you to: the *Times Herald-Record* of Middletown columnist Dave Buscema, *Newsday* Yankee beat writer Ken Davidoff, MLBradio.com host Seth Everett, *New York Times* Yankee beat writer Tyler Kepner, *Newsday* Mets beat writer David Lennon, WFAN Yankees beat reporter Sweeney Murti (who spoke to me for 45 minutes on what was likely his only night off in October), *Newark Star-Ledger* baseball columnist Lawrence Rocca, *New York Post* baseball columnist Joel Sherman, and *Newark Star-Ledger* Mets beat writer David Waldstein.

Special thanks to Buscema and mlb.com's Kevin Czerwinski, who helped me collect quotes during the World Series, and the Bergen *Record*'s Pete Caldera, whose words of support during the "credential incident" in Toronto were much appreciated.

This is not an official Matsui biography, but the New York Yankees media relations department was as kind and cooperative as they could be, for which I cannot thank them enough. Thanks also to the media relations departments of the New York Mets and Toronto Blue Jays.

To the handful of friends who knew about this project from day one—Billy Altman, Bryon Evje, and my fellow first-time author and Hofstra graduate, Jeff Belanger—thanks for your words of encouragement and for keeping me away from sharp objects when it looked as if this wouldn't pan out.

An extra thank you goes out to Bryan Hoch, who also knew about this from the beginning and was an enormous help during the four months I spent writing the book. In addition to pinch-hitting for me at ESportsNY.com, Bryan provided research assistance, on-the-spot copy editing in the Shea Stadium press box and many, many laughs.

To 21, who told me exactly what to expect every step of the way and hasn't been wrong yet.

To the editors I work regularly with on freelance assignments, thank you for allowing me to lessen my workload or, in some cases, disappear entirely for a few months last summer and fall: Bob O'Rourk, Marie Murtagh, Lynn Allopena, Leah Duniaef, and Jane O'Sullivan at the Times Beacon-Record newspaper chain, Brendan Manley at the *Long Island Press*, Steve Downey at *New York Mets Inside Pitch*, Bryon Evje at EsportsNY.com, Dan Leberfeld at *Jets Confidential* and Tom Feliney at the *NCTFL Report*. An additional thank you to Brendan for securing me credentials to the playoffs and allowing me to write about the Yankees' run to the World Series for the *Long Island Press*.

Thanks to John Guerriero, who provided legal advice in return for a ride home from Game Seven of the ALCS, and to Denis and Jill for "the sign" and for the late-night chats that alternately kept my sanity and robbed me of whatever I had left.

Thanks to Gerry deSimas Jr., who, as sports editor of *The Register Citizen* newspaper in Torrington, Connecticut, gave me my first opportunity as a 17-year-old way back in 1990 and subtly reminded me over the next few years that I didn't yet know everything.

Thanks to my cats Casey and Maggie for the late-night companionship, even if one of them did scratch the screen on my brand-new laptop.

Most of all, I thank my friends and family—including my wife, Michelle, my parents, Maureen and Jerry, and the latest addition, my godson Matthew, born to my sister Eileen and her husband David in between the ALDS and ALCS—and all the teachers and editors I've had over the years. The list of friends, family and mentors to whom I am forever indebted could fill this entire book, but rest assured each of you, in one way or another, helped cultivate and encourage my love of reading and writing and inspired me to never settle for mediocrity.

I hope I've made you proud.

Leaving Paradise

Yankee Stadium has seen snow in April, home runs in November, and all sorts of dramatics in between. But in its nearly eighty years as the most storied and famous arena in all of sports, it had never before seen a player for the home team blast a grand slam in his first-ever game inside the House That Ruth Built.

Yet Yankee fans are conditioned to expect unpredictable dramatics, so the 33,109 cold and damp fans at Yankee Stadium for the 2003 home opener on April 8 stood and roared in anticipation as Bernie Williams trotted to first base in the fifth inning against the Minnesota Twins.

Williams, the Yankees' All-Star centerfielder, had just been intentionally walked by Twins pitcher Joe Mays in order to load the bases for the highly touted rookie left fielder, Hideki Matsui, who had grounded out and walked in his first two plate appearances.

Twins manager Ron Gardenhire decided to test Matsui's mettle right away. The skipper hoped Mays, a sinkerball specialist, could induce Matsui to ground into an inning-ending double play and keep the Twins within shouting distance of the Yankees, who led by two runs at the time. As for Matsui, his third-ever plate appearance at Yankee Stadium was an opportunity to not only provide an early return on the Yankees' investment—he had signed a three-year, $21 million deal to join the Yankees in January—but also to curry goodwill with baseball's most demanding fans.

Matsui's productive first week in pinstripes—he had a hit in each of the Yankees' first six games on the road against the Toronto Blue Jays and Tampa Bay Devil Rays—and his modest and hardworking demeanor bought him some time with the Yankee faithful. One fan even paid homage to Matsui—long nicknamed "Godzilla" in Japan for his prodigious power-hitting feats—by dressing up in a Godzilla costume.

But honeymoons are short in the stands of Yankee Stadium, where the fans, spoiled by 26 World Championships—the most in North American sports—have little patience for anybody's learning curve. A year earlier, Jason Giambi, a former American League MVP who had been the Yankees' key signing following the 2001 season, was booed in the midst of an 0-for-5 performance in his home opener on April 5, 2002.

During spring training, Giambi—aware that Matsui used to receive standing ovations in Japan even when he struck out—recalled to a *Newsday* reporter how he told his new teammate: "That's gone. That's over with. Get used to it. I got booed the first month."

But Matsui had already won a warm round of applause from Yankee fans following a standout play on defense in the fourth inning. With runners on first and second and one out, Torii Hunter lofted a shot into the left-center gap. Matsui raced over, reached above his head, and cut the ball off, which limited the speedy Hunter to a double and limited the Twins to one run on the play.

Still, memories were short in the Bronx. So would a Giambi-like fate await Matsui if he failed to prolong the fifth inning?

As Matsui stood almost perfectly still in the batter's box, his elbows cocked and his bat coiled parallel to his left shoulder,

Yankees radio announcer John Sterling dramatically intoned that the scene was set for yet another memorable Stadium moment.

The tension grew as Mays and Matsui engaged in a protracted and suspenseful six-pitch battle. With the count full, the fans roared as Mays received the signal from catcher A. J. Pierzynski. Mays fired a changeup toward home plate.

However, the pitch remained up in the strike zone, right in the "wheelhouse" of the left-handed hitting Matsui. The sound of bat meeting ball echoed throughout Yankee Stadium, which then echoed a collective gasp, as the ball soared into the air and headed for the right-field fence.

The Twins' Hunter and Michael Cuddyer raced towards the wall, but it was a futile chase. The fans in the right-field bleachers were already jumping up and down in celebration and clamoring for position as one of the most historic home runs in the history of Yankee Stadium began its descent.

Matsui's blast cleared the fence by plenty. Delirious fans stood, stomped, and screamed, while Matsui's cheering teammates raced to the top step of the dugout.

About the only calm person in the Stadium was Matsui himself, who exhibited no outward signs of emotion as he dutifully put his head down and rounded the bases. Inside the Twins dugout, Rick Reed—a 37-year-old hurler known throughout baseball as one of the game's no-nonsense individuals—was so impressed by Matsui's professionalism that, according to the *Newark Star-Ledger*, he nodded his head in approval in spite of the fact that his teammate had just given up a game-altering grand slam.

Matsui stepped on home plate and exchanged greetings with Williams, Nick Johnson, and Giambi, all of whom had scored ahead of him on the homer, and on-deck batter Jorge Posada. He continued to jog into the dugout, where he was mobbed by teammates before making eye contact with manager Joe Torre.

Torre had witnessed his share of unforgettable moments and heard his share of raucous ovations. He knew the only way to finally acknowledge the appreciative roar was to send Yankee Stadium's newest icon out for a curtain call.

"You knew the fans wanted it," Torre said after the game. "He must have done that before. He didn't need much coaxing."

The Yankees went on to win the game 7-3, and those in attendance went home in the raw drizzle energized by yet another unforgettable Yankee Stadium moment—a moment that had its genesis on the opposite end of the country almost exactly six months earlier, when the Yankees' pursuit of yet another World Championship came to a stunning and premature halt against the Anaheim Angels.

The Yankees enjoyed one of the greatest and most historic runs in the history of baseball from 1996 to 2001, when they won five American League pennants and four World Series. But it took just five days for the seven-season reign to fall completely apart at the hands of the upstart Angels, who borrowed the Yankees' blueprint to beat the Yankees at their own game, three games to one, in the 2002 American League Division Series.

The Yankees of old overwhelmed postseason opponents with a patient lineup, effective starting pitching, and dominant relief pitching. But this time, it was the Angels' patient lineup working the Yankees' starters deep into counts and chasing the Yankees' All-Star caliber starters—Roger Clemens, Andy Pettitte, Mike Mussina, and David Wells—before the conclusion of the sixth inning. The Angels' batters then teed off on the Yankees' subpar middle relief corps, while the Angels' outstanding bullpen closed the door.

By the end of the Angels' dominant series victory, it was clear the Yankees desperately needed to reload. The bullpen needed to be revamped, the lineup needed an infusion of familiar patience, and the clubhouse needed to be cleansed. The professional likes of Paul O'Neill, Tino Martinez, and Scott Brosius policed the Yankees' locker room during the championship reign, but observers were beginning to think new additions such as Jeff Weaver and Raul Mondesi were ill-prepared to handle life as a Yankee, on or off the field.

Reloading wouldn't be easy, even for a team armed with a seemingly infinite payroll and an owner obsessed with winning.

Finding players skilled enough to contribute to the Yankees was one thing, but unearthing those who had both the talent and the toughness necessary to thrive in the most demanding and bottom-line oriented organization in sports was quite another.

However, the Yankees had long ago identified the one player who fit perfectly into their master plan, even if most of the club's high-ranking executives had yet to meet the object of their desires.

His name was Hideki Matsui, and he was the perfect fit for reasons beyond his abilities on the diamond.

Matsui was Japan's most famous player, a three-time Central League Most Valuable Player, and a power hitter of legendary proportions who was coming off the greatest season of his career (a .334 average with 50 homers and 107 RBI). He was also the most beloved player in the land, adored by fellow players, fans, and the media for his fundamentally sound approach to the game, the gentle and patient demeanor he maintained in the face of unyielding public attention, and, most of all, his ability to hit mammoth home runs on a regular basis.

"They love the home run over there," said Kansas City Royals pitcher Darrell May, who spent four seasons in Japan, including two as Matsui's teammate with the Giants. "They bring foreigners over to hit home runs. And he was a Japanese product who could do that."

Matsui's contract with the Yomiuri Giants expired at the end of the Japan Series, which the Giants won for the third time in Matsui's nine years with the club. And with those nine seasons under his belt, he was, for the first time in his career, truly a free agent, allowed to negotiate with any team on the planet.

Rumors of Matsui's departure had begun as early as 2001, when Japanese native Ichiro Suzuki tore up the American League on his way to becoming just the second player ever to win both the Rookie of the Year and Most Valuable Player awards in the same season.

It became clear America was in Matsui's long-term plans following the 2001 season, when he signed a one-year deal (for a record $4.7 million) with the Giants instead of the lucrative six-year, $64 million deal the club offered. "When he turned down the big contract offer, I think that pretty much sealed it that he's going to be coming to the States," May said.

And if Matsui was coming to the States, the Yankees wanted to make sure he ended up in Pinstripes.

The Yankees, more than any other team in Major League Baseball, had tapped into the international free agent market. Sometimes the Yankees added a foreign free agent because they were simply overwhelmed by his talent, as was the case with Cuban pitcher Orlando "El Duque" Hernandez, who was 9-3 with a 2.51 ERA in the postseason for the Yankees from 1998 to 2002, or Alfonso Soriano, who was signed out of Japan's Central League in 1997 and had evolved into an annual threat for 40-40 (40 homers, 40 steals) by 2002.

And other times the Yankees signed a foreign free agent because owner George Steinbrenner simply couldn't resist the urge to add another "toy"—no matter how misplaced—to his collection. Japanese pitcher Katsuhiro Maeda received a $1.5 million signing bonus in 1996 but became better known for his dyed hair and never pitched above Double-A. Cuban third baseman Andy Morales never played in the bigs and was released by the Yankees after they learned he was at least four years older than his listed age. Cuban pitcher Adrian "El Duquecito" Hernandez, nicknamed as such because he was compared in Cuba to Orlando Hernandez (no relation), had just a couple brief stints in the majors.

Perhaps the most infamous Japanese import of all was Hideki Irabu. He wasn't technically a free agent acquisition: The San Diego Padres had originally acquired the rights to Irabu in January 1997, but Irabu, a former star pitcher for the Chiba Lotte Marines of Japan's Pacific League, said he would only pitch for the Yankees. Eventually, the Yankees sent outfielder Ruben Rivera and minor league pitcher Rafael Medina to the Padres in April 1997 in exchange for Irabu.

Unfortunately for the Yankees, Irabu turned out to be an unqualified bust. The man dubbed the "Japanese Nolan Ryan" went 29-20 with a 4.80 ERA in parts of three seasons with the

Yankees and angered management and teammates alike with his aloofness and aversion to conditioning, the latter of which inspired Steinbrenner to call him a "fat, pussy toad" after Irabu failed to cover first base during a spring training game in 1999.

"I don't know why the Yankees built him up so big, that was a little bit too much, obviously, for him to live up to," said *Newsday* reporter David Lennon, who covered the Yankees for the newspaper in 1997.

Those who knew Matsui in Japan were certain he was the anti-Irabu. But the Yankees, understandably, had to find out for themselves before they began pursuing Matsui. As costly a mistake as Irabu was, a misstep with Matsui would be considerably more expensive.

Back in the early 1990s, the Yankees were merely the best-known franchise in the world—but the team was not truly a global enterprise. That all changed in 1997, when Steinbrenner signed a lucrative long-term sponsorship deal with Adidas, acquired the NBA's New Jersey Nets and NHL's New Jersey Devils under the "YankeeNets" ownership group, signed a marketing deal with the planet's premier soccer team, Manchester United, and formed his own television network, the YES Network, which carried 120 Yankees games in 2002.

A deal with a Japanese player would further broaden the Yankees' sphere of influence, but a mistake of Irabu-like proportions would be doubly magnified. Hence, the Yankees did their due diligence and then some with Matsui, who was scouted in August 2002 by Yankees vice president Jean Afterman.

If anyone could tell the differences between Irabu and Matsui, it would be Afterman, who had coincidentally helped pave the way for Irabu to join the Yankees in 1997. In the midst of heated negotiations with San Diego, Afterman, an assistant to Irabu's agent Don Nomura at that time, said Irabu "will never sign any contract with San Diego—ever."

As impressed as Afterman was with what she saw of Matsui on the field, she was more pleased with what she saw of Matsui off it.

"He's a very grounded person, really a mensch," Afterman told reporters. "He manages to keep his sanity when there's insanity around him."

By the time the Yankees concluded the 2002 regular season with a major league–best 103-58 record, it was clear Matsui was in their sights. After all, overwhelming success had never deterred Steinbrenner from tinkering with the mix: Following a 1998 season in which the Yankees won an American League–record 114 regular season games and the World Series, Steinbrenner acquired future Hall-of-Fame starting pitcher Roger Clemens from the Toronto Blue Jays.

However, the resounding loss to the Angels in the playoffs left Steinbrenner doubly determined to bolster the Yankees' offense and remind everyone that the Yankees were still the brand-name franchise of the sporting world. Matsui filled both needs: Not only could he create valuable off-season headlines, but also he could serve as an upgrade at either left or right field. Rondell White, who struggled throughout 2002, had been the Yankees' ninth different Opening Day left fielder in as many years, while right fielder Mondesi had failed to meet expectations following his midseason arrival in 2002.

The American competition for Matsui officially began, ironically enough, on Halloween, when the player dubbed "Godzilla" held a press conference in Tokyo and announced his plans to go overseas. "It was painful to tell my coaches, but my personal desire to go over there and play didn't go away," Matsui told the throng of more than 100 reporters.

Despite the years of speculation surrounding Matsui's long-term plans, his decision to leave for America still shocked Japan. After all, playing in Japan had made him rich beyond his wildest dreams and famous beyond all comprehension.

"If you took ten people, nine of those thought he would stay," teammate Koji Uehara told American reporters.

A Japanese scout told *Newsday* that Matsui's departure was "mind-boggling to me. Nobody leaves the Giants. Everybody usually signs their last contract with the Giants."

May, a teammate of Matsui's with the Yomiuri Giants in 2000 and 2001, said no player in America is as popular as Matsui was in Japan. The Americans who traveled to Japan in November 2002 for the All-Star series between the two countries in 2002, meanwhile, could only compare Matsui to the biggest pop culture icons in the Western Hemisphere.

Florida Marlins first baseman Derrek Lee, whose father Leon spent 10 years in Japan with three different teams, said, "Fans love [Matsui]. He's like Michael Jackson over there. It's amazing."

MLBradio.com host Seth Everett, meanwhile, said Matsui was "10 times the star of anybody else. The guy is the reincarnation of The Beatles in their heyday."

Everett, May, and *Newark Star-Ledger* reporter David Waldstein, the latter of whom covered the All-Star Series in Japan in November 2002, agreed a pair of key reasons for Matsui's overwhelming popularity was the fact he played in Tokyo for the Giants, whose games were regularly telecast throughout the country

"It's just [a] different fan mentality over there," May said. "It's a lot different. You're talking about a guy that's on national TV every night and for the most popular team in Japan and is very, very, very successful over there. Fans are just crazy in love with him. He's expected to produce and he did."

Said Everett: "He's a contact hitter that has home run power, but they make him out to be Babe Ruth, and mostly it is because of the fact that he played for the Giants and the Giants were on television the most."

"He plays for the Giants, that's key," Waldstein said. "I mean, the Giants are the Cowboys and the Yankees and Manchester United combined."

The Giants have often been called the "Yankees of Japan," a claim May called "absolutely true." May, who returned to America in 2002 and has spent the last two seasons with the Kansas City Royals, said the similarities between the Yankees and Giants range "from Tokyo being the largest city [in Japan] to the atmosphere at the ballpark to [being] expected to win."

For the Giants and Yankees, nothing else sufficed. Sadaharu Oh hit a world-record 868 home runs for the Giants during his career, yet he was fired as their manager after leading them to just one pennant from 1984 to 1988. Yankees owner George Steinbrenner, meanwhile, is known as the most hard-to-please executive in sports. In 1980, he fired Dick Howser after the Yankees won 103 games but lost to the Kansas City Royals in the American League Championship Series. And even though Joe Torre led the Yankees to four World Series crowns from 1996 to 2000, he spent most of 2003 on the hot seat because of the Yankees' three-season World Championship drought.

The Giants and Yankees each regularly drew sellout crowds both home and away. Jason Giambi has often said that being a member of the Yankees is like being part of a rock group, which is remarkably similar to the terminology Reggie Smith—a former Los Angeles Dodgers outfielder who spent two years overseas with the Giants—used to describe life with Japan's most popular team.

"I couldn't believe it," Smith said in Robert Whiting's book *You Gotta Have Wa.* "The Giants would go into towns around Japan and the young girls would start screaming and falling down. You wave to them and say 'Hi' and they pass out. It was like being a member of a rock band."

Like the Yankees, the Giants spared no expense when pursuing the objects of their desire. May's impressive performance against the Giants in 1998 not only won over his employers, the Hanshin Tigers, but it also led the Giants to make May—determined at the time to leave Japan—an offer he couldn't refuse after he left the Tigers following the 1999 season.

"[The] Giants contacted my agent and I said, 'Tell them I'm not interested,'" said May. "[May's agent said], 'Let's just look at what they have to say.' He talked to them [and] he said 'Well, they want to know what it would take for you to come back over.' So we came up with something that I thought it would take to get me to come back over, and they did it."

And like the Yankees, the Giants spare no expense to make players and their families feel wanted and secure both inside and outside Yankee Stadium. Before Mike Mussina's introductory press conference following the 2000 season, the Yankees presented his wife, Jana, with roses. And on May 26, 2003, the morning of Clemens' first attempt at his 300th career win, the Yankees dispatched a security guard to Clemens' Manhattan apartment to ensure he got safely to Yankee Stadium.

May recalled how the Giants flew his wife and her family into Tokyo for a surprise visit. "The Giants [were] such a great organization, they really take care of you so well," May said. "My family [and] my wife's family came over [and] I didn't even know about it. They had already arranged limos to take them to Mt. Fuji and to tea gardens and stuff like that.

"They really took care of me and my family," May said. "Obviously, they felt that would help me in my performance and make things a lot easier for me."

The effort seemed to pay off: May helped the Giants win the 2000 Japan Series, and he led the Central League in strikeouts in 2001. Overall, he went 22-15 with a 3.55 ERA in his two seasons with the Giants, as opposed to the 10-16 record and 3.83 ERA he posted with the Hanshin Tigers in 1998–1999.

As for Matsui, though, despite all the money and luxury offered by the Giants, he was determined to head off to America in order to play on the world's biggest stage, though he wasn't quite as obvious about his intentions as Ichiro Suzuki had been in 2000.

"Everybody knew Ichiro wanted to come to the States," May said. "He'd come over [to the United States in the off-season], he'd work out with the Mariners, so they knew."

May said Matsui "never would publicly say" whether he was leaning towards staying or going. "He always kept it quiet," May said. "He always avoided the questions about it."

Said Lennon, who covered the All-Star Series between American and Japanese All-Stars for *Newsday*: "He was pretty good at not revealing where he might want to go. He just spoke generally about wanting to prove himself in the major leagues, because it's the biggest stage in the world and it was time for him to try that. [He refrained from] specifying where he would want to play."

Before Everett could interview Matsui prior to Game Seven of the All-Star Series, he had to go over his questions with Matsui's interpreter to ensure there would be no questions about the Yankees. "At the time, he hadn't signed with the Yankees, and he would not hint [where he was going to sign]," Everett said.

Added Everett: "Even though it was implied. It was no secret he was [going to sign with the Yankees]."

The Yankees retained a poker face during the first few weeks of the off-season. As usual, executives talked about cutting the team's payroll, a "promise" greeted with almost universal skepticism.

"We have to be very cautious and make sure what we do is sensible," Yankees general manager Brian Cashman told the *Newark Star-Ledger*. "Really, that's no different from any other year. We always have a budget."

It became clear the Yankees budget included room for Matsui on November 6, when Bernie Williams and Jason Giambi—two players whose long-term deals likely will tie them to the Yankees for the remainder of their careers—arrived in Japan as part of the Major League Baseball All-Star team that was scheduled to play several games against a Japan League All-Star team featuring Matsui.

The presence of the two Yankees was noteworthy for several reasons. The Yankees were popular in Japan, thanks to their overwhelming success and the fact Irabu, a Japanese pitching icon, had played for the club from 1997 to 1999.

"The predominant teams over there [were] the Dodgers, because of [Japanese pitcher Hideo] Nomo, the Mets, because of Bobby Valentine [who had managed in Japan in 1995 prior to taking over the Mets in 1996], and the Yankees, because they're the

Yankees and everybody there knows the Yankees and knows the number of World Series they've won," Lennon said.

In addition, there was an air of mystery around the Yankees because Steinbrenner had never before allowed his players to participate in these postseason goodwill junkets. "It was the first time [in] a long time that a couple of guys from the Yankees have been [allowed to travel to Japan]," Williams said.

But Williams and Giambi were there this time, both as representatives of and recruiters for the Yankees. "Of course, the rumor mill is saying that [Matsui] wants to be a Yankee," Giambi told reporters. "I know from the Yankees' point of view, we would definitely be excited to have him."

Matsui's declaration, along with the presence of the two Yankees, turned the goodwill All-Star series between the two teams into a media circus. Several American newspapers covered the series, including three New York–area papers: the *Daily News, Newsday,* and the *Newark Star-Ledger.*

The New York papers were there partially because Met second baseman Roberto Alomar was on the American team, which was skippered by new Mets manager Art Howe. "There were a lot of [angles]," Waldstein said.

Mostly, though, the New York papers sent reporters overseas to cover Matsui, who remained a mystery to most area readers even as he appeared destined to join the Yankees.

Lennon had seen Matsui play once before in 2000, when the Yomiuri Giants faced the New York Mets in an exhibition game prior to the season-opening two-game series between the Mets and Chicago Cubs in Tokyo. But back then, Matsui wasn't even the most noteworthy Matsui in Japan. That honor belonged to Kaz Matsui, the shortstop for the Seibu Lions who had also made noises about eventually leaping to America.

"With [Hideki] Matsui [in 2000], there wasn't much speculation or talk about him playing in the United States yet," Lennon said. "He was still under contract for a few more years, so I think he just kind of went by the boards. He wasn't somebody that I remembered there being much of a focus on."

Matsui would not be nearly so anonymous this time. "The interest in [Matsui] was really ramping up around that time because the Yankees had been talked about as one of the main suitors since the [previous] summer," Lennon said.

Lennon said the buzz in America was about "Just who was this guy? Because everybody back in the States was pretty much in the dark about him."

The superstar outfielder, already accustomed to daily press gatherings with Japanese reporters, added a daily session with American reporters to his busy schedule. Not surprisingly, the three New York–area newspapers ran lengthy feature stories on Matsui during the early days of the trip.

In a column he penned for mlb.com, Warren Cromartie—a former major leaguer who starred for the Yomiuri Giants for seven years—wrote "[Matsui] . . . can't sneeze without it being on the front page of the papers."

Meanwhile, reporters from both sides of the globe cornered Williams and Giambi at every opportunity in hopes they would reveal some morsel of information regarding the Yankees' pursuit of Matsui. Williams said he and Giambi were asked about Matsui "a lot, pretty much [everyday]" by both the Japanese and American reporters.

And tongues wagged whenever Matsui was seen talking to Williams and Giambi at the batting cage or admitting that he had asked Giambi to go to dinner with him in Tokyo.

Even those who were not associated with the Yankees found themselves besieged by Japanese reporters, all of whom wanted to know what the Americans thought of Matsui's ability to succeed in the States.

Lee said he and the rest of the players were "asked . . . everyday 'How many home runs do you think [Matsui will] hit in America? How do you think he'll do?' We were peppered with that question."

"They ask you the question 'How's he going to do?' but you never know how he's going to do [until he goes to America]," Chicago White Sox second baseman Roberto Alomar said.

"I must have been interviewed like 15 times," Everett said.

"The Japanese reporters were pretty worked up over the possibility of him becoming a Yankee," Lennon said. "They talked to us everyday [and asked], 'Do you think he'll sign with the Yankees?' They really valued our opinion on what [Matsui] would [do]. They were always asking us daily about, 'How many home runs do you think he'll hit? How many RBI [will he have]? Did we think he would play for the Yankees?' "

Being a part of the American traveling party had its share of advantages, though. With a laugh, Everett recalled how the mere mention of the word "Matsui" helped bridge the language gap.

"When we were trying to talk to people—like [the] concierge who didn't speak the [English] language or something—all we would say is 'Matsui' and they would gravitate towards us," Everett said. "They thought you knew him."

As for the Yankees, their pursuit of Matsui grew even more public later in the All-Star series when a gaggle of executives—Cashman, team president Randy Levine, general partner Steve Swindel, and vice president of international and professional scouting Gordon Blakely—traveled to Japan. The purpose of the trip, according to all involved, was to announce a "working agreement" with Matsui's former club, the Giants, who were often dubbed the "Yankees of Japan."

Like the Yankees, the Giants were the Japan League's most powerful and tradition-rich franchise. The Giants had won twenty championships and became the first Japanese franchise to acquire an American player in his prime when they signed Cromartie in 1983.

Under the terms of the agreement, the Yankees and Giants would swap scouting reports on players in the United States and Japan, and exchange nonplaying minor league personnel. The Yankees would assist the Giants in scouting and developing players in Latin America while the Giants would help the Yankees scout and develop players in Asia.

The Yankees' quartet retained poker faces throughout their visit, as did Matsui. "The only reason I'm in Japan at this time is to finalize a working agreement with the Yomiuri Giants," Cashman told reporters upon arriving in Japan.

"I have not engaged the player. At this point I wouldn't even know how to go about doing it, who I would contact or what."

"I have no plans to meet anyone from the Yankees," Matsui told reporters the day before the arrival of the Yankees' executives. "I have received no messages."

Still, most observers were fairly certain the Yankees' business in Japan went far beyond the "working agreement" with the Giants. Asked which team he thought Matsui would sign with, Tsuneo Watanabe, the Giants' chairman of the board, told the *Newark Star-Ledger,* "Probably the Yankees. Could be another team. I don't really know for sure."

Said Everett: "From a media standpoint, it was the worst-kept secret that [Matsui] was going to the Yankees. Seeing Brian Cashman in the hotel [made it obvious]."

Ken Davidoff, the Yankees beat reporter for *Newsday,* said, "I think [Matsui] was signed, sealed, and delivered" long before he officially signed with the Yankees.

"It was never in doubt," Waldstein said.

Cashman was only slightly less pursued during the All-Star series than Matsui. "The Japanese reporters there knew the hotel that some of the Yankees officials were staying in, and they would follow them around in cars," Lennon said. "They were there when Brian Cashman arrived at the airport."

Cashman told the *Newark Star-Ledger* that "there were 45 cameras in my face" documenting his Far East arrival. "They followed me off the plane, to the baggage carousel and through customs. The taxi driver thought I was a Formula One [race car] driver."

Finally, after an hour of hedging during the November 16 press conference announcing the deal, Cashman gave a glimpse of his real intentions.

"Upon the conclusion of the series, if appropriate, I would like to meet [Matsui], if that's possible," Cashman said.

Later that evening, Cashman watched the game between the American and Japanese All-Stars from a seat in a Giants' luxury box. Not coincidentally, Japan manager Tatsunori Hara switched Matsui from his usual center field to right field, a position he could play for the Yankees if they traded Mondesi.

"I want to show he's well-rounded, that he can play anywhere," said Hara, who added he shifted Matsui to right partially to appease the fans in the right field bleachers.

As for Matsui, who had already sent letters via FedEx and email to all 30 major league teams informing them of his intentions, he said he was not "particularly concentrating on the Yankees. I'm on the receiving end and I have to wait for responses, but if I get an offer like that, of course I would meet with them."

Matsui endured an emotional and difficult All Star series. He appeared overwhelmed on the field, as well, where he struggled to the tune of a .161 average in 31 at-bats and suffered a lopsided defeat at the hands of Barry Bonds in a home run derby prior to the fifth game of the series.

Following the first game of the series, the sellout crowd at the Tokyo Dome—Matsui's home stadium the last nine years—roared for half an hour until Matsui, engulfed by photographers, ran back onto the field and bowed to the fans three times.

Such a sight floored the Americans, who finally began to under-stand the depth of Matsui's popularity in his home country. "Just go by the [reaction of the] fans, forget the media [coverage] for a second," Everett said. "The guy had a brutal series, and because it was his last game in the Tokyo Dome, the entire crowd stayed. The game had ended and they just waited for him to come out and acknowledge them."

Williams told the *Newark Star-Ledger* he raced on to the field to capture the scene with his video camera. "I filmed the whole thing," Williams said. "It was obviously very emotional and special for him and the fans."

Afterwards, Matsui was so overcome he didn't meet with reporters, a rarity indeed for Matsui. For the first time in his life, the unyielding attention seemed to be wearing on Matsui, who admitted he was feeling the pressure of playing in his final series in Japan.

Those who were seeing Matsui for the first time were beginning to wonder what the fuss was all about. "He didn't really impress over there too much," said Chicago White Sox pitcher Mark Buehrle, whose stint in Japan was ended when Matsui hit a line drive off his left (pitching) shoulder. "I think he only had like [five] hits off us, then [in] the home run derby [against Barry Bonds], he didn't really do much."

Said Everett: "He had an awful series. I went out on a limb [and said] I thought he was going to be a big bust [in America]. If he's saying something like 'The pressure got to me' in an exhibition series, what would an 0-for-21 string in New York do?"

"I think it was [a matter of] pitchers he'd never seen before and the pressure of him trying to put on a show every time he was out there in all these arenas in Tokyo," Lennon said. "I'm sure [it] weighed on him. As well as he handled things outwardly, I think he put a lot of pressure on himself internally. And you could tell [by] the way [he looked] at the plate—there were a lot of weak ground balls, there were strikeouts, he just didn't look anything like he was billed to be."

Of course, as Matsui's first-time observers would realize during the trip, the spotlight he was under during his final series in Japan was far brighter than anything he'd experience in New York or anywhere else.

"That's what we learned," Everett said. "He literally carries the weight of a nation on his shoulder. And as much as there's pressure to play in New York, we don't fathom what his real life is like. He's almost on holiday [in America]."

"It's not an exaggeration to say the guy is really a national treasure over there," Lennon said. "Matsui is the most recognizable name in baseball over there. It would be the same thing as saying Ted Williams or Babe Ruth [or] Barry Bonds [in America], but [with an] even great response [from] them, considering this is somebody they considered their prized baseball player."

"Maybe he was putting too much pressure on himself and trying to do a little bit too much to impress people," Alomar said.

Everett and the rest of the American traveling party were amazed at how well Matsui handled the constant attention. "There's a lot of interest in everything he does, and the sheer volume [of requests for his time] is overwhelming," said Everett, who got one interview with Matsui, but only after daily reminders to the Japanese All-Star team's media relations contacts. "So everything has to be really organized for him to be able to just do his job and get his work in [and] make his experience as normal as humanly possible, as [normal as] anything could be for him.

"I can't imagine what a typical day is for him, you know what I mean?"

"He essentially held two separate press conferences on the field everyday for 10 straight days, during the height of speculation about where he would go and what team he would sign with and what were his thoughts about playing in the United States," Lennon said. "He dealt with those questions everyday and not once did you see him appear upset or annoyed or irritated by the whole process, which, in my view, makes him a pretty special player and [a] pretty special person to be able to handle it as well as he did."

Said Buerhle: "There was a lot of media attention there, and it seemed like everywhere he [was], they're following him around."

In the end, a most unlikely source helped Matsui relax. During his home run derby with Matsui, Bonds—never the most sociable sort on or off the field—apparently sensed the stress Matsui was under and began rubbing his rival's shoulders. The scene was more than a bit ironic: Bonds, the textbook surly superstar who has chafed at life in the spotlight almost from the moment he exploded on to the scene with the Pittsburgh Pirates in 1986, trying to loosen up Matsui, who had never before indicated a discomfort with his fame.

"I think [Bonds] wanted Matsui to win it," Waldstein said. "He was really trying to help him out."

Whatever Bonds did or said seemed to work. Matsui hit four homers after the impromptu massage, and Lennon said Matsui appeared more relaxed the remainder of the series, even if it didn't necessarily show up in his statistics.

"It really wasn't until he had that home run derby with Bonds that he started to lighten up," Lennon said. "Bonds just joked with him and really tried to loosen him up, and Matsui started hitting home runs [in the derby]. The pressures seemed to come off him."

Not surprisingly, Matsui's subpar performance was the talk of the country: One daily newspaper ran a front page cartoon that pictured a frightened-looking Matsui dwarfed by Bonds, who hit .367 with five homers and 13 RBI during the All-Star Series.

And regardless of how the Japanese team fared, the lead story everyday was Matsui. Everett said Japanese starter Koji Uehara performed admirably in the first game of the All-Star Series, but "all they wanted [to talk about was] Matsui."

"Everybody that showed up to see these games was there to see Matsui," Lennon said. "Everybody else was in a secondary role. Fans just rushed down to the front to get a glimpse of him."

In addition to dealing with the overwhelming coverage of his final series, Matsui said he had difficulty adjusting to the craftsman-like nature of the American pitchers. Not only do Japanese pitchers typically throw slower than their American counterparts, but they also don't throw nearly as much "off-speed" stuff and they rarely throw the same pitch more than once in an at-bat. But most of the American pitchers Matsui faced threw the proverbial "kitchen sink" at him.

"They worked on the corners, inside and out," Matsui said during the series. "The pitchers have such good command and the changeups they throw is something that I'm not used to. They don't throw those in Japan. I had some awkward moments."

After the series, Hara, who was also Matsui's manager with the Giants, told reporters that "For some reason, [Matsui] played to about 20 percent of his ability in the series. It's a shame the major leaguers didn't see him play the way he did all season."

Most of the Americans were considerably kinder in their assessment of Matsui. "It was November—you're not usually playing baseball in November," Lee said with a grin. "People are tired [at that point]. I don't think you [can put too much] weight on that series. It was just an exhibition."

"I think he was just going through a bad stretch at that time," Waldstein said. "[The Giants] had just won the championship and I bet he had turned it down a little bit."

"I think Matsui is putting a lot of pressure on himself trying to do good," said Matsui's future teammate Williams. "That's obviously understandable. But over the long run, his talent is going to show up."

The short run, however, was not satisfying for Matsui and his countrymen. His final at-bat in Japan was anything but storybook.

With two outs in the ninth inning of Game Seven, a runner on third and Japan down by two runs, Matsui stepped to the plate against the Los Angeles Dodgers' flame-throwing closer Eric Gagne. But instead of lofting a dramatic game-tying home run, Matsui hit a meek series-ending groundout to second base.

The fireworks would have to wait a few months.

Culture Clashes

iji Sawamura was just 18 years old, but he was already used to this: A fan waving to get his attention and extending to him a piece of paper. Such autograph requests were common on both sides of the Pacific for Sawamura, a pitcher who had led the Dai Nippon Tokyo Yakyu Kurabu—or The Great Japan Tokyo Baseball Club—to a 93-9 record against American minor league and semi-pro teams in 1935.

But this . . . this request was different. Sawamura noticed the small print written in a foreign language on the piece of paper. He showed the document to his friend, Sotaro Suzuki, who could read and speak English.

And what Suzuki read inspired a colorful reaction in two different languages. The "fan" who offered the piece of paper to Sawamura wasn't a fan at all; he was a scout for the Pittsburgh Pirates. And the piece of paper was actually a major league contract.

Suzuki handed the contract back to the scout and gave him an earful in the process. And it was just as well, because Sawamura had zero interest in playing in America.

"My problem is I hate America, and I can not make myself like Americans," Sawamura said in a magazine article partially reprinted in the book *You Gotta Have Wa*. "I'm not good at the language, I can't eat as much rice as I wish when I'm there and the women are too haughty. In America, you cannot even tie your shoestrings if there is a woman around. People like myself can not possibly survive in an environment where such uncomfortable customs exist."

Hideki Matsui was just 18 years old, but he was already used to this: Thousands of people screaming his name and millions more listening intently on the radio. In his autobiography, *Slugging It Out in Japan*, former Japanese baseball star Warren Cromartie recalled the summer afternoon when he rolled down the window in a cab and found every other car in the area was tuned to the same event: the National High School Baseball Championship.

It was the premier amateur sporting event in Japan—in his book *You Gotta Have Wa*, Robert Whiting wrote the tournament receives more coverage than the Japan Summit—and in 1992, it served as the backdrop for Matsui's elevation from mere icon to legend. In one game, he was intentionally walked by Meitoko High School five times.

Matsui's power had been the stuff of legend since his grade school days, when he was noticeably taller and broader than his classmates. Athletic greatness ran in the family—Matsui's mother excelled at volleyball—and Matsui won a sumo tournament and obtained a first-degree black belt in judo before he began winning acclaim on the diamond, where the right-handed hitter displayed so much power that he actually began batting left-handed in order to level the playing field.

Matsui's prodigious home runs at Seiryo High School—during one practice, he supposedly hit a ball 113 meters (371 feet) onto the roof of his manager's house—earned him the nickname "Godzilla" and an unprecedented amount of respect from opposing teams, who pitched around Matsui long before Meitoko never let him take the bat off his shoulders in that 1992 tournament game.

"He got walked every time in Little League and high school," Cromartie said. "They wouldn't pitch to him. It was all about [his] power. Once you establish the power, word spreads pretty quickly in Japan about the next potential phenom to come up."

In return, Matsui displayed an unprecedented amount of patience. He had exhibited anger only once in his entire career, when he threw his bat after yet another intentional walk in junior high school.

His coach immediately slapped him in the face—on the field, in front of everyone. "It was a valuable lesson for me," Matsui told the Asian edition of *Time* magazine. "From that day on, I resolved never to lose control of my emotions in a game again."

Such restraint would prove especially valuable during adulthood for Matsui, who was drafted by Japan's most popular professional team, the Yomiuri Giants, weeks after his high school graduation. For the next 10 years, he would be the most scrutinized person in the country, more recognizable than the prime minister and more popular than anybody else could possibly imagine.

And after all that, he'd become even more famous by becoming the 17th Japanese player to sign a contract with a Major League Baseball team in America. And yet even in following others, Matsui was blazing new trails.

Never before had a Japanese hitter known for his power attempted to make it big in America. Those who had preceded Matsui were either slap-hitting leadoff types (Ichiro Suzuki), mediocre journeymen (Tsuyoshi Shinjo), or pitchers (Hideo Nomo, Kazuhiro Suzuki, Hideki Irabu, Shigetoshi Hasegawa).

And never before had a position player attempted to make it big in America with the nation's preeminent franchise: the New York Yankees.

But Matsui, much more open-minded and learned than Sawamura, was eager to adapt to a new language and a new culture. And while Sawamura cringed at the thought of America's "challenging environment," Matsui left for the Yankees emboldened by the knowledge that he'd already survived the most challenging environment possible as the most popular member of the Giants.

Cromartie, who spent seven years with the Giants, said, "Playing for the Giants is like playing for the Yankees and [Los Angeles] Dodgers—at the same time."

Challenging environment? America?

That'd be a breeze.

When nothing else linked the countries together, Japan and America always shared a mutually passionate love affair with baseball.

Baseball as it is currently played was invented in America in 1845, and the only problem the Japanese had with that was they didn't think of it first. "Baseball is perfect for us," a Japanese writer said in *You Gotta Have Wa*. "If the Americans hadn't invented it, we probably would have."

Several college teams and all-star squads comprised of American minor leaguers conducted barnstorming tours of Japan during the first two decades of the 20th century. Victories for the Japanese were few and far between, but the often-lopsided losses made them even more determined to beat the Americans. After Waseda University lost a three-game series to the University of Chicago by a combined score of 44-6 in 1910, second baseman Suishu Tobita quit the game and, according to *You Gotta Have Wa*, promised he would "beat Chicago if I have to die to do it."

Tobita eventually became Waseda's manager, and in 1925, skippered his alma mater to three 1-0 wins and a 3-3 tie in four games against Chicago. For this, Tobita became known as the "Japanese Connie Mack"(Mack won an all-time record 3,731 games during his 53-season managerial career.) Upon his death in 1965, he was honored by Japan's emperor for his contributions to sport and his cultural achievements.

But Tobita might have earned acclaim from the emperor even if he hadn't directed Waseda to wins over its American rival. In Japan, amateur baseball was the most beloved sport in the land—so much so that it took until 1936 for a professional league to begin play.

The Japanese cherished the purity of amateur baseball. Wrote Whiting in *You Gotta Have Wa*: "The idea of playing for money struck many Japanese as somehow profane."

In America, professional baseball had existed in some form since 1871. It was one of many ways in which the American game differed from the Japanese game.

For instance, a tied baseball game in America was almost unheard of, as evidenced by the furious uproar raised when the 2002 All-Star Game ended in a 7-7, 11-inning tie because both leagues ran out of pitchers. Commissioner Bud Selig was lambasted by fans and media for signing off on the decision to end the game while managers Joe Torre and Bob Brenly were criticized for using their pitchers so liberally.

And this was an exhibition game.

Regular season games never ended in ties, and on the rare occasion a game was tied when it was called due to inclement weather, the stats counted and the game was made up in its entirety later in the season.

In Japan, however, tie games were commonplace. If two teams were deadlocked after nine innings, the game was over. One season, Cromartie's Giants lost the pennant to the Hiroshima Carp even though the Giants won more games. The Carp had more ties and fewer losses and a higher winning percentage, though, so they finished first.

In *You Gotta Have Wa*, Bill Madlock, a four-time National League batting champion who spent the 1988 season in Japan, said the Japanese were "satisfied with ties." Former Pacific League president Shinsuke Hori didn't disagree.

Hori said in *You Gotta Have Wa* that ties "suited the Japanese character. That way, nobody loses."

In 1931, Major League Baseball sent an all-star team overseas for a series of exhibition games against a Japanese squad comprised of collegiate all-stars. The Americans, which future Hall of Famers such as Lou Gehrig, Mickey Cochrane, and Lefty Gomez, beat the Japanese 17 straight times.

Three years later, another American all-star team went over, but this time it had the world's most popular player in tow: Babe Ruth. Hundreds of thousands of people turned out to see Ruth, who hit 14 homers in the 17 games—once again the Americans won every game—and became a Japanese icon in the process. A statue was built outside Koshien Stadium in Osaka in honor of Ruth. It still stands today.

Ruth was so popular in Japan, the United States government almost asked him to broker a peace agreement between the two countries near the end of World War II. The government actually devised a plan in which it would fly Ruth to Guam, where he'd deliver a radio broadcast to the Japanese imploring them to surrender or face the consequences.

In the end, the United States decided against Ruthian diplomacy and instead dropped the atomic bomb on Hiroshima.

More than four decades later, in 1989, Cromartie tended to agree with a writer who theorized Japan's sportswriters were pressured to elect Cromartie as the Central League Most Valuable Player in order to soothe relations between the United States and Japan, which at the time were frosty due to various economic disagreements between the countries.

Wrote Cromartie in *Slugging It Out In Japan*: "In fact, a newspaper article suggested that the Foreign Ministry had applied pressure on the sportswriters to cast their ballots for the gaijin because of deteriorating relations between Japan and America."

Ironically, times were never better for Americans who wanted to play overseas. Japanese teams were always eager to add foreigners, preferably hitters with power, and with Major League Baseball owners conspiring to artificially dry up the free agent market, many American players were more willing than ever to change countries.

Arbitrators eventually found Major League Baseball owners guilty of collusion between 1985 and 1987 and forced them to pay

$280 million to affected free agents such as Andre Dawson, Tim Raines, Steve Garvey, and Kirk Gibson, the latter of whom actually turned down a deal to play in Japan in 1987 in order to re-sign with the Detroit Tigers.

Alas, most of the big names traveling to Japan were either over the hill or the antithesis of the Japanese ballplayer. Madlock was 37 when he went to Japan and lasted just one season. Ben Oglivie, a former American League home run champ, had to be begged and bribed by the Kintetsu Buffaloes in order to return for a second season at age 39 in 1988.

Larry Parrish hit a total of 70 homers in 1989 and 1990, but he was cut by the Yakult Swallows following the 1989 season because of his inability to bunt. It was a fact of Japanese baseball: When the leadoff batter in an inning reached base, the next batter bunted, even if he was a power hitter. About the only player exempt from this rule was Matsui.

And then there was the tale of Bob Horner, who earned acclaim in America in 1978, when he went straight from Oklahoma State to the big leagues with the Braves and won the NL Rookie of the Year even though he played in just 89 games. In 1986, he became just the 11th player ever to hit four homers in a single game.

It seemed as if Horner could roll out of bed and hit 400-foot homers, and judging by his rapidly expanding frame in the 1980s, it appeared rolling out of bed was the extent of his exercise regiment.

After the 1986 season, Horner was one of several players who refused to sign a below-market deal to remain with his club, and he eventually signed a one-year deal with the Swallows. His arrival was huge news in Japan: In *You Gotta Have Wa*, Robert Whiting wrote "Most Japanese put Horner's arrival in the same category as the Second Coming of Christ."

Horner was assigned uniform number 50 by owner Hisami Matsuzono, a not-so-subtle reminder of how many homers Horner was expected to hit. Fifty homers looked like a modest estimate when Horner blasted six homers in his first week with the Swallows. By the end of his second week, he had already been the subject of an hour-long prime-time television special, and by the end of his first month, Horner was one of the most popular advertising pitchmen in the country.

Unfortunately for Horner, the honeymoon was brief. Teams stopped throwing fastballs against him and began pitching around him, which angered Horner almost as much as the unyielding media attention.

During the Swallows' first meeting of the season against the Yomiuri Giants, cameramen and writers surrounded Horner and Cromartie in order to record every last detail of what transpired between the history-making duo, who were the first players to leave America in their prime in order to play in Japan.

In *Slugging It Out In Japan*, Cromartie recalled the camera-interrupted conversation he had with Horner behind the batting cage:

"I don't believe this shit," [Horner] said.

Flash! Pop! Whirr!

"Horns," I said, *"You ain't seen nothing yet."*

The Japanese were even more impatient with Horner, who battled a severe cold and a nagging back injury during the summer. Horner's biggest problem, though, was his reluctance to participate in marathon pregame batting practice sessions, which did not go over well in a country so obsessed with practice that Cromartie wrote it provided players with "a means of emotional fulfillment."

Wrote Whiting in *You Gotta Have Wa*: "That Horner could be expected to succeed without even working up a sweat before a game was somehow sacrilegious. It went against the whole Japanese philosophy on baseball and life."

No one was surprised after the season when Horner turned down a three-year, $10 million offer to remain in Japan in order to sign a one-year deal with the St. Louis Cardinals for just $950,000 with the chance to earn another $500,000 in bonuses.

Said Darrell May, who spent four years in Japan with two different teams before he came back to America with the Kansas City Royals prior to the 2002 season: "If you go over there to work hard, to do the job, you're going to get along fine. If you're going over there just to make the money and try to skate through things, then you're going to find it more difficult, because [the Japanese] work hard, there's no doubt about it. They work hard, and if they see that you work hard, you're not going to have that hard of a time."

No athletes in the world worked as hard as Japanese baseball players. The workouts endured in the 19th century by the players on the First Higher School of Tokyo team were dubbed "Bloody Urine," because legend had it players actually urinated blood after practice.

Workouts were only slightly less strenuous in the 20th century. There is no such thing as an off-season in Japan, whereas major leaguers get a four-month break followed by a six-week spring training, which, at least for established veterans, is more luxurious than it is strenuous. Workouts end long before nightfall, which gives players the chance to spend almost as much time on the golf course as on the diamond, and stars rarely play an entire game during the exhibition season.

During the regular season, Major League Baseball players participate in pregame stretching and a 45-minute session of batting and fielding practice. Most players do some sort of additional exercise—whether it be running, weight-lifting or extra hitting in the cage—but they are encouraged to save their best and most concerted efforts for the game itself.

But in Japan, Cromartie is convinced teams "believe in practice more than playing the game." So-called off-days were actually packed with workouts.

As a high-priced foreigner, Cromartie was allowed to devise his own workout schedule, but as he described in *Slugging It Out In Japan*, the rest of his teammates had to endure marathon pregame exercise sessions: "My teammates, on the other hand, would be out there every afternoon in the god-awful heat, doing an hour of running laps, calisthenics, and whatnot before even beginning their hitting and fielding practice."

Said Leron Lee in *You Gotta Have Wa*: "There's such a thing as too much work. In Japan, pregame practice is like running a marathon before a twelve-round boxing match. They are exhausted by the middle of the season, especially the pitchers. The players would be a lot better, if the coaches wouldn't wear them out on the practice field."

No team anywhere ever went through what the Seibu Lions endured after the 1984 season, when manager Tatsuro Hiroka put most of his team through a 59-day "autumn camp." Wrote Whiting in *You Gotta Have Wa*: "[The workouts] consisted of an average of nine hours of daily drills, including 600 swings a day for each batter, 430 pitches a day for each pitcher, as well as swimming and aikodo—a kind of self-defense—session."

In *You Gotta Have Wa*, American Steve Ontiveros recalled a team meeting Hiroka held with the Lions during a season in which they did not win the pennant. When the players told Hiroka they weren't having fun under him, the manager "shot back and said that 'Baseball isn't supposed to be fun.' He said, 'It's your job and it's your duty to do it well.'"

And they were expected to do it no matter what kind of physical or mental anguish they might be experiencing, as symbolized by two of the most famous players in the country's history.

Hiroshima Carp third baseman Sachio Kinugasa played in every game of his 18-season career—2,215 games overall. Along the way, he suffered five broken bones, including a broken shoulder blade, but never left the lineup. After taking into account all the extra workouts Kinugasa participated in, Cromartie and Rich Lancelotti—a teammate of Kinugasa's in 1987—each figured Kinugasa played the equivalent of 4,000 straight games.

When the father of Giants manager Sadaharu Oh died, Oh did not attend the funeral, even though Oh was so close with his parents that he brought them on to the field after he broke Hank Aaron's worldwide record for career home runs. Instead, the morning after his father died, Oh took a plane to Tokyo, appeared at his father's noontime wake, and then took a bullet train back to Nagoya in time for the Giants' game against the Chunichi Dragons.

In *Slugging It Out In Japan*, Cromartie recalled Oh's brief speech to the Giants following his father's death: "This is a private matter, and it has nothing to do with baseball. I plan to go on as before. We will still take each game one at a time, and there will be no more days off until the end of the season."

The Japanese were shocked when American Randy Bass left the Hanshin Tigers during a pair of family crises. In 1984, he went home to be with his dying father. Upon his return, he was criticized by the Japanese, who, as Whiting writes in *You Gotta Have Wa*, thought Bass was "irresponsible and self-centered."

A shocked Bass told Whiting in *You Gotta Have Wa*: "How the hell can you put a game ahead of someone you love?"

In 1988, Bass requested an unpaid month-long leave of absence in order to take his son, Zachary, back home for surgery on a neck tumor. When Bass took longer than expected tending to his son, the Tigers released him. Bass eventually sued the Tigers for breach of contract and reached a settlement with the club, but Bass, one of Japan's great power hitters of the 1980s and a two-time winner of the Triple Crown, was blacklisted out of Japanese baseball.

Most Japanese agreed with the Tigers' treatment of Bass. In his autobiography, Cromartie recalled reading a "magazine survey [which stated] 70 percent of Japanese company workers thought Bass had done the wrong thing."

Major League Baseball, meanwhile, created a "bereavement list" in 2003 for players who had to leave the team due to family matters.

As far as the Japanese were concerned, playing through the pain was just one of the many ways a team maintained its *wa*—its harmony. Wrote Cromartie in *Slugging It Out In Japan*: "Americans would find the power of the Giants' coaches and the deference the players showed them hard to understand. It was mind-blowing to me, but it reflected how the society as a whole was run. Harmony came first, the individual second; seniority ruled."

Japanese players were reminded of their unyielding commitment to the game even when they did well: After the Giants won the 1989 Japan Series, they were "rewarded" immediately afterward with a two-week training camp in Palm Springs, California.

Former American League All-Star Julio Franco, who played with the Chiba Lotte Marines in 1995 and 1998, said the Japanese "can practice bunt plays for hours. There's no time limit for fundamentals. There's no room for mistakes over there. You make a mistake and tomorrow you're working on it. You make an error today and you're working on that tomorrow."

Still, even if an American worked hard, there was no guarantee he'd be accepted in Japan. Indeed, for most of the *gaijin*, playing in Japan was like a fraternity Hell Week that never ended: No matter how hard they worked, no matter how well they played, they always seemed one misstep away from earning scorn from their hosts—especially when they threatened to break long-standing Japanese records.

In 1986, Bass hit .389—the highest single-season mark in Japanese history, six points higher than the previous mark, set by Isao Harimoto—and won his second straight Triple Crown. But he lost the MVP to pitcher Manabu Kitabeppu, who went 18-4 with a 2.93 ERA for the first-place Hiroshima Carp. In addition, the Matsutaro Shoriki—awarded to "the most outstanding baseball figure of the year"—was given to Masaaki Mori, the manager of the Japan Series champion Seibu Lions.

And when Bass left Japan in 1988, a front-page story about him in *Nikkan Sports* failed to mention his record-breaking batting average two years earlier.

In 2002, Alex Cabrera, a former big leaguer, tied Oh's single-season mark of 55 home runs during the final week of the season. His Seibu Lions faced the Daiei Hawks—managed by Oh—after Cabrera tied the record, and Cabrera never got a chance to hit the tie-breaking homer.

"They didn't want me to get the record," Cabrera told ESPN.com. "The last 20 at-bats of the season, I think I only saw one strike. All records are for the Japanese."

In 2001, the Kintetsu Buffaloes' Karl "Tuffy" Rhodes, a former big leaguer from Ohio, tied Oh's single-season record of 55 homers with five games to play. He never got the record-breaking homer, because Oh's Hawks pitched around him.

According to the Associated Press, the Hawks' Keizaburo Tanoue threw 18 pitches against Rhodes, just two of which were strikes. Oh said he was "out of the loop" regarding the decision to pitch around Rhodes.

Said Darrell May, a current member of the Kansas City Royals who played for the Yomiuri Giants in 2001: "[He was] talking with some of the Japanese guys [and they told May] it was reported in the paper that the players took it upon themselves to pitch around him. Now whether that was true or not, out of respect for the manager [May isn't sure]. That was kind of the thought [to make sure foreigners didn't break the record], which to me is tough to swallow."

Ironically, the exact same thing occurred when Bass threatened Oh's record in 1985. Bass had 54 homers with two games left on the schedule.

Both games were against the Giants, who were managed by Oh.

In those final two games, Bass drew six walks in nine plate appearances. Five of those were intentional, and during the season finale, Bass took pitches so far off the plate that, in the words of Whiting, "even a boat oar would not have helped him hit the ball."

Afterwards, Oh said he did not order his pitchers to walk Bass. But Whiting reported in *You Gotta Have Wa* that Keith Comstock, a former major leaguer pitching for the Giants, told Bass a Giants coach had threatened to fine pitchers $1,000 every time they threw Bass a strike.

Asked if the willingness to pitch around Americans pursuing Japanese records was a sign of the country's reluctance to fully embrace foreign-born players, Hide Sueyoshi—the Seattle Mariners' Assistant Director of Professional and International Scouting and a native of Japan—said, "I don't know. But of course, nobody wants their names to [be associated] with the history [that's] made. It's the one thing they just try and avoid."

Conversely, in the United States, Seattle Mariners outfielder and Japan native Ichiro Suzuki became just the second player in history to win both the Rookie of the Year and Most Valuable Player award in the same season in 2001. He was the third Japanese player to win Rookie of the Year after Hideo Nomo (National League, 1995) and Kazuhiro Sasaki (American League, 2000).

In 2003, the two Baseball Writers Association of America writers who refused to vote for Matsui in the Rookie of the Year balloting because of his Japanese experience—Jim Souhan of the *Minneapolis Star-Tribune* and Bill Ballou of the *Worcester* (Mass.) *Telegram & Gazette*—were harshly criticized for their show of protest, especially because it may have determined the race.

Matsui finished second in the balloting, just four votes behind Angel Berroa. Had Souhan and Ballou placed him second on their ballots—points were awarded on a 5-3-1 system—Matsui would have won the award.

The pressure on foreign-born players in Japan was unyielding.

"They expect you to be a big impact on the media, on the fans, on players," Franco said. "They see it like, 'This guy can teach us something that we don't know. We can teach him some things that he doesn't know.' And they import you over there because they want you to be their home run hitter, [and a] leader on the team.

"They want you to make them win."

In 1985, Cromartie hit .309 with 32 homers and 112 RBI. But as Whiting wrote in *You Gotta Have Wa*, when Cromartie struggled during a September series against the Hanshin Tigers, one of his coaches, Toshimitsu Suetsugu, called Cromartie's performance "a first-degree crime."

A year later, Cromartie hit .363 with 37 homers and 93 RBI, and 14 game-winning hits. Yet Whiting recalled in *You Gotta Have Wa*, that "a commentator lamented on TV, 'It's too bad he doesn't hit like Bass.'"

Cromartie hit .304 with 28 homers and 92 RBI in 1987. But prior to the 1988 season, he was lambasted in a magazine article (partially reprinted in *Slugging It Out In Japan*) that ended with this harsh and seemingly unfair criticism: "Four consecutive years of batting .300 or more give him a high rating, but home run total dropped. 1987 was his first year under 30 homers. RBIs dropped to 92. Inadequacies including defense remain."

Wrote Cromartie in *Slugging It Out In Japan*:

I was a bum again.

But I was used to it.

Said Cromartie last year: "It's easy for the press to get on Americans over there because it sells papers. Everyone wants to read about the foreign guy instead of their own guy. We made more money than other players, that was a [source of] jealousy as well.

"Also, [the Japanese] consistently try to change [foreign] players to conform to the Japanese style," Cromartie said. "We don't try to dictate how Korean or Japanese guys play. We try to help them in many ways, but we don't dog them or talk [bad] about them. A lot of that goes on in Japan."

It wasn't easy, but it was still a pretty good living, especially for players who had yet to receive an extended opportunity in America's major leagues. Foreigners regularly made two or three times as much money as the natives, and they weren't paid to sit on the bench.

"Guys like to go over there [to] prove themselves, and maybe they like to [obtain] the financial security," Sueyoshi said. "Minor leaguers [in America] don't get paid that much. So their determination going to Japan is different from [the] Japanese player coming over here. [The Americans] like to get secure financially, they like to [play] everyday at a higher level rather than [being] stuck in the minor leagues."

Big-name imports such as Bass, Rhodes, and Lee never received regular playing time in the majors. May had appeared in just 41 games with three different teams between 1995 and 1997 when his agent helped convince him a year abroad with the Hanshin Tigers was better than another year in the minors in America.

"Actually, I didn't even really want to go," May said. "Basically, what it boiled down to is I ended up being the 26th guy on a 25-man roster [with the] Anaheim [Angels]. I was out of options, so they were going to try to sneak me through waivers and be the guy that they brought up and down if somebody got hurt. The year before, I was kind of in that similar role . . . [and I] didn't enjoy it too much.

"[The Angels] said there was a Japanese team interested in me—I had no interest in going to Japan," May said. "I talked to my agent [and] decided to see what they had to say. I didn't realize how good the money was to go over there. And we sat down, talked to them, heard their initial offer, and thought about it. [I] thought about it a lot and said, 'Hey, it'll be a good opportunity to help my family financially for one year. Why not?'"

One year turned into four for May. And for Cromartie, who had been a regular with the Montreal Expos for seven seasons prior to leaving for Japan, one year turned into seven. Cromartie was considered the first American player to depart for Japan in his prime yet ended up earning far more acclaim and money in Japan than he ever did in America.

"For me, it was about [making] a couple million dollars," Cromartie said. "I didn't go over there to meet friends. I wasn't planning on staying two years, I wound up staying seven."

The most famous American refugee turned out to be Cecil Fielder, albeit for what he accomplished after he returned to America. Fielder, a 25-year-old power-hitting first baseman, signed with the Hanshin Tigers in 1989 because he couldn't get an extended look with the Toronto Blue Jays, who were committed to Fred McGriff at first base.

Fielder hit 38 homers for the Tigers, after which he signed a two-year deal with the Detroit Tigers. He paid immediate and hefty dividends for Detroit when he blasted 51 homers in 1990. Fielder was the first player to hit 50 homers in a season since George Foster with the Cincinnati Reds 13 years earlier.

The year 1990 marked the first of four straight 30-homer, 100-RBI seasons for Fielder, who for a short time in 1993 was the highest-paid major leaguer in history. His success in America legitimized Japanese baseball almost as much as the success of the Japanese who eventually thrived in America.

"I tell you what," Franco said. "Japan was a great country for baseball. If you can hit in Japan, you can hit up here. The question is when [is a player going to get the opportunity]? You don't get the opportunity, so you go to Japan instead of being in Triple-A. You go to Japan and play good baseball, make good money and get an opportunity to come back here and succeed."

Franco had done pretty well for himself during a decade-plus career in the major leagues—he was named the MVP of the All-Star Game in 1990 and won the AL batting crown in 1991—but with the future of American professional baseball in doubt following the strike that canceled the 1994 World Series, he chose to sign with the Chiba Lotte Marines in 1995.

Franco, whose career would eventually also take him to Korea and Mexico, had no trouble adapting to the Japanese style of baseball and was embraced far faster than most of his predecessors. He returned to America with the Cleveland Indians in 1996, but after the 1997 season, Franco was out of work again in the bigs and returned to the Marines, where he made history by becoming the first foreigner elected as captain of a Japanese team.

"I liked it so much—my family liked it, I liked the experience," said Franco, who told the Japanese edition of *Playboy* in 1996 that he would eventually return to Japan. "The second time they offered me [a contract] in Japan [that an American team] didn't offer me here, so I went there."

Those who stuck it out long enough eventually earned the respect of the Japanese. Before his unceremonious departure in 1988, Bass was one of Japan's most popular celebrities and pitchmen.

And Cromartie, who enjoyed playing for Oh so much that he named his third child Cody Oh Cromartie, was embraced by fans after he led the Giants to the Japan Series championship in 1989.

He struggled for most of his final season in Japan in 1990, yet he was the top vote getter among outfielders in the fan balloting for the All-Star Game.

The highest compliment, though, was issued by Oh. During an unbelievable hot streak early in the 1989 season—Cromartie was hitting as high as .452 on May 25—Cromartie had dinner with Oh, who had been fired as the Giants manager the previous season.

In *Slugging It Out In Japan*, Cromartie recalled Oh lifting his glass of sake for a toast. "Congratulations, Cro," Oh said. "You've mastered Japanese baseball."

Nearly 15 years later, Cromartie admits he "was floored by that. I still am. It was a very emotional time for me."

Cromartie said that after five seasons in Japan, he began "having fun. I figured something out. I figured out the Japanese customs, the ways, the whole game of baseball . . . when you say something like ['he mastered the game'], that's the whole ball of wax."

No matter how well Americans did overseas, though, the urge to return to the majors remained. May turned down a $5 million offer from the Yomiuri Giants following the 2001 season in order to sign a one-year deal with the Kansas City Royals for $375,000. May turned into the Royals' staff ace in 2002, when he went 10-8.

And yet even after Oh bestowed upon him the highest praise any ballplayer could receive in Japan, Cromartie chose to play one more season in America following his retirement from the Giants in 1990. Cromartie signed with the Kansas City Royals and hit .313 in 131 at-bats in 1991.

Soon, plenty of Japanese superstars would follow Cromartie's lead.

Any athlete likes to play in the higher level [at] the competitive level, and once they establish their status in Japan, [they have the] desire to play here, which is the highest level of baseball. I don't think they come here to prove [they belong] here, they just want a challenge.

— Hide Sueyoshi, Mariners assistant director, Professional and International Scouting

It took just one fantastic, headline-grabbing season for Hideo Nomo in 1995 to prove to the rest of Japan's professional ballplayers that it was indeed possible to make a successful leap to America.

But he wasn't the first Japanese player to play major league ball. That honor went to Masanori Murakami, who reached the bigs with the San Francisco Giants as a 20-year-old in September 1964. At the time, it seemed as if Murakami would be the historic trendsetter.

Murakami, who was one of three members of the Nankai Hawks allowed to play for a Giants farm team for one season as a "goodwill" gesture intended to improve American-Japanese baseball relations, went 11-7 for Fresno, the Giants' Triple-A affiliate, and earned the California League Rookie of the Year. During his month in the big leagues, he went 1-0 with a 1.80 ERA, one save and 15 strikeouts in 15 innings.

The Giants, understandably excited at the promise displayed by Murakami, exercised a clause in the contract that allowed them to keep one of the three players. However, officials in Japanese baseball believed they had loaned Murakami to the Giants for the 1964 season only.

The two sides argued bitterly and vehemently until it was finally agreed that Murakami would spend the 1965 season with the Giants before returning to Japan. After going 4-1 with eight saves and a 3.75 ERA for the Giants, Murakami went back home and compiled a 103-82 mark over the next 17 seasons.

And for the next 30 years, Murakami stood alone among Japanese players. No one else made the move west—until 1995, when a salary dispute between star pitcher Hideo Nomo and the Kintetsu Buffaloes allowed Nomo to make a trend-setting defection.

Nomo, just 26 years old at the time, was already one of the greatest pitchers in Japan. In 1988, he led Japan's baseball team to a silver medal performance in the 1988 Summer Olympics. A year later, he was Kintetsu's first-round pick in the amateur draft. Nomo—armed with a nasty split-fingered fastball and a deceptive delivery in which he turned his back to the plate—won the Pacific League's MVP and Rookie of the Year awards in 1990 and led the

Pacific League in wins and strikeouts every season between 1990 and 1993. By the end of 1993, Nomo had reached 1,000 career strikeouts faster than any pitcher in Japan's history.

But he battled shoulder problems in 1994 and won just eight games. Following the season, he and Kintetsu became embroiled in a bitter contract battle.

History suggested Nomo had no choice but to eventually play for the Buffaloes. After all, with just five seasons under his belt, he was barely halfway to the nine years of service time needed for free agency.

But then Nomo and his agent, Don Nomura, discovered a loophole: A player who retired could play wherever he liked. It was an ironic loophole, but it was good enough for Nomo, who, in the prime of his career, announced his "retirement" and, on February 13, 1995, signed a deal with the Los Angeles Dodgers for the major league minimum plus a $2 million signing bonus.

Not surprisingly, Nomo's decision to jump the shores did not go over well in Japan. "Voluntary retirement should mean he had the will to quit baseball," Central League executive Masaaki Nagino told *USA Today Baseball Weekly*.

According to a 2002 article in *Sports Illustrated,* Nomura's stepfather—former Japanese star catcher Katsuya Nomura—and his mother were so mad at their son for brokering Nomo's deal that they refused to speak to him anymore. Nomo's parents were in hysterics as they begged him to change his mind, while the Kintetsu general manager stepped down from his post.

"At the time, people said, 'He's a traitor to Japanese baseball,'" Oh told *Sports Illustrated*.

Such sentiment didn't stop his countrymen from passionately tracking his progress in America, though. According to *USA Today Baseball Weekly*, 30 Japanese reporters showed up for Nomo's first day of spring training workouts. The Dodgers issued 85 extra media credentials when Nomo made his Dodger Stadium debut on May 12, 1995.

In a scene that would become familiar to all the Japanese stars who ventured abroad, Nomo had his every move chronicled, from pregame stretching to the postgame press conferences that took place in a separate room in order to handle the overflow of interest. And Nomo's games, most of which started at 4 A.M. Tokyo time, were telecast live on the NHK public television network.

Those who got up early had to love what they saw. Aided by the NL's unfamiliarity with his unorthodox style, Nomo immediately became one of the most dominant pitchers in the game. In his first 12 starts, he posted nine wins, a 1.91 ERA, and 168 strikeouts in 136 innings. He was named to the NL All-Star Team and won the NL Rookie of the Year award after finishing the season 13-6 with a 2.54 ERA and a league-leading 236 strikeouts.

Along the way, he went from martyr to icon.

"It's very important that he does well," *Sankei Shinbun* sportswriter Jin Setoguchi told *USA Today Baseball Weekly*. "He could be a pioneer for other Japanese who want to play in the majors."

He didn't have to succeed in order to be a pioneer. As angry as the Japanese were when Nomo bolted for the Dodgers, they were also impressed by the courage it took to leave.

"There is a Japanese stereotype," Nomo's interpreter, Michael Okumara, told *USA Today Baseball Weekly*. "No one wants to be the pioneer because no one wants to fail."

Following the pioneer was a different matter entirely.

Japanese players began trickling over during the next few seasons, the most famous of which was Hideki Irabu. In January 1997, the San Diego Padres had worked out a deal with the Chiba Lotte Marines in which they acquired the rights to Irabu, who had been dubbed the "Nolan Ryan of Japan" thanks to his 100-mph fastball.

But Irabu said he would never play for the Padres and demanded a trade to the Yankees, who eventually traded two prospects and $3 million to the Padres in exchange for Irabu and two minor leaguers. Shortly thereafter, the Yankees signed Irabu to a four-year, $12.8 million deal that included an $8.5 million signing bonus.

It didn't take long for the Yankees to realize they'd made a huge mistake. Irabu, who was just 59-59 during his career in Japan, went 29-20 with a 4.80 ERA with the Yankees and chafed underneath the heavy scrutiny placed upon him by the American and Japanese press corps. He was traded to the Montreal Expos prior to the 2000 season and, after a brief stint as the Texas Rangers' closer in 2002, Irabu went back to Japan and joined the Hanshin Tigers.

The departure of each player was greeted with the same mixture of sadness and anticipation—until 2001, when Tsuyoshi Shinjo, a career .249 hitter for the Tigers, had an impressive rookie season with the New York Mets. The Japanese were more alarmed by Shinjo's success than they were by that of Ichiro Suzuki, the former Orix Blue Wave outfielder who became the first position player to sign a major league contract (beating Shinjo by less than a month) and promptly won the AL Rookie of the Year and Most Valuable Player awards for the Seattle Mariners.

"[Shinjo] came over and people saw he had success over here, even though he wasn't a great player [in Japan]," May said. "[He] saw a lot of Japanese players thinking, 'Wow, I could probably go over there and be successful,' and I think that was kind of the thought process throughout Japan: Fear of losing a lot of our talent to the States."

And no departure was feared more than that of Hideki Matsui's.

Japan had waited forever for someone like Matsui: A homegrown power hitter armed with the durability, work ethic, and modesty of a mere mortal in the factory.

And he was a member of the Yomiuri Giants, the most beloved franchise in the land.

On his deathbed, the Giants' founder, Matsutaro Shoriki, wished the following: "May the Giants always be strong, and may they always be gentlemen."

That was Matsui, who appeared as if he was programmed for superstardom with the Giants from childhood. It was a path he obediently followed.

Look at his batting stance: He's almost perfectly still inside the batter's box, aside from a few twitches of his right elbow. Look at that swing: Quiet, efficient, yet compact, and powerful to all fields.

Such a nondescript stance was far different than what Americans had gotten accustomed to out of their swinging-from-the-heels power hitters, but it was exactly what the Japanese—and the Giants in particular—wanted. In *You Gotta Have Wa*, Whiting writes that Tatsunori Hara, who was the Giants' premier power hitter of the 1980s, had been told "what to do all his life; first his father, then a long succession of Giants instructors, all of whom believed that form, orthodox form, was all important. Hara had learned how to bat and field by the numbers. He looked like a carbon copy of every other player in Japan."

But Matsui was different than the rest. He indicated as much upon signing with the Giants in 1992, when he requested and received uniform number 55—in honor of Oh, the all-time Giant great whose single-season mark of 55 homers Matsui hoped to match or break.

"I think I have a chance at tying or breaking Oh-san's record one of these years, but it would be a career year when I get off to a good start and everything goes right," Matsui told the *Tokyo Weekender* in 2001.

Matsui, already wildly popular due to his exploits at Seiryo High School, was beloved from the moment he donned a Giants uniform. He played in every game between 1993 and 2002—1,250 games in all, the second-longest "Ironman" streak in Japanese history—and followed every instruction given to him by Giants management. Among those requests: No flashy attire, no living outside the team dormitory and no dating, at least during the first few years of his career.

He was also unfailingly polite and patient with both fans and the throng of media that tracked his every move. "I asked for this life," Matsui told *Time* magazine's Asian edition in 2003. "Nobody forced it on me, and I have a duty to the people who put me here. When I was 14, I promised my father that I would always be nice to people and I have done my best to keep that promise. Sure, sometimes, I get upset. I get mad like anybody else. But I try to hold it in."

The Giants, whose games are regularly telecast nationwide, won three Japan Series titles in Matsui's nine full seasons. He hit 332 home runs, including a career-high 50 in 2002, and drove in 100 or more runs five times.

As a result of his hitting exploits, Matsui became the most popular person in the nation—even if he may not have been the best all-around player in his own game.

"Ichiro is an MVP—[Matsui is] not an MVP," said MLBradio.com host Seth Everett, who used to host the Seattle Mariners' postgame radio show and covered the All-Star Series between America and Japan following the 2002 season. "In Japan, [Matsui] is, just because [of the] coverage [he received]. He was a Giant—a Yomuiri Giant.

"Look at 'Little Matsui,' " Everett said, referring to shortstop Kazuo Matsui, who signed a contract with the New York Mets prior to the 2004 season. "[He] could be a better player [than Hideki Matsui]. He plays for the Seibu Loins, he hits .330 [with] 30 homers, plays shortstop. He's the package.

"But again, he's just known as 'Little Matsui,'" Everett said. "This guy hits 30 home runs and he's known as 'Little.' [Hideki] Matsui's not a giant, he's just the biggest guy there."

And Japan felt its icon slipping away following the 2001 season.

Matsui, just a season away from free agency, was offered a record six-year, $64 million deal by the Giants. But Matsui turned it down, accepting instead a one-year deal for 2002 for a club-record $4.7 million, and everyone began to prepare for the inevitability of Matsui's departure.

The Giants' owner, the powerful Tsuneo Watanabe, had previously spoken out against Japanese players who left for America. He spoke to Matsui after the season in hopes of changing his mind, but to no avail.

Matsui was going, and he was as heartbroken about it as the rest of his countrymen, many of whom wept when he concluded his Japanese career following the All-Star Series against Major League Baseball in November 2002.

Bill Bickard, who was the English public address announcer during the All-Star Series, told ESPN.com that, "Matsui has always been a class act, and that's why he is so loved. When he came back on the field [following his final game at the Tokyo Dome], the woman who does the Japanese p.a. next to me had tears in her eyes.

"We don't have a parallel like this for American baseball to lose a player like Matsui," Bickard said. "The Giants are the national team. They're like the Yankees and Cowboys rolled into one."

Matsui opened the press conference announcing his departure with a 40-minute speech in which, according to *Time* magazine's Asian edition, he "apologized profusely to team management, teammates, and the fans."

Said Matsui: "I hope people don't think I'm a traitor."

He had nothing to worry about.

With Japan's economy spiraling downward and the national mood as low as it had been in decades—ironically, America was in the throes of a similar countrywide malaise—the idea of Matsui starring on the American stage enthused the Japanese. "Such people make us recall the confidence we have lost and make us believe that maybe we can make it through these hard times," sportswriter Midori Masujima told *Time* magazine's Asian edition.

Most important of all, though, the most powerful figure in Japanese baseball approved of his nation's best players making their way to America.

"Now if you're a good player, people ask, 'Why don't you go to the United States?'" Oh told *Sports Illustrated* in 2002. "Why not? I wish I had the chance to go."

In 2003, he, and the rest of Japan, could live through Matsui.

Tampa Crush

As Matsui found out in the weeks following his final appearance on a Japanese diamond, he didn't have to play in his homeland in order to remain Japan's biggest headline-maker.

The day after the All-Star series finale, Matsui announced he would retain an agent for his American contract negotiations. That came as good news to the high-powered agents who traveled to Japan for the All-Star series, especially those who had ties to the Yankees and/or Japanese superstars: The International Management Group (which represents Derek Jeter), Scott Boras (who represents Bernie Williams), and Tony Attanasio (who reps Seattle Mariners stars Ichiro Suzuki and Kazuhiro Sasaki).

On December 3, 2002, Matsui selected Arn Tellem, who had negotiated big-buck deals the previous two winters for Yankees Mike Mussina and Jason Giambi, the latter of whom spent a lot of time in Japan with Matsui and recommended he choose Tellem as his agent. Tellem also helped well-known Japanese agent Don Nomura when the latter negotiated a contract for Hideo Nomo—the first well-known Japanese player to depart for America—in 1995.

With his agent in tow, Matsui could finally begin the process of determining his next employer. Even though his future was the source of constant debate during the All-Star Series in Japan the previous month, David Lennon, a *Newsday* reporter who covered the Series, said, "Nobody really knew the inside information on [Matsui's future], per se. This guy was still trying to sign with an agent. He still had that hurdle to get over before he could actually start negotiating with the Yankees and get a contract done."

Tellem chatted with a handful of teams over the next two weeks, including the Yankees' bitter crosstown rivals, the Mets, but absolutely no one was surprised when word leaked out on December 19 that the Yankees and Matsui had reached what the Yankees dubbed an "understanding" with Matsui on a three-year, $21 million deal.

"I think people just assumed that the Yankees would be the ones that would offer him the most money," Lennon said. "And he wanted to play in a big city. I think the Yankees fit the bill on both those details."

Or, as one unnamed American League official had told the *Newark Star-Ledger* upon learning Matsui had retained the services of Tellem: "If you didn't think the Yankees were the favorites to get him before, you can write it down in ink and underline it now."

After agreeing to terms with the Yankees, Matsui held yet another packed press conference in Tokyo. "The Yankees have a great tradition and great players," Matsui told reporters. "It's the ball club that would most challenge me. That's where I wanted to show my abilities."

"We have high hopes for him. We're excited about what he presents, both as a player and in terms of the buzz that surrounds him," Yankees general manager Brian Cashman told reporters.

The Yankees were so excited, in fact, that they immediately began selling jerseys with Matsui's name and number (55) on their official website. The *Newark Star-Ledger* reported the jerseys were priced at $200—far more than the jerseys of incumbent star first baseman Giambi, whose jersey could be purchased for $149.95. The Yankees had to stop selling the jerseys, though, after being informed by Major League Baseball that the team could not sell Matsui merchandise until he passed his physical.

Due to the holidays, Matsui didn't travel to New York for his physical and introductory press conference until the middle of January. And the scene upon his arrival looked like some hybrid of The Beatles' movie *A Hard Day's Night* and a Tom Clancy spy novel.

Matsui was scheduled to arrive at an airport in Newark, New Jersey, around 4 P.M. on January 9, 2003. Long before his plane landed, there was a crowd of 150 reporters and cameramen—most of whom were from Japan—waiting to chronicle his first steps on American soil.

Matsui's arrival was so hotly anticipated that the *New York Post* reported Japanese photographers took pictures of the terminal—before Matsui's flight even landed.

Alas, those waiting to capture Matsui left disappointed. The flight—a Continental flight 0008—landed at 4:01 P.M., and a few minutes later, a passenger on the plane walked into the terminal and, according to the *New York Post*, announced, "He's coming! He's on his way!"

But Matsui never appeared. An hour later, according to the *New York Post*, Continental Airlines spokesman Gavin Darrugh invoked the spirit of Elvis Presley when he dramatically announced, "Ladies and gentlemen, Mr. Matsui has left the building. That's all I can tell you."

The security personnel inside Newark Airport were no more cooperative in helping the reporters determine Matsui's location. One policeman told the *Post,* "They didn't tell us" where Matsui went. Another told the newspaper Matsui did "not [go] through here."

As it turned out, much to the chagrin of the reporters gathered to document his arrival, Matsui had been squired away by the Yankees' suffocating security corps, who designed an anonymous arrival at the airport and an unencumbered trip to his midtown Manhattan hotel.

"[Matsui's] arrival [at] the airport was not well-choreographed by the Yankees," *New York Times* Yankees beat writer Tyler Kepner said. "They could have been better-prepared for that, in terms of giving us the heads-up as to what he was going to do."

Rumors abounded that Matsui would be staying at the Waldorf-Astoria, but the Japanese reporters who camped out there did so for naught, because Matsui ended up arriving at a different hotel via an underground entrance. Yankees security hurried Matsui up to a seventh-floor suite, where he met with Yankees owner George Steinbrenner and assistant general manager Jean Afterman, the latter of whom had scouted Matsui during the 2002 season.

"He's thrilled to be here," Afterman told the *New York Post*. "Who wouldn't be?"

The Yankees didn't seem thrilled to see the *Post* outside Matsui's hotel. The *Post* reported that Yankees security "tried to shoo away" reporter Michael Morrissey and his photographer, while hotel personnel tried to convince the newspaper duo that Matsui was resting following his 13-hour flight and planned to stay in his room for the night.

"He's in the nest and he's not coming out," a doorman told the *Post*.

Twenty minutes later, Matsui walked out.

The *Post* reported he was dressed in a beige turtleneck and dark winter coat and generally looked as if he were tired from his long flight. But he gave an indication he was just as polite and good-natured as advertised once Morrissey hollered, "Welcome to New York, Mr. Matsui."

The typical superstar would either ignore and/or glower at reporters camped outside his hotel, but Matsui turned towards the reporter and quietly said, "Thank you" as he bowed his head. Matsui then got into the passenger seat of a Suzuki Grand Vitara and sped off to enjoy a private night out on the town.

His next public appearance would be considerably less secretive.

The delay between Matsui's signing and his introductory press conference was probably just as well, since the Yankees' PR department no doubt needed every extra second to prepare for a media gathering that was enormous even by Big Apple standards.

The interest in Matsui was so great the Yankees had to move the January 14 press conference from the team's offices in the Bronx to the Marriott Marquis hotel in midtown Manhattan. "This is the biggest news conference the Yankees have ever had," Yankees media relations director Rick Cerrone told reporters. Such a proclamation was pretty impressive indeed considering the Yankees had been the king of free agent signings for more than a quarter-century.

By dawn, Japanese reporters were already gathering outside the seventh-floor banquet hall housing the press conference. By 9 A.M., the hallway was packed. And by the time the press conference started at noon, more than 300 reporters, nearly 30 television crews and dignitaries ranging from Yankees manager Joe Torre and ace pitcher Roger Clemens to New York City Mayor Michael Bloomberg showed up at the Marriott Marquis to greet Matsui.

New York Post columnist Mike Vaccaro described the scene as some combination of "the Beatles arriving at JFK back in '64. This was Sinatra at the old Paramount, clogging the streets with crazed bobby soxers. This was every massive media photo op you've ever seen, multiplied by 40."

WFAN Yankees beat reporter Sweeney Murti also found the scene Beatles-esque. "The place was just bonkers," Murti said. "I remember going around [as a] couple of people walked in. They had a big dais up on the stage [and] I said, 'Hey can you point out to me which one is [Beatles drummer] Ringo [Starr]?' It was just an amazing scene, trying to see exactly what was going on."

Bloomberg, who grew up rooting for the hated Boston Red Sox and was currently a fan of the crosstown Mets, opened the festivities. "Those who compete in New York City are at the top of their game," Bloomberg said. "And as the famous song goes, 'If you can make it here, you'll make it anywhere.'"

It didn't take long for Matsui to get a taste of New York's demanding ways. The first question he received after stepping to the podium came from a television reporter who asked Matsui how he felt following his subpar All-Star series performance in November.

"I would just accept the result," Matsui said through interpreter Bob Norton. "I will try hard when I get here to show what I can do here."

Matsui could do no wrong during his first day in the big city. He spoke poignantly about Ground Zero, which he visited prior to the press conference. "I still can't believe something like that happened," he said. "It does hurt my heart."

He also spoke reverentially about the Yankees and fabled Yankee Stadium. "I cannot wait to stand in the batter's box at Yankee Stadium, where very honorable players and very famous players have stepped in," he said.

Few of those players had the advance hype and billing of Matsui, who was expected to pay huge dividends for the Yankees on and off the field. Torre, who interrupted his annual Hawaiian vacation in order to personally greet his new left fielder—"I thought it was important for me to be here; this is not someone coming from a different team, he's coming from a different country"—was hesitant to estimate how much Matsui would play or where he would play.

"Left field, right field, I don't know—Raul Mondesi is a pure right fielder," Torre said. "We have a lot of things to do . . . right now, I haven't got a clue."

While most scouts and observers didn't expect Matsui to approach his Japanese gaudy home run totals in America—where the baseballs are larger and less tightly wound than in Japan—Cashman was confident Matsui's plate patience and ability to spray the ball into the gaps would make him "the type of player we like to build our offense around."

Even more importantly, Matsui was the type of person the Yankees could build a marketing campaign around. "We can capitalize on this from a baseball perspective, and we can capitalize on it financially as well," Cashman told *Newsday*. "Because a lot more revenue sources are going to open up if we handle it correctly."

The Yankees had nothing to worry about when it came to Matsui's ability to handle the media crush. Despite the constant clicking of cameras and rat-a-tat-tat pace of the questions, Matsui appeared at ease throughout the press conference and on an appearance later in the evening on *The Late Show with David Letterman*, where Matsui read a "Top 10" list titled: "Reasons I, Hideki Matsui, signed with the New York Yankees."

The number one reason? "Dude, this city never sleeps!"

Referring to the press coverage, Matsui said, "It's pretty much the same in Japan. If I can somehow work out a good relationship with the media, it will be best for me and for the media."

Most of the American reporters had never seen Matsui play in person, but that didn't stop the Japanese reporters from swarming their American brethren and asking them how they thought Matsui would fare with the Yankees.

While Torre hadn't seen nearly enough of Matsui on the field to know whether or not he could help the Yankees, he'd seen enough at the press conference to know Matsui could handle life as a marquee player on baseball's marquee team. "I'm not saying he's going to be successful," Torre said, "but if he fails, I don't think it's going to be because he can't handle it emotionally. That's a big part of what goes on in New York—the expectations, the media—and it will only be enhanced with the Japanese media."

A month later, Torre would find out just how enhanced it would be.

Matsui arrived in Tampa, site of the Yankees' spring training facility, February 10—less than 90 minutes after he arrived on a flight from Newark, six days before position players were supposed to report and eight days before the Yankees' first full squad workout.

He'd never even swung a bat in the Western Hemisphere but he was already almost as famous in Tampa as the NFL's

Buccaneers, who had won the Super Bowl less than two weeks earlier. Upon landing at the Tampa airport, Matsui was greeted by a sign reading, "Tampa Bay, Spring Training Home of the New York Yankees, Welcomes Hideki 'Godzilla' Matsui, Japan's Home Run Champion!"

After some jogging and coordination drills, Matsui told the *New York Post* that he felt "a little anxiety because this is my first experience in trying to become a major league player."

And with Matsui came the Japanese press corps, which, in the estimate of *Newsday* columnist Jon Heyman, momentarily doubled the number of year-round Japanese residents in the Tampa-St. Petersburg area. Yankee players had been told what to expect in terms of the increased media attention, but what they saw in Tampa still surprised veterans and newcomers alike.

Shortstop Derek Jeter and catcher Jorge Posada were the only Yankees to arrive at Legends Field before Matsui. "We were practicing in the minor league complex, and then [Matsui] comes around," Posada said. "And he's got 100 people following him. We thought, 'This is gonna be a fiasco. It's gonna be really tough.'"

Those who arrived in the subsequent days expressed similar sentiments. "I thought it was a zoo around here before," Yankees pitcher Mike Mussina said. "[And now it's] twice the zoo."

"It was amazing, the media coverage that follows that team to begin with," said relief pitcher Jason Anderson, who was traded to the Mets for Armando Benitez July 16. "And then you throw in the Japanese reporters on top of that, and it's just a lot of people in one clubhouse. It almost smothers you sometimes."

"We always have a lot of media, [but] it was probably [double the normal coverage during the spring]," said Yankees centerfielder Bernie Williams, who has been with the club since 1991.

Japanese media often camped outside the condominium complex housing several Yankees and the reporters who covered the team. One of those reporters, WFAN's Murti, saw Matsui a few times at the condominium's gym, and Murti felt it necessary to clarify he was there to work out, not to follow Matsui around.

"I remember going up to him one day [inside the Yankees club-house] and through his interpreter telling him, 'Listen, I know there's a lot of people who follow you [around],'" Murti said. "'I don't want you to think I'm one of them. I just happen to live in this complex in spring training, too. I'm just [at the gym] working out. I don't want you to think I'm following you from the ball-park to the gym to every place else.'

"He got a good chuckle out of it," Murti said. "Both of us [got] a chuckle at the way that he's reported."

One hundred Japanese reporters chronicled Matsui's every move in matters as minor as his first-ever batting practice session on February 11, which was carried live back in Japan at 2 A.M. Cameras clicked and pens scribbled as Matsui first hit balls the opposite way before he finally tried going for the fences. On his 32nd swing, Matsui finally hit a home run. Many of the Japanese reporters whispered, "Ichigo," which means "first" in Japanese.

The extra attention was nothing new to Matsui, who told reporters "this is a normal thing" back home. "There's always a lot of media."

The *New York Post* reported that Jeter said, "This is unbelievable" as he observed the throng around Matsui. "Are you guys coming everyday? How do you say 'everyday' in Japanese?"

Said Murti: "I just remember everybody being kind of fascinated by the number of media there watching his batting practice and basically counting the number of home runs he hit in batting practice, which is just ridiculous."

With a laugh, Murti added, "But I did it myself."

The attention paid to Matsui was remarkably similar to the attention received by the Seattle Mariners' trio of Japanese stars, outfielder Ichiro Suzuki and pitchers Kaz Sasaki and Shigetoshi Hasegawa, during their inaugural season with the club. Following Sasaki's bullpen sessions—i.e. glorified games of catch—in the spring of 2000, Mariners catcher Dan Wilson would field numerous questions from the Japanese reporters.

Matsui immediately impressed the Yankees with his performance on and off the field. Reggie Jackson, the former Yankee slugger and current team executive, told *Newsday*, "I love his swing; he'll be successful."

"I thought that he certainly showed good power potential," Yankees infielder Todd Zeile said. "But his swing was not a typical power-like stroke as we're used to in the States. He hit a lot of balls straight away and to left-center, opposite field, and [it] seemed that he would be more conducive to [becoming] a doubles-with-power type of a [hitter].

"As he got more at-bats, I thought he had a great feel for situational hitting, which is not typical for a guy that's a power run producer," Zeile said. "And I thought he showed a lot of great fundamental skills in the outfield."

Matsui's new teammates, many of whom had grown tired of the Yankees' status as the most chronicled team in New York, were stunned at how easygoing Matsui remained in the face of the press corps that followed his every move.

According to newspaper reports, Matsui told Jeter—the Yankees' biggest incumbent star—that "wherever I go, a lot of Japanese media follow me. Please let me know if they bother you."

All this happened before the Yankees' first real workout of the season, scheduled for February 18, and Matsui's first official spring training press conference, scheduled for February 17. Upon arriving in Tampa, Yankees manager Joe Torre predicted spring training would be "mayhem. We're the Yankees. We're used to mayhem. It just increases the number of people who are interested."

Many of those people began filing into the Yankees clubhouse at 8:30 A.M. sharp on the morning of February 17. Five hours later, Matsui, Torre, and Matsui's interpreter, all surrounded by three Yankees security guards, made their way to a press conference underneath a tent on the grounds of Legends Field.

Even media members, long conditioned to expect a frenzied scene around the Yankees, were amazed by the scene surrounding Matsui. "I'd seen similar things with Japanese players, but never to that extent," said Kepner, who had covered the Mets during Tsuyoshi Shinjo's rookie year in 2001. "The first day press conference was huge."

Yet it was also orderly, thanks in large part to the meetings Yankees media relations director Cerrone held with members of the New York chapter of the Baseball Writers Association of America and the Japanese writers who were moving to New York to cover Matsui.

"I had two meetings with Rick Cerrone before spring training, one with a few other New York writers and one with some Japanese media, to kind of prepare ourselves for Matsui," said *Newsday* Yankees beat writer Ken Davidoff, who also doubles as the chairman of the New York BBWAA. "I credit Rick with the idea. We kind of went over everything and I think that helped. There's never been a problem."

The calm surrounding Matsui was a welcome change from the hysteria that engulfed big-budget Japanese pitcher Hideki Irabu in 1997. Irabu, whose rights were acquired from the San Diego Padres April 22, 1997, made just eight minor league starts before the Yankees promoted him to the big league club July 10, 1997.

Like Matsui, Irabu was trailed by a horde of Japanese media, but unlike Matsui, Irabu hated the attention. Irabu broke a photographer's camera, chucked a fastball just above the head of another photographer, and generally alienated the American reporters covering the Yankees—all within his first week in the major leagues.

Lennon, who covered the Yankees in 1997 for *Newsday*, said he believed "the Yankees didn't really know how to handle a player like" Irabu, whom he called "a little bit more of a pioneer" than Matsui.

"[Irabu] needs special treatment, he needs special considerations," said Lennon, who currently covers the Mets for *Newsday*. "I just think they didn't know Irabu. The Yankees had no idea how to help him adjust to life over here and playing baseball over here. And while [Irabu did] have some ability, he wasn't well-equipped to handle [the transition]. There wasn't much of a support group here for him, and I think that was the biggest problem that they ran into with him."

Fortunately for Matsui, Yankees management put to use the lessons they learned from the Irabu experience.

The Yankees helped ease their new star's transition by laying down the ground rules regarding Matsui's press availability. Japanese reporters were allowed in the clubhouse, but their best chance to speak to Matsui would occur during pregame and postgame press conferences outside the locker room. American reporters, meanwhile, could approach Matsui and his interpreter in the clubhouse.

"[The Yankees] kind of keep [the attention surrounding Matsui] a little bit separate from us," said Robin Ventura, who was the Yankees' third baseman until he was traded to the Los Angeles Dodgers July 31. "We don't see [the Japanese media throng] quite as much as he does. He has his own Japanese press conference and it's different [from what the rest of the Yankees deal with], obviously."

The Yankees strictly regimented the access to Matsui, but the Japanese reporters covering the team still had much more opportunity to see and speak to Matsui than they did in Japan. "In Japan, media people cannot come into the locker room," Matsui said. "So the time that [the] media is allowed to interview players [is] actually very limited. It's only right after the game [that] they can interview [players] on the field [and] on the way out of the stadium. But it seems like here, the media have a little more freedom as far as the access to the facility and to the players."

Matsui's transition would also be eased by his media-savvy manager, Torre, who asked the media throng of more than 140 at the first spring training news conference to "be patient" and to not read too much into his spring training maneuverings. "[Matsui] is obviously capable of hitting anywhere besides leadoff," Torre said. "But if I hit him fourth one day and sixth the next, that doesn't mean I didn't like the way he hit fourth the day before."

Said Murti: "Very early on in spring training, [during] his first couple press conferences with the Japanese reporters, [Torre] was asked about where Matsui was going to bat in the order in an intrasquad game—which is silly, but that was the news in Japan. Again, we're talking about having to cover one guy and all the news that goes along with that. And Torre had to say a couple of times those first couple of days 'this is what I do, I move guys around in the order because I want to see what it's all about. I don't know him very well; I want to know my team better by seeing where people fit in the batting order. It's not just him.'"

Torre's firm but patient ways with the media were a godsend for Matsui throughout his rookie season. Torre handled the media better than any other coach or manager in New York, partially because Torre was a born-and-bred New Yorker—he was in the stands at Yankee Stadium when Don Larsen threw a perfect game in Game Five of the 1956 World Series—and partially because Torre spent six years in the media as a broadcaster for the California Angels from 1985 to 1990.

Murti said Torre's dealings with the media are so smooth it's as if he's a "well-oiled machine. He knows exactly how to handle the media on a personal basis.

"He understands [dealing with the media is] part of his job very well," Murti said. "So I think he just saw this as an extension of that in that, sure, he'd have to answer more questions about Matsui and spend a few more minutes with reporters than he already does, just because [of] the extra numbers, [but] I think he did his best to try and set things up in the very beginning."

Torre's ability to patiently deal with the additional Japanese media and their unending thirst for knowledge on Matsui stood in direct contrast to the edginess displayed across town by Mets manager Art Howe, who seemed to chafe at repeated questioning about reserve outfielder Shinjo.

At one point, according to the *New York Times*, Howe told Japanese reporters the Mets might demote Shinjo, even though the Mets had no such plans at the time. Howe later apologized, saying he was just trying to make a joke.

Matsui, who appeared more at ease responding to questions from the Japanese reporters during the inaugural spring training press conference, made it clear the extra attention paid to him half a world away wouldn't affect his preparation or play. "I understand the fact that people in Japan have a lot of expectations," he said. "That, I have no control over. I only have control over myself."

The Yankees' postseason veterans said Matsui's spring training press coverage far exceeded anything any of them had ever experienced during the World Series.

"In getting to the playoffs and World Series," said Zeile, who played for the Mets in the 2000 World Series against the Yankees, "there's the typical focus, [a] different focus all the time—'Who was the guy [that was the story] that day and what do you expect out of him tomorrow?' and all those things. [Matsui is] giving, basically, daily updates. He's doing a diary for the whole country of Japan on a daily basis through the media."

Asked if he had ever seen anyone receive as much media attention as Matsui, Ventura, another member of the 2000 Mets team which fell to the Yankees in the World Series, said, "I think the only thing [that compares] was when [former NBA star] Michael Jordan was in spring training with the White Sox [in 1994]. That was about as close as I've ever seen."

As it turned out, the last thing the Yankees had to worry about during a distraction-riddled spring training was Matsui, who melted into the background as Yankee veterans Jeter and David Wells each sparred with hot-tempered owner George Steinbrenner.

"I think [Matsui] just wants to fit in," Yankees Senior Vice President of Baseball Operations Gordon Blakeley told *Newsday*. "I don't think he wants to be the big fish."

Matsui was certainly the center of attention during the Yankees' first workout of the spring on February 18. A crowd of 2,534—an increase of 83 percent over the crowd of 1,386 that showed up on the same day a year earlier—showed up to watch Matsui stretch and take batting practice with the rest of the Yankees.

No player had ever taken his first swings of spring under the gaze of so many watchful eyes. Torre and several members of the Yankees' front office stood behind the cage as Matsui stepped into the batter's box, and his swings were carried live on the NHK television network in Japan—where it was nearly two o'clock in the morning.

On his fourth swing against batting practice pitcher Roman Rodriguez, Matsui lofted a home run over the right-field fence, which was a good sign for a left-handed hitter who would spend half his season taking aim at the short porch in right field at Yankee Stadium.

"He looks like he knows where the right field fence is," Yankees scout Gene Michael told *Newsday*.

Matsui hit three more homers during the session and impressed the Yankees with his ability to hit line drives in all directions. Afterward, he worked on his defense in left field—he had played centerfield throughout his nine-year career in Japan—and took a few more swings in the cage before meeting with the American newspaper reporters who cover the Yankees.

"He handles himself unbelievably well," Yankees first baseman Jason Giambi told reporters. "He's like Jeter."

Jeter was easily the most visible Yankee—his Visa ad campaign with Steinbrenner, in which he and "The Boss" poked fun at their spring training flap over whether or not Jeter spent too much time on the town, became one of the most popular ads of the year—but the attention he received was nothing compared to the attention received by Matsui.

"Jeter has a lot of media demands, and he chooses to do a lot in terms of commercials and magazine covers," Davidoff said. "But I just don't think it compares [to Matsui]. I don't think it compares to the swarm of people writing every day just about you."

Asked if any other American athlete received as much attention in his home country as Matsui did in Japan, Davidoff said, "I don't cover [golfer] Tiger Woods. That's [the only American athlete] I can think of. It's extraordinary, just the way [Japanese reporters] cover [Matsui's] batting practice at the Yankees' minor league complex."

The attention failed to let up during the second day of work-outs, when Matsui faced star pitchers Mussina and Mariano Rivera during batting practice. Matsui wasn't quite as successful against Mussina, whose combination of mid-90s fastballs and wicked off-speed stuff annually makes him one of the hardest pitchers to hit against in all of baseball, and Rivera, whose "cut" fastball has broken bats and tortured batters for nearly a decade.

After Matsui faced Rivera, the *Newark Star-Ledger* reported that Ventura approached Matsui and said, "That's the best you're going to see. There's no pitcher in the major leagues who throws anything tougher than that."

Mussina and Rivera threw a total of 26 pitches to Matsui, 11 of which Matsui didn't even swing at. Of the 15 he did swing at, none left the park.

Afterward, Mussina found himself answering plenty of queries about a game that was no big deal "in the grand scheme of things."

"They asked [questions] but I didn't make too much [of it]," Mussina said. "[The game] wasn't important to me—I know it was important to them, I know it's important to him, and everybody's trying to make a good first impression. And it is a big deal that he's playing over here. But at the same time, it was [the] first [batting practice]."

It was a pretty big deal for Matsui, who told reporters, "It's been a while since I hit against a live pitcher."

> It was fun. Spring training, [the] first intrasquad game, it's real relaxed.
>
> — Jason Anderson

Maybe it is in 29 other camps. At Tampa's Legends Field, it's a worldwide event.

Matsui played a flawless left field during the Yankees' first intrasquad game February 24 and went 0-for-2 against minor leaguers Anderson and Alex Graman, who were cornered afterward by reporters even though they threw a total of just five pitches to Matsui.

For Anderson, who threw three of those pitches—"the first one was up and away for a ball, the second one, I think, was a fastball away [for] a strike and he took it, and the third pitch, we went in on him and he popped it up behind second base"—it was a crash course in life with the most famous and followed franchise in the world.

Anderson spent 15 minutes talking to reporters from both countries. "By the time I got in there [to the locker room], I think that was about the time [Matsui] was coming out of the game," Anderson said. "So I think all the reporters were going into the locker room waiting for him. There were probably 20 or 30 of them, and we just did a little interview."

This little interview covered plenty of topics, though. "They wanted to know what I thought of him, [did] I think he was going to be a good major league player and [could Anderson] compare him to other major league players," Anderson said.

With a laugh, Anderson, who hadn't yet pitched above Triple-A, said, "He was probably like the third major league guy that I'd faced, so it was tough to answer those questions."

Matsui told reporters he felt comfortable playing left field and "good playing the game" in general. "The more games I can play here, the more I can get the feel and be in better shape," he said.

The biggest Matsui-related news of the day, though, had nothing to do with what he did on the field. After the game, Matsui went to an area dentist. Matsui said he needed to have cavities filled, but Torre said Matsui was going in for a root canal. The Japanese media wondered if they'd have access to Matsui's x-rays.

Such attention to detail among the Japanese press corps was nothing new: Back when Yomiuri Giants slugger Tatsunori Hara missed a game following the removal of a wisdom tooth in the 1980s, a photographer wanted to take a picture of Hara's mouth.

It turned out Warren Cromartie, the American who spent several seasons as a star outfielder with the Yomiuri Giants, was right a few months earlier, when he wrote Matsui couldn't sneeze without it ending up on the front page of the Japanese papers.

The procedure turned out to be a root canal, and Torre gave Matsui the next day off to recover. That turned out to be bigger news in Japan than the root canal itself, because Matsui ended his career in Japan by playing in 1,250 consecutive games—the second-longest "Ironman" streak in Japanese baseball history.

The regular season was more than a month away, but Japanese reporters were already wondering if Torre would allow Matsui to begin a new Ironman streak. Torre believed in regular rest for his players, and no player had played in every regular season game in any of Torre's seven years as the Yankees' skipper.

It didn't sound as if Matsui would become the first Yankee to enjoy "perfect attendance."

"I like to rest pretty much everybody, because it's a tough grind," Torre told reporters. "The danger of having streaks like that is you tend to be handcuffed by it. When a day off would help him and the ball club, you hate to not to be able to do that."

As for the root canal, Matsui told reporters it was "no problem. Just one tooth. It didn't hurt as much as I thought."

Ironically, Matsui earned his first praise from Steinbrenner—who is typically less fun to be around than a root canal—during his day off, when the demanding Steinbrenner made an appearance at the Yankees' complex.

"We've got to be patient with him," Steinbrenner told reporters. "I couldn't be happier with him."

When the regular season began, Matsui would realize how fleeting happiness could be for "The Boss." But Matsui provided Steinbrenner an immediate return on his investment during the Yankees' Grapefruit League opener on February 27.

With Steinbrenner in attendance, Matsui capped a protracted nine-pitch battle with Cincinnati Reds pitcher Jimmy Anderson by hitting a two-run homer to right field. It was the only highlight for the Yankees in their 9-3 loss, and it left Torre gushing afterward.

"There's a lot of things that could make you say, 'The hell with this,' in spring training," Torre told reporters. "But he was locked in, and he really hit a rocket."

Matsui's presence created a sizable buzz in the air at Legends Field, which was filled to capacity with 10,169 fans, many of whom no doubt sampled the five types of sushi—priced between $7 and $9—available at the new Japanese food kiosk in the concession area.

Asked what he thought of the sushi bar by Dave Buscema, a columnist for the *Times-Herald Record* of upstate Middletown, Matsui laughed and said, "It's gone too far."

The game was also carried live in Japan, even though it started at 3:15 A.M. local time.

"I was very impressed," Torre told reporters. "Very impressed with his first day."

Matsui continued to enjoy an eventful spring. With executives from the Yomiuri Giants in attendance at Legends Field on March 3, Matsui went 3-for-3 with a homer and three RBI.

"I was happy to see them after a long time," Matsui told reporters.

Matsui wasn't quite as successful on the field on March 5, when he went 0-for-2 with a sacrifice fly and misplayed two fly balls in left field in the Yankees' 9-2 loss to the Minnesota Twins. However, it was still a day to remember for Matsui because his father, Masao, and his high school coach, Tomoshige Yamashita, were there to see him in person for the first time since he left Japan.

The elder Matsui and Yamashita remained in Tampa throughout the weekend, during which time Yamashita regaled the American reporters with recollections of Matsui's teenaged years.

"My house was across the road from our high school stadium," Yamashita told *Newsday* through an interpreter. "Hideki would hit home run balls and they would crash on my house—into the house. On the roof. He broke the windows. Many times he did this. And my house was 113 meters [371 feet] away."

The presence of his mentors seemed to soothe the always-calm Matsui, who was seen eating Japanese food at his locker before the Yankees' 7-4 win over the Twins on March 8. His father told *Newsday* that "I haven't seen him look so happy for years."

Matsui made news on both sides of the world on March 11. He missed an afternoon game against the Detroit Tigers with a stiff neck, which was noteworthy in Japan because of Matsui's well-documented durability.

Later in the evening, Matsui wowed the American press corps by going out to dinner with the 10 newspaper, website, and radio reporters who cover the Yankees on a regular basis. Matsui also regularly ate with reporters in Japan. Takahir Horikawa, a sportswriter for the *Asahi Shimbun*, told the *Newark Star-Ledger* that Matsui dined with writers partially because "he hates to eat alone."

Matsui, though, seemed to genuinely enjoy the company of those who covered him, which made him something of a rarity among major leaguers. Social interaction between writers and players is almost unheard of in America. where ballplayers are trained to maintain only the most limited of relationships with media members. Even Ventura, unfailingly polite and accommodating to reporters, expressed shock when the *New York Times*' Jack Curry asked him if he'd ever dine with a reporter.

"This is something [Matsui] didn't have to do," Murti said. "It was kind of a 'get to know you' type of gesture. It was fun. We talked about some baseball, we talked about other things in general."

Murti was most impressed by how interested Matsui appeared in actually getting to know the reporters on the Yankees beat. "I remember going around the table, everybody introducing themselves and him being very interested in what we do and who we work for," Murti said. "And from that day on, he knew every one of our names. I've had guys that I've walked up to and introduced myself to 50 times [and they] still don't know my name."

Matsui's new teammates, meanwhile, were continually impressed by his performance on and off the field. "He's very fundamentally sound," Anderson said. "I think he was always working on things. He was just trying to get adjusted to American pitching, and I'm sure there [were] other differences he had [to get used to], like the language barrier [and] being in a different country."

Most of all, the Yankees were impressed with Matsui's ability to fit into the clubhouse and remain composed despite his celebrity status. "I'm sure it was bothering him, I think it would affect anybody, having that much press and the expectations that were placed on him," Anderson said. "But he didn't show it. I think it was good for the team, and it showed us that if it wasn't a big distraction to him, then it shouldn't be a big distraction to us."

Matsui also curried favor with his teammates and employers with his generosity. According to the *Newark Star-Ledger*, he handed out toy Godzillas—in honor of his nickname—to the Yankees who had children. Later in the season, Matsui would be the only Yankee player to give general manager Brian Cashman a gift following the birth of Cashman's son.

Matsui spent the remainder of the Grapefruit League schedule in relative anonymity, at least by his standards. When the Yankees were showcasing 2002 left fielder Rondell White for a potential trade—he was eventually dealt to the San Diego Padres—Matsui saw some time as the designated hitter. Later in the spring, the Yankees put Matsui in centerfield—the position he played regularly in Japan—to gauge whether or not they could rely upon him as a fill-in for regular centerfielder Williams.

Matsui impressed Torre with a pair of nice running catches against the Twins on March 22 and the Tigers on March 24. "He gets a good jump," Torre said following the Twins game.

Matsui ended the Grapefruit League season with a .324 average, three homers, and 10 RBI. He led the Yankees with 22 hits and two triples. He also drew four walks and struck out just six times, the latter of which especially pleased Torre, who hoped the Yankees would drastically reduce their strikeouts in 2003. The Yankees struck out an American League-high 1,171 times in 2002.

Before the Yankees' regular season opener in Toronto, Torre told reporters he hoped his hotly hyped rookie could "get a couple of knocks and settle in," unlike White, who never got untracked in April 2002 and struggled throughout his only season with the Yankees.

"I am hoping he gets off to a good start, because in spite of the numbers we talk about and what he has done in Japan, this is a new league, a new year, a new club and we are all human," Torre told the *New York Post*. "We are not robots, and if you don't start out well, there is going to be more pressure. Rondell White last year was trying to be so good so bad that he put a lot of pressure on himself and had trouble relaxing."

Those who had covered Matsui throughout the spring predicted big things for him. "I remember guessing that he would hit about .305 with 25 home runs and 105 RBI," Murti said. "I remember thinking—and saying on the air—that he was going to knock in 100 runs by accident, just because [of] the people that were going to be batting in front of him: [Alfonso] Soriano, [Derek] Jeter, Bernie Williams, [Jason] Giambi.

"Giambi and Williams, they're on-base monsters, they're .400 on-base percentage guys," Murti said. "If Matsui was going to be batting fifth most of the time, he is, simply by chance, going to be walking up many times with one or both of those guys—or more—on base."

Perhaps the most complimentary assessment was offered by *New York Post* baseball columnist Joel Sherman, who wrote March 30 that he sees "a 2002 Anaheim Angel" in Matsui. The Angels, of course, had won the World Series the previous season with a fundamentally sound, team-first style of play.

"Tough at-bat, fouls off good pitches, excellent eye, able to hit a mistake with authority, hustles on the bases and plays solid defense," Sherman wrote. "In other words, a championship player. If I must be pinned to numbers, a .285 batting average, but more important, a .370 on-base percentage and a .470 slugging percentage to go along with 25 homers and 90 RBIs."

During a press conference the day before the Yankees' regular season opener against the Blue Jays in Toronto, Matsui said he "still can't anticipate my statistics. It would certainly be great if I could have some good results, but I just have to focus one game at a time."

Unfortunately for Matsui and the Yankees, their focus on the season opener was interrupted shortly after they arrived in Toronto, when they learned the Blue Jays marketing department had run a rather tasteless anti-Yankee ad in the city's newspapers. The ad pictured a Yankee cap soiled by two bird droppings. Above the cap were the words "Boo Matsui" written in both Japanese and English.

"To me, I thought it was tasteless, especially in the climate of what's going on in the world today," an obviously annoyed Torre told reporters. "I can understand fun and games and all that stuff, but I thought maybe it was a little too much."

Jim Bloom, the Blue Jays' director of consumer marketing, defended the ad by telling reporters it was intended to appeal to Yankee-haters and get a rise out of a Blue Jays fan base that had grown apathetic since the club's back-to-back World Series championships in 1992 and 1993.

"The advertising agency said, 'You have to wake people up,'" Bloom told reporters. "I have respect for the Yankees' legacy, but when the show comes to town, they have to expect people to use that to market their product. We aren't showing disrespect to Matsui, but he was the high-profile signing by the Yankees.

"When you lose 60 percent of your fan base, we have a big boulder to push up the mountain," Bloom said. "If it sells tickets, it accomplished what we wanted."

It also annoyed almost everyone on the Yankees, as the *New York Post* reported in its March 31 editions. Giambi told the paper the ad "went a little far; they could have done without that."

"Pretty weak," Ventura said.

"Stupid," Posada said.

The only person who didn't seem offended by the ad was Matsui, who, as expected, laughed off the controversy. The day the "Boo Matsui" ad appeared in the Toronto papers, Torre told reporters that Matsui "has a great personality. He seems to be having fun."

Regarding the "Boo Matsui" furor, Matsui told reporters "I'm a little happy that the fans were actually aware of my name."

It wouldn't take long for everyone to become aware of Hideki Matsui.

Earning His Stripes

One week into the season, there were two questions surrounding Hideki Matsui:

1.) Where's the power?

2.) Was it too early to already name him the Rookie of the Year?

Other first-year players got off to quick starts in the American League, but none did so with two countries watching their every move. And every day, it seemed, Matsui did something different to help the Yankees win a game.

On Opening Day March 31 in Toronto, Matsui laced the first official Major League Baseball pitch he ever saw from Blue Jays starter Roy Halladay into left field for an RBI single to drive home Derek Jeter with the Yankees' first run of the season in the top of the first inning.

Ironically, the Blue Jays had not used Halladay during spring training games against the Yankees in hopes of keeping him "under wraps" until the season opener.

"I was very happy to get a hit in my first at-bat," Matsui told reporters afterwards. "I was very excited as well. In any at-bat, I try to hit my pitch, even if it's early. The pitch I was looking for came in on the first pitch."

It was a first hit witnessed by millions of giddy Yankee fans in the tri-state area. Hours before the first pitch of the season, the YES Network, which was scheduled to carry more than 130 Yankee games during the regular season, and Cablevision, the cable provider for all of Long Island and much of Westchester County, reached an agreement to put YES on Cablevision systems.

The agreement ended a year-long impasse between YES and Cablevision, which used to carry Yankee games on its MSG Network until George Steinbrenner formed the YES Network prior to the 2002 season. Cablevision did not carry YES on its systems in 2002, ostensibly because Cablevision refused to offer YES on its basic cable stations, as YES demanded.

Unfortunately for Yankee fans, the settlement between YES and Cablevision, Matsui's first notable big league achievement and the Yankees' 8-4 win over the Blue Jays and future 22-game winner Halladay were overshadowed by the loss of Jeter, who separated his left shoulder during a third-inning collision at third base with Blue Jays catcher Ken Huckaby. At first, it was feared Jeter, the heart and soul of the Yankees since their championship run began in 1996, would miss the season, but he ended up missing just six weeks.

With Jeter out, manager Joe Torre said Matsui would be among those considered as candidates to fill in for Jeter in the second spot. "He could hit there, that's a possibility," Torre told reporters in Toronto.

Matsui certainly didn't hurt his cause by going 3-for-10 in the next two games, both Yankees wins, with two RBI and a double that grazed off the top of the left-field wall at Sky Dome and just missed becoming his first major league home run.

After sweeping the Blue Jays, the Yankees visited another AL East doormat, the Tampa Bay Devil Rays. Matsui, whose defense was often described as just adequate in Japan, made a key defensive gem in the first inning of the Yankees' 12-2 win April 4 when he caught Damion Easley's fly ball at the left-field wall. Had it cleared the fence, Easley would have had a three-run homer and the Devil Rays would have had a 4-2 lead.

The Yankees, who opened the season with four consecutive road victories for just the second time in team history, finally lost April 5, but Matsui was the best player on the field in the 6-5 defeat.

In the bottom of the fifth, with the Yankees and Devil Rays tied 2-2, Matsui fielded Aubrey Huff's double off the left-field wall. Carl Crawford scored easily on the play to give the Devil Rays a 3-2 lead, but Matsui fired the ball into shortstop Erick Almonte, who in turn threw to catcher Jorge Posada in time to nail Rocco Baldelli, who was attempting to score from first.

Matsui's broken bat single in the top of the sixth gave the Yankees a 4-3 lead. A few moments later, he displayed the natural baseball instincts the Yankees had been raving about for nearly a year.

Matsui attempted to score on Bubba Trammell's shallow single to centerfield, but the throw from Baldelli beat Matsui to the plate. However, Matsui evaded the tag of catcher Toby Hall by hooking his slide and touching home with his hand.

"We all marveled at how committed he was when he made the call on the ball that was hit," Torre told reporters. "That was a great read on his part. And he committed to that. He didn't start, stop, start, stop. Even if he was wrong, it's more important to be decisive."

Bernie Williams told reporters Matsui was "becoming a very important part of the team, just in the way he plays the game. He's very fundamentally sound."

The Yankees got back on track the following day with a 10-5 victory in which Matsui went 1-for-5. Six games into his career and Matsui already had a six-game hitting streak, even if some of the Japanese reporters following the team were beginning to wonder just when Matsui would hit his first major league home run.

Despite the lack of power, Matsui's teammates were impressed with his professional approach at the plate and his ability to deliver in key situations. "He quickly established himself as more than a power threat," Yankees infielder Todd Zeile said. "He hit the ball to the opposite field, he'd come up with base hits with men in scoring position. He did all the things as a hitter that you expect out of a situational-type hitter."

Still, his fans back home were concerned over Matsui's power outage. Complicating matters for Matsui was the fact eight other Yankees had already hit at least one homer.

"He looks to me like he's trying to hit a home run," Torre told reporters during the series against the Devil Rays. "And it's understandable. He wants to get in on all the fun."

Matsui, his fans, and those who covered him wouldn't have to wait long.

The Yankees' home opener, scheduled for April 7, was postponed by the time the club departed St. Petersburg, Florida, the afternoon of April 6. Heavy snow was in the forecast, and the Yankees, who had been criticized for playing the 1996 home opener during a steady snowstorm, played it safe by rescheduling the game for April 8.

Before the postponement was announced, Matsui expressed excitement over his imminent debut at Yankee Stadium. "I am really looking forward to it and I am really excited," Matsui told the *New York Post*. "The regular season has started, but I will have a special feeling for Opening Day at Yankee Stadium."

Ironically, the Yankees' home opener would be started by Andy Pettitte, who was also on the mound for the snowy 1996 home opener which remains a popular "Yankees Classic" staple on the YES Network.

There would be no snow this time around, but thanks to Matsui, the 2003 home opener would end up a "Yankees Classic" favorite as well.

Most of the 33,109 fans who poured through the Yankee Stadium turnstiles on this cold and drab Tuesday afternoon (gametime temperature was 35 degrees) had never seen Matsui play in person, but judging by the plethora of Matsui jerseys and t-shirts in the stands—and the one guy who showed up dressed as "Godzilla" in honor of Matsui's nickname—he was already one of the most popular players on the team.

The only two jerseys shown on the Yankees' website store were Jeter's number 2 and Matsui's number 55. *Newsday* reported that The Sports Authority, a local sporting goods franchise, had sold 80 percent of its Matsui t-shirts and 50 percent of its Matsui jerseys by April 3, four days before the Yankees' scheduled home opener. His merchandise was selling at a much higher rate than that of Tom Glavine, the future Hall-of-Fame pitcher who had recently signed a free agent deal with the Mets.

"[Matsui's popularity is] very uncommon," The Sports Authority market sales manager Terry Goldstein told *Newsday*. "When Jeter was in his rookie year, we were close to sell-outs."

Other Matsui memorabilia was hot as well. According to beckett.com—the bible of sports collectibles—a baseball autographed by Matsui was going for as much as $379, considerably more than baseballs autographed by all-time single-season home run king Barry Bonds ($279), popular home run hitter Sammy Sosa ($279), Jeter ($269), and superstar Alex Rodriguez ($119).

The Yankees' promotion schedule at Yankee Stadium featured a Matsui bobblehead doll day July 22. He was the only rookie in Major League Baseball with his own bobblehead doll day.

Overseas, Matsui's replica Giants jersey was selling for $380 on sportsjapan.com, which was also selling t-shirts and hand towels ($39 each) and figurines ($24).

By nightfall Tuesday, those prices were probably even higher.

I n retrospect, perhaps everyone should have known Matsui's first magical Yankee moment would occur against the Minnesota Twins. On May 17, 2002, in the middle of a drenching rain, Jason Giambi, the Yankees' heavily-hyped free agent acquisition, ended six weeks of heavy boos by the Yankee faithful with a 12th inning walk-off grand slam home run against the Twins.

The dramatic blast jump-started Giambi, who entered play May 17 hitting a pedestrian .286 with eight homers and 24 RBI. From May 17 through the end of the regular season, though, Giambi hit .325 (132-for-406) with 33 homers and 98 RBI. Eventually, Giambi would refer to his grand slam against the Twins as the moment in which he earned his stripes as a Yankee and earned acceptance from Yankee fans.

And so here were the Twins again, unwilling participants in Yankees history.

Before his historic grand slam, Matsui had almost melted into the background from the moment he arrived at Yankee Stadium shortly after 11 A.M. He was one of the first Yankees at the park, so early, in fact, that there were only a handful of diehard fans hanging out near the players' entrance, which is typically mobbed hours before first pitch.

Inside, the *Newark Star-Ledger* reported Matsui sorted through fan mail and answered countless questions about the weather, how he had slept the night before, and his superstitions.

On the field, Matsui's first two at-bats—a ground out to second in the second inning and a walk in the fourth inning—came and went without much fuss. But he had won acclaim from the notoriously hard-to-please Yankee fans in the top of the fourth inning, when he hustled to cut off Torii Hunter's shot into the left-center gap and limited Hunter to a double and the Twins to one run on the play.

A buzz enveloped Yankee Stadium in the bottom of the fifth, when, with the crowd chanting "Mat-soo-ee," Matsui strode to the plate with two outs, the bases loaded and the Yankees leading 3-1.

As he watched from the dugout, Robin Ventura—a player with his own flair for the dramatic; he was the active leader in grand slam homers with 16—had a premonition something unforgettable was about to happen.

"I just have this eerie feeling," Ventura reportedly said to the teammate seated next to him, Roger Clemens.

Matsui made Ventura look like a genius and made the fans at Yankee Stadium deliriously happy—when he crushed a full-count changeup from Joe Mays and hit a no-doubt-about-it *manruidan* (grand slam) into the bleachers beyond right-center field.

It marked the first time in the 80-year history of Yankee Stadium that a Yankee newcomer had hit a grand slam in his first home game. In addition, Matsui was only the fifth player in team history to hit a grand slam for his first major league home run and the first since Horace Clarke in 1965.

"This is going to make a huge star out of the guy," Ventura told *Newsday* afterward.

Matsui slowly trotted around the bases, seemingly oblivious to the frenzy around him. The words "home run" appeared on the Yankee Stadium scoreboard in both English and Japanese. The crowd continued to stand and roar even after Matsui walked into the dugout, where Torre motioned for him to go out and accept his curtain call.

"It didn't take much coaxing," Torre told reporters. "He must have done it before."

Another singularly grand moment for a new Yankee.

"Special players do big things," Twins manager Ron Gardenhire told *Newsday*. "Jason did the same thing to us.

"A special moment in New York. What's new?"

The next day, Matsui's accomplishment was splashed across the back *and* front pages of all three New York tabloids, which was no small feat considering America was at war with Iraq. *Newsday*'s front page "skyline" featured a picture of Matsui following through on his grand slam with the words "Grand Opening: Matsui Slam Leads Yanks to Victory in Stadium Debut," while the back page pictured Matsui doffing his cap and the words "Monster Mash."

Even longtime Yankees, so used to the magical moments which had engulfed Yankee Stadium the previous seven seasons—two no-hitters, two perfect games, and countless goosebump-inducing moments during the postseason—were amazed at Matsui's flair for the dramatic.

Pettitte, the winning pitcher in the home opener, told reporters "It seems like every year something special happens that amazes you, like Hideki hitting that grand slam."

"It was a lot of fun to see that," Posada said. "We were on the road [for the first week] and he didn't hit a home run. He was pressing a little bit. And then he gets home and hits a grand slam to help us win the game in the pouring rain. It takes a lot of concentration to do what he did."

"It was great, it was fun, [a] great moment for him, and I was happy for him," Zeile said. "That was great, to be able to endear himself [to] the city and the fans the way he did from the first day."

Matsui appeared pleased yet far from overwhelmed after the game, which didn't surprise those who had seen him during his days in Japan. "By no means does he overlook [the history of the Yankees]," said MLBradio.com host Seth Everett, who covered the All-Star Series in Japan in November 2002. "He's not in awe of Yankee Stadium."

Maybe not, but Matsui knew enough to invoke the history of the hallowed place during his postgame interviews. He told the *Newark Star-Ledger* that he "had the feeling it was going to be a home run" when it left his bat but that he "didn't feel like I hit it by myself. It was like there was other energy, other power helping me hit it."

Prodded further, Matsui told the questioner that "other power" was provided by the rabid Yankee fans and the legendary Yankees who were immortalized in Monument Park beyond the left-field fence.

Matsui said his parents and brother, who were in the stands for the game, were happier about the home run than he. But he did admit, "When I look back [on the grand slam], I may say this was the moment that made me feel comfortable as a member of the Yankees."

Matsui's special moment would be preserved forever in the National Baseball Hall of Fame, which requested the bat Matsui used to hit the grand slam. It would be displayed along with several other artifacts from the 2003 season.

And his special moment was viewed on Channel 2, the local CBS affiliate, by more than 500,000 viewers. The game drew an 8.0 rating, an increase of 16 percent from 2002 and the highest rating for a Yankees' Opening Day in at least five seasons.

By the next day, who knows how many of those couch potatoes were telling folks they'd seen Matsui's grand entrance in person? As *Newsday*'s Marty Noble wrote: "60,000 will say they saw it all."

And in his eighth game, Matsui went hitless.

Matsui's first week in pinstripes was so impressive that it was noteworthy when he finally endured the first "0-fer" of his big league career against the Twins April 9. But the 31,898 fans at Yankee Stadium, still abuzz over Matsui's fireworks the day before, applauded him throughout the evening.

"So we had a good game," Gardenhire told *Newsday* following the Yankees' 2-1 win. "We got Matsui out."

The Twins weren't nearly as fortunate the following afternoon, when Matsui's two-run opposite field double in the third inning accounted for all the offense in the Yankees' 2-0 win. Matsui went 3-for-4 with two other opposite field singles, and he would have been 4-for-4 if not for the nifty bare-handed play Twins pitcher Rick Reed made on Matsui's grounder up the middle in the first inning.

"He's an aggressive hitter," Torre told reporters afterward. "He has an idea what he wants to do, but he's still learning. He's facing pitchers he's never faced before. The one thing that surprises me is that he doesn't swing and miss."

"I haven't been able to adjust yet to hit home runs, so what I'm concentrating on is to just make contact and hit the ball properly," Matsui told reporters. "Hopefully, as time goes, I'll hit more home runs."

The Yankees were getting to the point where they were no longer surprised by anything Matsui did. After a Grapefruit League season in which he spent most of his time pulling the ball to the right side of the field, Matsui hit the ball the other way with impressive regularity during the first two weeks of the regular season.

"[In Japan] I pulled [the ball] more, but a lot of the pitches [thus far] are away, so I'm focusing on hitting the ball as hard as I can, and they go in the opposite direction," Matsui told reporters.

"He's a very good clutch hitter," Posada said. "He's a very good guy when [it] comes to [hitting with] guys in scoring position and two outs. [He] gets the key hit."

His RBI opposite field single with two outs in the bottom of the ninth inning lifted the Yankees past the Devil Rays, 5-4, April 12. The game-winning hit was quickly dubbed a "sayonara hit" by the New York media.

The "sayonara hit" also proved Matsui's resiliency: Two innings earlier, with the bases loaded and the game tied 4-4, Matsui hit into an inning-ending double play.

"You don't get too many opportunities to redeem yourself in the same game," Torre told reporters. "He took advantage."

Matsui told reporters he was "relieved to get that hit at the end."

With a laugh, he added, "Maybe if I didn't get a hit there, I wouldn't have come back alive."

Nobody in baseball was quite as alive as the Yankees, whose 9-1 record through April 12 tied the franchise's best 10-game start ever. And in those 10 games, Matsui had become an indispensable member of a team which already featured an ace pitcher barreling towards 300 wins (Clemens), the most exciting young player in the game (Alfonso Soriano), and numerous potential future Hall-of-Famers (Williams, Giambi, Jeter, and Mariano Rivera)

"[Matsui is] such a calm individual," Torre told reporters. "His calm and professionalism give him a presence on this ball club. But it was important, I think, to get a couple of key situations the first home stand and be able to deliver both times."

Matsui delivered yet again April 15, when, on a frigid night at Yankee Stadium, he hit a tie-breaking three-run homer in the sixth inning to propel the Yankees past the Blue Jays, 10-6. His homer landed in the upper deck above, ironically enough, an advertisement for the Far East industrial equipment company Komat'su.

The Blue Jays had played the Yankees just five times and still had 14 games to play against the Bronx Bombers, but the Blue Jays were already alternately numb to and impressed by Matsui's apparent mastery of them. "Whew, he can rake," Blue Jays infielder Orlando Hudson told the *New York Post*. "He can flat-out hit. That's a good hitter, very patient at the plate. It helps that he's in a great lineup. He's patient like the rest of them, and [he] always hits the ball square.

"He fits perfectly in the puzzle over there."

Matsui wasn't done tormenting the Blue Jays. Two nights later, Matsui capped his first Yankee Stadium home stand by hitting a two-run double in the 43-degree cold to help the Yankees beat the Blue Jays, 4-0. Matsui hit an impressive .313 (10-for-32) during the home stand with four extra base hits (two homers and two doubles) and a blistering 12 RBI.

"When you move somebody from one culture to another, you wonder if his ability is going to translate," Torre told reporters after the game. "I think he's answered the question very quickly."

Asked to explain his early success at home, Matsui once again gave a lion's share of the credit to the general aura at Yankee Stadium, just as he did following his grand slam April 8. "I think it's just the support of the fans and the magic of the Stadium," Matsui told reporters.

The Yankees went 7-2 during the home stand to extend their overall record to 12-3. With the season not even one-tenth complete, observers were already comparing the 2003 Yankees to the 1998 club which was recognized as one of the best teams of all-time following a 114-win regular season and a four-game sweep of the San Diego Padres in the World Series.

Many of those observers viewed Matsui as the missing link, the player the Yankees lacked when they disappeared from the playoffs in a shocking first-round loss to the Anaheim Angels six months earlier. *Newsday* columnist Johnette Howard noted on

April 18 that the players most responsible for the Yankees' sizzling start were Matsui, second baseman Soriano, and pitchers Mike Mussina and Jeff Weaver, none of whom had been with the Yankees when they won four World Series in six years between 1996 and 2001.

In addition, Matsui solidified a position that had always been a weakness: He was the Yankees' 11th Opening Day left fielder in as many seasons.

The best compliment may have been a wordless one offered by Posada, who had harshly criticized his teammates following the Yankees' elimination in 2002. Howard reported Posada "just smiled . . . at the mere mention of Matsui's name."

Matsui's popularity outside the locker room, meanwhile, could best be measured this way: He was already an icon in local memorabilia circles.

The *New York Post* reported April 6 that Grandstand Sports & Memorabilia, which commissioned Matsui to sign 48 baseballs for purchase, sold its entire stock within the first week . . . at $359 a ball, no less.

The Yankees continued their winning ways by winning the first six games of a 10-game road trip to Minnesota, Anaheim, and Texas. The 18-3 mark after 21 games was the best in Yankees history and put the Yankees on pace to win an amazing 139 games.

That, of course, wasn't going to happen, but New Yorkers were still giddy over the Yankees and what they might do once star shortstop Jeter and Hall of Fame–caliber closer Rivera returned from the disabled list. *New York Post* columnist Kevin Kernan wrote these Yankees might be a "once-in-a-lifetime team."

But the Yankees' magic carpet ride was about to come to a crashing halt.

The Yankees were in the midst of one of the greatest stretches in team history, but owner George Steinbrenner, who seems to thrive on self-created chaos, sent the Yankees—and, in particular, beloved manager Joe Torre—into disarray April 20, when Steinbrenner ordered general manager Brian Cashman to send struggling Cuban pitcher Jose Contreras—the player Steinbrenner inked to a four-year, $32 million deal Christmas Eve—to the Yankees' Single-A affiliate in Tampa, where Contreras would work with Yankees organizational pitching coach Billy Connors.

Torre was livid—as mad as he's ever been at Steinbrenner, no small feat considering he had worked under the volatile owner since 1996—because Torre said Steinbrenner had told him he could determine Contreras' minor league destination. Torre told reporters he had informed Contreras he'd be heading to Triple-A Columbus, and Torre said the change of heart by Steinbrenner left the manager feeling like "a liar."

"My problem with this is that I sat in my [hotel] room with this young man and told him where he was going," Torre told reporters. "Now it turns out that I was a liar. That, I'm not crazy about. I take pride in my honesty. When that gets questioned, especially when you're dealing with a communication problem, then I have a problem there."

The "problem" between Torre and Steinbrenner dominated New York's back pages for several days, which, in an odd way, was fortuitous for Matsui, because it meant he could endure his first-ever American slump in relative anonymity.

Matsui could do no wrong during his first three weeks in the bigs, but he began falling into an extended funk during the Yankees' four-game series at Minnesota. Coincidentally or not, Matsui's slump started immediately after Torre gave Matsui a "day off."

Matsui, who was eager to maintain the consecutive games streak he'd begun in Japan, wanted nothing to do with a day off. But Torre, who liked to give his starters regular rest, compromised with Matsui by holding him out of the starting lineup April 20 but inserting him into the game as a pinch-runner in the sixth inning.

"In Japan, I never experienced this," Matsui told reporters before the game. "But whatever the Yankees need for me to do for the team, I will follow."

The fact Matsui got some rest during a game was headline-worthy news in Japan. According to the *Newark Star-Ledger*, Matsui had not missed an inning of play since August 1999. Since then, he had played in every single inning in 477 consecutive games—460 games in Japan and 17 games in America.

"I feel very strongly about playing every game," Matsui told reporters.

The Yankees won the game, 8-2, and Matsui ended up getting a hit in his only at-bat, which raised his batting average to .314 and gave him at least one hit in 16 of the Yankees' first 18 games. But Matsui went 0-for-5 the following afternoon to begin a nine-game stretch in which he batted just .150 (6-for-40) with no homers, three RBI, three walks, and eight strikeouts.

The slump dropped Matsui's overall average to .255 by the end of April. "I'm not really satisfied," Matsui told the *New York Daily News*. "Maybe there are some spots where I haven't been able to adjust well to the pitching."

Matsui's skid occurred in relative anonymity in America, though, because the Yankees finished April with a sparkling 21-6 mark. In eight series between March 31 and April 27, the Yankees won seven and split one.

Tougher times were ahead for the Yankees, though. And this time, Matsui would be the target of Steinbrenner's venom.

Godzilla Meets Ichiro

They're the Beatles of Japan.

—JEFF NELSON

I magine the Super Bowl, World Series, and NCAA men's basketball Final Four all rolled into one, and you might have an idea of what the two Yankees-Mariners series in late April and early May meant to the baseball fans of Japan. The country's two most famous baseball exports, the Mariners' Ichiro Suzuki and the Yankees' Hideki Matsui, were finally going to meet on an American diamond.

Jeff Nelson, who opened the season with the Mariners before he was dealt back to the Yankees in August, uttered perhaps the understatement of the century when he said the meeting of the two players was "big for Japan."

Takeo Nakajima, a television analyst in Japan, told the *New York Post* that the Matsui-Suzuki meeting "will be one of the biggest moments in Japan baseball history."

One Japanese baseball executive went even further than that when he told the *Bergen Record* that "[Matsui and Suzuki], together in America, is the biggest thing since Matsui signed with the Yankees.

"And that was the biggest thing ever."

For fans on both sides of the globe, the six games between the Yankees and Mariners in late April and early May provided an opportunity to watch two vastly different players and people.

"It is not fair yet to compare Matsui with Ichiro," Fox TV analyst Tim McCarver told the *New York Post*.

Of course, that's exactly what people were doing on both sides of the globe.

Suzuki was the blazing fast spark plug who could do almost anything at the plate—his teammates, coaches, and managers in Seattle were convinced he could hit 20 homers a season if he wanted to—on the basepaths (he led the AL in stolen bases during his rookie season in 2001) and in the field.

It took just a week in America for Suzuki's cannon-like arm to become the stuff of legend: During the Mariners' eighth game of the season April 11, 2001, Oakland's Terrence Long tried to go from first to third on a single to right field. But Suzuki fired an on-the-fly strike to Mariners third baseman David Bell, who tagged out a stunned Long.

Matsui, meanwhile, was certainly talented, but less flashy and more workman-like than Suzuki. Though he played centerfield, Matsui's defense was considered nothing more than passable, and his speed on the basepaths was almost nonexistent.

"Ichiro, I think he's 10 times the player, just because he can hit to all fields and he can basically do anything and he's got speed," said MLBradio.com host Seth Everett, who used to host the Mariners' postgame radio show. "But Matsui's a gamer. Matsui maximizes his talent. [They're] just totally night and day type of [players and people]."

Charles Gipson, a reserve outfielder who played with the Mariners from 1998 to 2002 and spent the first two months of the 2003 season with the Yankees, told the *New York Daily News* that Suzuki once mentioned his goal was to hit .400.

"I wouldn't doubt he could do it, with his focus, the way he runs and [the way] he hits to all fields," Gipson told the *Daily News*. "People don't understand how good he is. He's a Gold Glove outfielder, he's got a good arm, he's a leadoff guy and can hit with a little power if he wants to and steal bags. He's a tone setter, like [Yankees leadoff man Alfonso] Soriano is. He can hurt you anytime."

Still, Matsui was immeasurably more popular than Suzuki, which chafed Suzuki to no end. "I could hit .400 and still Matsui would get more attention," Suzuki once said.

"Like many baseball fans, regardless [of] whether [they're in] the United States or Japan, they love guys that can hit home runs," said *Newsday* reporter David Lennon, who covered the All-Star Series in Japan in November 2002. "They become folk heroes, and that's what Matsui became by hitting so many home runs. [Japanese fans] could certainly appreciate [it] and loved Ichiro for what he could do hitting-wise, the way he could hit for average and his speed and his defense. [But] Matsui they admired for his home run–hitting ability."

Matsui attained superstar status in Japan during his days at Seiryo High School, when he hit a record 60 home runs in his career and earned the nickname "Godzilla" for his powerful exploits. By the time he was a senior, Matsui was so legendary that one opponent, Meitoku High, intentionally walked him five times in a single playoff game.

In June 1992, the 18-year-old Matsui was drafted first overall by the Yomiuri Giants. Matsui had a quiet rookie season (he hit .223 with 11 homers and 27 RBI in 57 games) but began evolving into the nation's premier power hitter in 1994.

Matsui's feats garnered greater acclaim because he played in Japan's Central League—the larger and more scrutinized of the country's two baseball circuits—for the Yomiuri Giants, who were the most popular and tradition-steeped team in Japan.

Suzuki, meanwhile, spent most of his professional career in Japan in relative anonymity. He wasn't selected until the fourth round of the 1991 draft, and he didn't reach the Japanese big leagues for good with the Orix Blue Wave of the lesser-known Pacific League until 1994.

In fact, Suzuki had to move to America in order to attain icon status in his home country. "Once Ichiro came [to America], MLB International started broadcasting Mariner games in Japan," Everett said. "So he was on TV more when he was with the Mariners than he was when he was with the Orix Blue Wave.

"Ichiro's popularity grew to rock star status [when he succeeded in America]," Everett said. "He was [already] a legend in baseball circles, and then he became a rock star once he came to America, because he was the first [position player] to do it."

Everett called Suzuki "Elvis," and Suzuki certainly struck a distinctive pose with his sideburns, his snazzy play, and desire to be called by his first name only (in fact, his Mariner uniform reads "Ichiro" instead of "Suzuki"). Matsui, on the other hand, more easily melted into a crowd, which was a good trait to have as a member of one of the few teams in baseball that did not put the names of its players on the back of its uniforms.

There was also an intriguing aura around the reluctant superstar Suzuki, who at one point during his rookie season in 2001 refused to talk to the Japanese reporters who had followed him halfway around the world. By the 2003 season, he had relented somewhat: He'd talk to Japanese reporters, but every reporter had to ask him at least one question.

Suzuki wasn't much more accessible to American reporters, either: One person went so far as to tell *Newsday* that an appointment was needed merely to talk to Suzuki's back.

"Certainly, Ichiro has that air of mystery around him [because] he's very unapproachable," *New York Times* Yankees beat reporter Tyler Kepner said. "But Matsui is refreshingly approachable."

Said WFAN Yankees beat reporter Sweeney Murti: "Everybody who [had] previous experiences [with Suzuki] felt that [Matsui] was better [to deal with] than Ichiro."

Suzuki had plenty in common with the reticent likes of Barry Bonds, Nomar Garciaparra, and Pedro Martinez, superstars who usually refused to talk to the media. "We're used to Major League Baseball players over here, to a large extent, kind of shunning the media attention or turning their backs to the fans on occasion and just being overwhelmed with it," Lennon said.

Those who observed Suzuki on a daily basis said his apparent aloofness was more a matter of his business-like approach to the game and his reluctance to subject teammates to the scene that followed him wherever he went.

"Ichiro's not a bad dude," Everett said. "Ichiro would not ride on the team bus out of respect for his [teammates], because he knew how mobbed the bus would have been [by reporters] had he been [on the bus]. He took his own [transportation]. That was out of respect."

Said Nelson: "Ichiro [has] just one time [when] he'll talk to the media [on game day] and that's it. He's not a guy that wants to sit there [and] spend a lot of time with them. He'll talk to them and answer all the questions, but that's it. Hideki just seems like he'll accommodate a little bit more."

Indeed, almost anyone who approaches Matsui via his interpreter finds Matsui willing to chat on any number of topics at any time. "I think it's a responsibility, as a player, when you're asked something, to make sure you answer," Matsui told *Newsday*. "Everybody has their own way of approaching things, and that's my perspective."

Matsui welcomed the coverage, so much so that Kepner said, "it's almost like he enjoys it.

"He's incredibly patient," Kepner said. "He should win the 'Good Guy Award' [given to the player who cooperates most with the media], in my opinion, because he has to put up with so much more media and so much more scrutiny than everybody. And he handles it with so much class."

Lennon said, "The thing that struck me the most [and the] other American reporters" during the All-Star Series in Japan "was the fact that he really dealt with [the coverage] incredibly well. There's really no one in the United States who compares with the type of attention that Matsui received on a daily basis [in Japan]."

"Matsui is different in that Matsui took the writers out to dinner when he came to New York," Everett said. "I think that helped. He embraced what the coverage was, rather than run away from it. It's all-encompassing."

Matsui frequently joked with reporters, even those who wrote for Japan's sensationalistic sports papers. Takuya Mizoguchi, who covered the Yomiuri Giants for nine seasons for *Tokyo Sports*—the most ribald paper in Japan—told the *Newark Star-Ledger* that "When [Matsui] has trouble answering questions about baseball, he likes to make [off-color] jokes. The other papers can't use it, but we do, and he thinks it's funny. You can ask him anything."

Sometimes, the treatment of Matsui by Japanese reporters bordered on reverential. Before he departed for America, Matsui made an appearance at his high school in Kanazawa, where reporters presented him a uniform in a bag. The lettering on the bag spelled out the words "Lucky Bag." Japanese reporters were seen during the 2003 season giving gifts such as compact discs to Matsui.

Before a Mets-Yankees game at Shea Stadium, a Japanese reporter approached Matsui and gave him a handful of CDs. And later in the year, a Japanese reporter declined to be interviewed for this book because it was not an authorized biography.

The fondness between Matsui and the Japanese reporters appeared genuine, but the cozy relationship between the parties was, in Everett's opinion, at least partially a matter of self-preservation on the part of the reporters since Matsui is "the only reason why [they're] here."

"It's just that they need him," Everett said. "Because if you're a reporter and you can get Matsui to say anything—if you're a television reporter and you can get Matsui to be on your show, even if it's for a 10-second sound bite, that's All-World to you."

Matsui's generosity with the media may have helped increase his popularity in Japan. Most reporters will agree it's human nature to write kinder and more extensive prose on a player who is more accommodating to the press.

"He is friendlier, that helps [in terms of his popularity]," Lennon said. "[Matsui] was more approachable and he seemed a warmer person to people that followed the sport and fans of the sport than Ichiro, who didn't have that same expressiveness."

The big leaguer with the most unique perspective on Suzuki and Matsui was probably Nelson, who signed a free agent contract with the Mariners following the 2001 season and had a first-hand glimpse at "Ichiro Mania" until he was traded to the Yankees August 6, 2003.

Nelson, who also played for the Yankees from 1996 to 2000, during which time he observed the difficulties of Japanese pitcher Hideki Irabu, said Suzuki and Matsui are vastly different on and off the field but similar where it mattered most to their teammates: In the locker room.

"Both of them are great guys in the clubhouse, very easy to talk to," Nelson said.

So much so, in fact, that Nelson said, "I want to learn Japanese as much as they want to learn English."

Nelson said when he arrived in New York, he immediately heard from others that Matsui was the best player to come from Japan, just as he had heard from others in 2001 that Suzuki was Japan's greatest baseball export.

"It's funny: You play in different places, you get kind of the same stories about both players," Nelson said. "[He hears] 'Oh, Hideki is the best player in Japan,' and then [in] Seattle [he hears] 'Oh, Ichiro's the best player in Japan.' Obviously, they're both very good players, they're superstars over there."

Such superstars, in fact, that it's difficult to compare them to any sporting icons in America. Nelson said he's heard both players called "the Michael Jackson of Japan."

And while Nelson believed Suzuki received more attention during his rookie season than Matsui, he was amazed at how well both men dealt with the overwhelming media attention.

Nelson said being "focused on all the time" in New York can "wear on [players] after a while," which made him even more impressed by the patience displayed by Suzuki and, especially, Matsui.

"I don't know how those players do it, as far as every single day [having] to answer questions to the media, no matter what they do [during the game]," Nelson said. "I don't know how they stay focused. You're going to have a bad game, and obviously you're not going to be too happy with it and not want to talk to the media, but it's amazing how they stay focused [and how] they accommodate the media and still do a great job on the field.

"You've got superstars over here that hate [talking to the media], and they just blow off the media," Nelson said. "And [Suzuki and Matsui] can't do that. That makes their job out on the field, I think, a lot tougher."

For the Mariners, the series against the Yankees served as a six-game trip in a time machine back to the first two years of the decade, when their every move was chronicled by the throng of Japanese media covering Suzuki and relievers Kazuhiro Sasaki and Shigetoshi Hasegawa.

"I remember it being pretty wild the first couple years—[a] lot of media attention," Mariners catcher Dan Wilson said. "And [it] seemed like every time Kaz pitched, even on the side in the bullpen, there was a lot of attention. I think people got used to it. I think [the attention is] maybe a little bit more intense than the American media."

Like the Yankees with World Series experience, the Mariners who had played on baseball's biggest stage for other teams—Seattle has never appeared in the World Series—said the attention their Japanese teammates got on a daily basis far surpassed anything they had ever experienced in the Fall Classic.

"In the World Series, maybe it would be [only] the superstar guys [getting all the attention], because they get most of the focus," Mariners first baseman John Olerud said. "But these guys, especially [Hideo] Nomo and Ichiro, they've had all that focus on them all year long."

Nelson said the increased attention was more noticeable in Seattle because the Mariners never received much coverage prior to the arrival of the Japanese superstars. "The American media that covers the team [is] a very small amount—five or six people," Nelson said. "And then, all of a sudden, you have the Japanese media, so obviously you notice it more."

However, the presence of another Japanese superstar in America—and in America's biggest media market—lessened the amount of coverage received by the Mariners and their trio of Far East stars. "Because a new player came here, [Japanese reporters] kind of shifted attention to [Matsui]," said Hide Sueyoshi, the Mariners Assistant Director of Professional and International Scouting. "But certainly, Japanese baseball fans pay attention to Sasaki and Ichiro and the other Japanese players also."

Mariners utility man Mark McLemore said the coverage in 2003 was "a little bit less" than it was in 2000 and 2001. "The first year Kaz was here [2000], it was an awful lot of attention," McLemore said. "Then when Ichiro got here, it was that much more. But I think it has tapered off a little bit."

Said Olerud: "There's probably a little less [coverage], but there's still an awful lot. They still have a big crowd of guys, beat reporters that follow them everywhere. I'm sure it's probably a little less [than it was in 2000 and 2001], but I think it's still pretty significant coverage."

In addition, the "buzz" surrounding Sasaki and Hasegawa had faded over the past few years. While both hurlers were still All-Star caliber pitchers—Sasaki racked up 119 saves in his first three seasons while Hasegawa took over closer duties with the Mariners when Sasaki missed much of 2003 after he injured his ribs lifting his wife's luggage—the Japanese had long ago shifted their attention to their everyday players.

"As far as Sasaki and Hasegawa, they get hardly any [coverage]," Nelson said. "They get a little bit, but not as much. Here, just like [everywhere else], offense is the big thing in this league. And [Suzuki and Matsui are] offensive players, they're on the field all the time, so they're looked at all the time. As far as the American media and the Japanese media [are concerned], they wanted to see how [the everyday players] do more than everybody else."

In the days leading up to the long-awaited reunion, everyone, it seemed, was talking about it . . . everyone, that is, except Matsui, Suzuki, and Suzuki's teammates and fellow natives of Japan, Sasaki and Hasegawa.

At first, Suzuki refused numerous interview requests about Matsui in the days leading up to the first meeting between the teams April 29 at Yankee Stadium. "I'm not comfortable talking about other players," Suzuki told the *Newark Star-Ledger*.

Suzuki eventually granted an interview to *Newark Star-Ledger* baseball columnist Lawrence Rocca but gave him nothing resembling a substantive answer. "I don't see any games on TV or read any newspapers," Suzuki said. "I don't know anything about him. I don't care what any player does."

Suzuki's refusal to say anything interesting publicly was hardly shocking, but teammates were surprised by his reluctance to talk about Matsui even within the private confines of the locker room. Suzuki, described as "normally chatty with his teammates on any topic" by the *Star-Ledger*, clammed up around the Mariners when the topic was Matsui—as did Sasaki and Hasegawa.

"They're weird," Nelson told the *Star-Ledger*. "You ask them what they think about Matsui and they don't say anything. They won't answer."

In fact, when Sasaki arrived at Yankee Stadium for the opening game of the series April 29, he put signs around his locker reading "I will not talk about Matsui."

Sasaki and Hasegawa were only slightly more talkative with Rocca a week earlier. Sasaki, a former pitcher for the Yokohama BayStars who owned Matsui during their individual matchups— Sasaki limited Matsui to just two hits in 25 at-bats, a puny batting average of .080—claimed he didn't have any recollections of his battles with Matsui.

"It's been so long and I've faced so many other guys," Sasaki said through his interpreter. "Nothing stands out."

Hasegawa, who reached the major leagues with the California Angels in 1997, faced Matsui just once in Japan and said it wouldn't be a big deal to face him at Yankee Stadium or Safeco Field. "It was a much bigger deal when I faced Ichiro, because that was the first time a Japanese hitter and a Japanese pitcher played against each other in the big leagues," said Hasegawa, who was still with the Angels when he faced Suzuki for the first time April 13, 2001.

The typically talkative Matsui was unusually evasive when asked about Suzuki as well. "As a fellow ballplayer, I would like it if we both had good seasons," Matsui told reporters. "But in the end, I think the Yankees will win out."

However, those who covered Matsui believed part of his reluctance to talk about Suzuki was rooted in the Japanese custom of respecting one's elders. Wrote *New York Daily News* Yankee beat writer Anthony McCarron: "Matsui, 28, wasn't going to say anything controversial about the 29-year-old Suzuki."

As for Suzuki's reluctance to talk about Matsui, Nelson said it was a reflection of Suzuki's general aloofness with the media and not his personal feelings for Matsui. "[With] the media, [Suzuki gives] a lot of straightforward answers, and [he's] not going to elaborate on a lot of things," Nelson said. "That's just the way he is. He's a very private person as far as when it comes to the media, so I think that's probably more him not saying very much or [not] wanting to say too much."

In addition, Nelson theorized that Suzuki may not have had much to say about Matsui simply because he didn't know him that well. The two men played in different leagues in Japan—Matsui starred for the Tokyo Giants of the Central League while Suzuki played for the Orix Blue Wave of the Pacific League. Interaction between the two leagues was limited to the playoffs and exhibition games, and Matsui and Suzuki played against each other in Japan just once, during an exhibition series called the Nippon Series in 1996.

Nelson said there was considerably more attention paid to the Yankees-Mariners meeting at Yankee Stadium than the series a week later at Safeco Field in Seattle. "It wasn't as big a deal when [the Yankees] came out to Seattle," Nelson said. "But when [the Mariners] went to New York, obviously, [the press] made a big deal out of it. [The papers] had the back [page reading] 'Godzilla vs. Ichiro' and all that. And then [after] every game, [the papers] had how each other did. So it was a big deal."

So much so that the Yankees issued well over 100 media credentials to Japanese writers, photographers, and cameramen, most of whom stood and formed a semi-circle between the dugouts. *Newsday* reported that a sign in the press dining room read, "Tonight on the buffet table: Sushi." Most of the sushi was gone before the first pitch.

Yankees infielder Todd Zeile said the media throng was "more than spring training. But they both [were] certainly accustomed to it."

Interest in the inaugural meeting between Matsui and Suzuki went far beyond those covering it. The Yankees welcomed a healthy weeknight crowd of 38,724 through the turnstiles. Many of those fans shelled out $22.50 for a t-shirt picturing the two players and the words, "The Showdown in the Bronx."

Upon hearing how much the shirts cost, Suzuki grinned and asked reporters, "What percent do you give me?"

Overseas, where the Japanese were in the middle of a week-long holiday called Golden Week, the game was watched by millions who got up early for the 8 A.M. local time start. In the New York area, meanwhile, the *New York Post* predicted 335,000 homes would tune into the game on the YES Network.

Matsui proved to be a master of the understatement when he told reporters, "The Japanese fans are probably really excited about this matchup."

How excited? So excited that Japanese baseball icon Shigeo Nagashima, who managed Matsui in Japan, traveled to Yankee Stadium to witness the historic matchup in person.

Matsui was thrilled to see Nagashima, whom he told reporters was "bigger than the emperor" in Japan.

Nagashima, meanwhile, told reporters via an interpreter that the Matsui-Suzuki meeting "should only enhance the dreams of American youth."

Another indication of how excited Japan was over the Yankees-Mariners series: According to the *Newark Star-Ledger*, about 5,000 of the fans at Yankee Stadium were Japanese.

One of those, Yuka Ito of Tokyo, told the *Newark Star-Ledger* it was worth the long plane rides and the layover in Hong Kong, which at the time was consumed with worry over the SARS illness.

"It was worth it to take a flight through Hong Kong," Ito told the paper, her voice cracking. "It was worth the risk of SARS to see this. I feel so lucky to be here physically, right in the middle of this atmosphere."

Yankees assistant general manager Jean Afterman, who laid the groundwork for Matsui's signing when she scouted him in Japan the previous summer, viewed the game as a watershed cultural event. "I think what the city of New York is hoping is that the more people in Japan that see this, that people will want to take their vacations here," Afterman told *Newsday*.

The moment people on both sides of the globe were waiting for occurred during batting practice prior to the first game at Yankee Stadium April 29, when Matsui and Suzuki met behind the batting cage. The two Japanese icons shook hands and chatted briefly as cameras clicked, tape recorders whirled, and pens scribbled.

"I remember seeing or feeling the buzz created when those two guys just basically shook hands and said 'hi' to each other in batting practice," Murti said. "Even though they're not particularly close, they just both happen to be Japanese. It touched off a little buzz because that was the story, that was the photo op for the day."

"It's the biggest moment in Japanese baseball history, especially [since it occurred] at Yankee Stadium, the House That Ruth Built," Fuji TV commentator Yoshi Fukushima told reporters.

Still, the two players did their best to downplay the moment. Suzuki, as usual, declined to speak to reporters before the game, while Matsui told reporters it was "the fans and media that are placing special significance on this. We don't look at it as any special significance. We're not representing a country."

The next morning, pictures of and stories about the Matsui-Suzuki meeting appeared in both the sports and news sections of many New York–area newspapers. A photo of Matsui meeting the Japanese media appeared on the front page of *Newsday* along with the headline "American League East: Japanese Stars Center Stage at Yankee Stadium."

Oh, and as for the game? The Mariners won, 6-0, behind the brilliant pitching of Gil Meche, who tossed 7.2 innings of six-hit ball. Neither Matsui nor Suzuki snapped out of his slump—Matsui entered the game hitting .252 while Suzuki entered with a .257 average. Matsui went 1-for-4, but the hit was a ninth-inning single off his fellow countryman Hasegawa. Suzuki went 1-for-5 with a bunt single in the seventh inning.

Suzuki was cheered throughout the evening, which was a unique experience for someone used to hearing all sorts of profane catcalls from Yankee fans. "I felt a little strange, awkward, because I heard some cheering from the fans, too," Suzuki told reporters.

Suzuki and Matsui remained the story throughout the six games between the two teams during the final week of April and the first week of May. The Yankees took two out of three in each series, and those wins were especially valuable for a club that went a decidedly un-Yankee-like 12-18 between April 29 and May 31.

As for the two players themselves, it had become clear neither would ever admit to trying to top the other. And maybe they weren't. But was it a coincidence each experienced a mini-surge during their series against one another?

Suzuki hit .296 (8-for-27) in the six games with three RBI and a stolen base. Matsui had a hit in each of the six games and batted .346 (9-for-26) in the series with one home run and five RBI.

He had two hits and one RBI in each of the three games at Seattle from May 6 to 8, and the two-run homer he hit in the Yankees' 7-2 win on May 7 not only ended a homerless drought spanning 23 days, 20 games, and 85 at-bats but also made huge news back home because he hit it just over the outstretched glove of—that's right—Suzuki in right field.

"It was too far," Suzuki told reporters in typically aloof fashion.

"I don't think there's a player who doesn't feel good about hitting a home run," Matsui told reporters.

The surge against the Mariners extended Matsui's hitting streak to eight games—a season high—and lifted his average to .270. "He's gotten some big hits," Yankees manager Joe Torre said. "I'm sure he's not hitting as well as he'd like, but the situational hitting he's done has been outstanding."

Matsui's homer beyond Suzuki's outstretched glove was also noteworthy because it marked one of the few times in the six games that the two countrymen "crossed paths" on the diamond. Neither player hit a ball to the other during the three games at Yankee Stadium, but Suzuki hit a two-run single to Matsui in left field in the second inning and flew out to Suzuki in the eighth inning of the Mariners' 12-7 win on May 6. Two days later, in the Safeco series finale, Matsui flew out to Suzuki in right field in the fourth inning while Suzuki flew out to Matsui in left in the fifth inning of the Yankees' 16-5 win.

The irony of exclusively covering two men in the ultimate team sport wasn't lost on Murti. "I remember just thinking about the fact that this wasn't [NBA stars] Patrick Ewing versus Hakeem Olajuwon," Murti said. "It wasn't a one-on-one matchup, but that's the way people were looking at it in terms of the attention that it got. This wasn't [NBA stars] Michael Jordan going up against Kobe Bryant on a basketball court, it wasn't [NBA stars] Magic [Johnson] and Larry Bird."

But half a world away, it was even bigger than that.

"I remember talking about it but not really understanding, in some respects, what [the media was] trying to create," Murti said. "Because this wasn't basketball, they were never going to go up against each other. I remember saying there was a great possibility that the two can do things in the game that don't involve either one, and that's a perfect example: Ichiro never hit a ball to Matsui the entire series [at Yankee Stadium] and Matsui never hit a ball to Ichiro.

"Yet everything they did on the field was very important in its own way to the people that were covering it."

CHAPTER

6

Sinking Yet Centered

ideki Matsui's surge during the Yankees' six games against the Seattle Mariners seemingly snapped him out of the slump he had been in during the final days of April. Matsui batted just .121 (4-for-33) in the seven games prior to the Yankees' first game against Seattle April 29, but he hit .346 against the Mariners and had a 10-game hitting streak between April 29 and May 9, which lifted his average from .252 to .283.

Matsui continued to exhibit a knack for the clutch hit at the plate and, much to the surprise of everyone who had heard about the supposed tepidity of his defense, a flair for the dramatic play in the field. Against the Oakland Athletics on May 3, Matsui fielded Ramon Hernandez's two-out double and fired a perfect relay strike to Erick Almonte, who threw home to Jorge Posada to catch Miguel Tejada trying to score from first. The defensive gem kept the game scoreless in a contest the Yankees would eventually lose, 5-3, in 10 innings.

The next day, Matsui encountered the game's nastiest curveball artist, Barry Zito, and managed to notch one of the Yankees' four hits in their 2-0 loss to the Athletics. Afterward, Matsui told reporters the break on Zito's 12-to-6 curveball "might be the best I've faced."

Matsui's fundamentally sound ways had long ago earned approval from teammates, opponents, and fans alike. An area newspaper, *Newsday*, even used a picture of Matsui sliding feet-first into a base in a story about sliding techniques employed by big leaguers. The text above the Matsui picture read, "Trainers and coaches consider a feet-first slide to be far safer than a head-first slide."

New York area fans, meanwhile, continued to show their appreciation of Matsui by snapping up his memorabilia. The *New York Post* reported on May 11 that an autographed Matsui ball went for $350 at a charity auction benefiting the Christopher D. Smithers Foundation. In comparison, a golf bag used by Tiger Woods—who happened to be one of the few American athletes whose popularity in his native country rivaled that of Matsui's—went for $500.

However, even fundamentally sound players suffer through extended funks, as Matsui was about to learn. The slump Matsui endured between May 10 and June 3 was odd in many ways. He had six multi-hit games in that span—only Derek Jeter and Alfonso Soriano had more, with seven apiece. He had three mini-hitting streaks of three games and never had more than two hitless games in a row.

Overall, though, Matsui hit just .214 (18-for-84) with no homers and six RBI in the 22 games between May 10 and June 3. The slump began with consecutive hitless games in Oakland on May 10 and 11. In the latter game, a 5-2 loss to the Athletics, Matsui struck out twice with runners in scoring position. It was his sixth multi-strikeout game of the season and his fourth in a span of 14 games dating back to April 26.

And unlike his slump in late April, which Matsui endured in relative anonymity because the Yankees continued winning, his struggles this time received plenty of attention in New York, where fans were aghast over the Yankees' poor play.

The Yankees followed their blistering 18-3 start with a 30-game stretch in which they went a tepid 11-19 and generally played worse than they ever had before under manager Joe Torre. Following a 5-1 loss to the Texas Rangers at Yankee Stadium on May 18—a defeat which capped the Rangers' first-ever sweep of the Yankees at Yankee Stadium—Yankees general manager Brian Cashman was so angry he told reporters: "In a nutshell, we stink right now."

Two days later, *New York Post* baseball columnist Joel Sherman publicly challenged Matsui to begin displaying the power that earned him his "Godzilla" nickname overseas. Wrote Sherman: "OK, no one expected 50, like Matsui hit last year for the Yomiuri Giants. But no one expected that a quarter into the season that the great singles hitting Japanese export Ichiro Suzuki would be out-homering Matsui 4-3."

As always, the criticism did not faze Matsui, who told Sherman, "I feel like I can do a little more. I think it would be ideal to reach that point [of more regular power]. But there is still a lot to get used to and absorb."

The fact Matsui continued to exhibit the same low-key demeanor and continued to play a sparkling left field throughout his "absorption" process at the plate impressed those around him.

"He's always been the same," Yankees catcher Jorge Posada said. "No matter what, he's always been even-keeled and always ready to go. [His] emotions are always the same.

"You've got to understand that it's a long season," Posada said. "You've got to understand that there's going to be hills and valleys, and you've got to be able to take the moment and adjust. And I think he's been able to adjust."

Torre told reporters "Right from day one, you put [Matsui's] composure on a level and he's kept it there. He hasn't spiked. He's extremely stable. He's in the game. He knows how to win. But I think the mental stability has been a great addition to our club."

And unlike many players, Matsui never let his troubles with the bat carry over into his performance in the field. Against the Rangers on May 16, Matsui momentarily saved the Yankees from defeat when, with the score tied 5-5 in the 10th inning, he made a nifty catch of Carl Everett's line drive and then fired to second base to double up Ryan Christenson. The Rangers eventually won, 8-5, in 12 innings.

Torre went so far as to say Matsui was the key element in the best defensive outfield he'd fielded since he took over as Yankees manager in 1996. Matsui wasn't dazzling in left field, but he got to every ball and exhibited almost perfect instincts for the position, no small feat considering he hadn't played left field at all during his career in Japan.

Matsui's technically sound and efficient defense gave the Yankees a stability and competency they had lacked the previous seven seasons, during which defensively challenged castoffs such as Darryl Strawberry, Luis Polonia, and Tim Raines had treacherously navigated left field.

"We never heard about his fielding," Posada said. "When he came over, we heard about his power, heard about how good of a hitter he was. He comes [into] spring training [and] he's a very good outfielder. [He's] got a very good arm, he gets rid of the ball and he's always in the proper position. All the things that you don't hear from him, we were seeing."

Matsui saved his most dazzling plays for two of the Yankees' biggest games in May. Matsui helped preserve the 299th win of Roger Clemens' career on May 21, when, with one out and the Yankees nursing a 4-2 lead, he made a sliding catch with a runner on second.

Five days later, in Clemens' first attempt at his 300th win, Matsui made a marvelous diving catch of Kevin Millar's bases-loaded liner in the top of the third inning. Nomar Garciaparra tagged up to score on the play, but Matsui's play robbed the Red Sox of at least one more run. The Yankees, though, lost the game, 8-4.

Matsui managed to impress the Yankees even when he made the rare mistake in the field. He committed two costly errors against the Rangers in a 5-2 loss May 17. On the first one, Matsui ran down Michael Young's sinking liner into the left-center gap, but he failed to hold on to the ball and two runs scored.

Torre told reporters afterward it "was unfair to give him an error" on the play. "He had to run a long way," Torre said. "I was surprised he caught up with it to begin with."

An inning later, Mark Teixiera lofted a fly ball to Matsui, who lost it in the sun as Teixiera ended up with a double.

"That ball went right in the sun," Matsui told reporters.

The sun had made infrequent appearances during New York's unusually cloudy and rainy spring, so Torre was willing to give Matsui a pass on that miscue as well. "It's the first time we've had nice weather," Torre told reporters.

And during a 4-2 loss to the woebegone Detroit Tigers on May 31—the Tigers would end up with 119 losses, one shy of the post-1900 mark set by the 1962 New York Mets—Matsui turned the wrong way as he attempted to field Ramon Santiago's fly ball leading off the seventh. Santiago ended up with a double.

The errors committed by Matsui may have cost the Yankees those games against the Rangers and Tigers, but his teammates remained impressed by how willingly Matsui took the blame for his mistakes and his refusal to make excuses. After the game against the Rangers, Matsui told reporters the error he made on Young's fly ball "was completely my mistake. I felt like I could catch up to the ball, but when I put out my hand, I had my hand too far out and it hit the palm."

Matsui also could have blamed the howling wind in Detroit for his error against the Tigers, but he said it was his mistake for not being prepared enough. His attitude stood in marked contrast to that of the Yankees' losing pitcher on May 31, Jeff Weaver, who ignored his own grotesque numbers (he was 3-4 at the time with a 5.17 ERA) and groused that the Yankees always seemed to play badly whenever he pitched.

Matsui's ability to leave his plate difficulties behind once he jogged into the outfield came in handy, especially later in May, when he had to readjust to centerfield on the fly due to the extended absence of Bernie Williams. With Williams nursing a chronically sore left knee, Torre started Matsui in centerfield—the position he played throughout his nine-year career in Japan—May 18 against the Rangers.

"I've seen enough of him as an outfielder to know he can play centerfield," Torre told reporters. "He's a special player."

It marked Matsui's first start for the Yankees at a position other than left field, and at the time, both Torre and Matsui believed it would be a one-day assignment for Matsui.

"I had no problems," Matsui told the *New York Post* after he flawlessly handled four chances in the Yankees' 5-1 loss to the Rangers. "But I don't think I'll be playing there regularly."

But he'd end up spending most of the summer there.

Four days after Matsui's "one time only" appearance in centerfield, Williams underwent an MRI that revealed a sobering surprise: He had a torn meniscus in the left knee that would necessitate surgery and put Williams on the disabled list for 4 to 6 weeks. The Yankees immediately announced Matsui would play centerfield for the duration of Williams' DL stint.

Matsui would prove to be a more-than-capable fill-in for Williams, but the latter's absence still presented a challenge for the Yankees, who lost the first five games he missed following his diagnosis.

Entering the season, Williams had batted .300 or better in eight consecutive seasons and had driven in at least 90 runs in seven consecutive seasons. He had also averaged 143 games a season since 1995.

In addition, Williams' extended absence exposed the Yankees' lack of depth in the outfield. The Yankees began the season with Bubba Trammell and Chris Latham as their backup outfielders, but Torre exhibited little trust in the duo, each of whom were no longer with the Yankees by midseason.

As a result, the Yankees needed Matsui to snap out of his troubles, which were similar to those suffered by other rookies and other players who had switched leagues. "[It was] much more the exception to find somebody not having struggles in their first year in the major leagues," Yankees utility man Todd Zeile said. "Whether they've got experience somewhere else or not."

Yankees third baseman Aaron Boone was hitting .273 with 18 homers and 65 RBI for the Cincinnati Reds before he was traded to the Yankees July 31, but he hit just .218 with one homer and 13 RBI during his first month in pinstripes.

"You move over [to a different league], it is a huge adjustment, not only learning the new pitchers [but also] learning a new guy everyday," Boone said. "That is a huge adjustment."

"You see it from the National League guys coming over to the American League [and] American League guys going over to the National League," said pitcher Jeff Nelson, who opened the season with the Seattle Mariners before he was traded to the Yankees August 6. "It still takes them some time for them to get adjusted, and they've been in the big leagues over here for a long time."

Matsui admitted he had trouble hitting the two-seam fastball and cut fastballs thrown by so many American pitchers. The two-seam fastball, better known as the sinker, was thrown slightly slower than a regular four-seam fastball but either dipped away from or towards the hitter at the last possible instant. A hitter fooled by the pitch usually hit a weak grounder. The cut fastball, or "cutter," bore in on hitters and often resulted in broken-bat grounders.

"He was really getting adjusted to the cutter [and] sinker and pitchers that he'd never seen," Zeile said.

For a while in April and May, Matsui was Mr. Groundball. During a three-game series against the Red Sox from May 19 to 21, *Newsday*'s Ken Davidoff observed that Matsui put the ball on the ground in 10 of his 13 plate appearances. Those ground balls resulted in three singles and seven groundouts.

"It seemed like every ball he hit was a ground ball to second base," WFAN Yankees beat reporter Sweeney Murti said. "I think it was [former outfielder] Andy Van Slyke [who] one time joked that he was having the 'Summer of 4-3' because he'd grounded out to second base all the time. That's what Matsui was doing all the time.

"He became 'Groundzilla.'"

Matsui told *Newsday* his struggles were not an indication that he "[hasn't] been able to adjust" to the new pitchers and pitches he was facing but was instead a problem with his swing. "I think the difficult part is being able to bring my swing, the swing that I have, against pitches that are thrown," Matsui said. "The first thing I think about is making contact. I haven't been able to really bring my swing into things."

But as a foreign-born player who had never before played baseball at any level in America, Matsui's struggles were also decidedly unique. After all, those who change leagues only had to adapt to new pitchers and new ballparks, not an entirely new culture and language.

"[Adapting to a new] language, everybody would have assumed that to be an aspect of [his struggles]," Zeile said. "But he seemed like he was certainly mature enough to handle all those things."

"You're getting used to the cities, you're getting used to the ballparks," Nelson said.

Added Boone: "All the other things [Matsui had to go through]—being in a completely different country, trying to learn [the language and customs] and meet people and [get to] know your teammates and not even speaking their language, I think [it] takes a special person [to do that]."

In addition, Matsui carried the added weight of an entire country on his shoulders. Those who covered Matsui were beginning to worry not only about the lack of power exhibited by Matsui but also by the possibility that he'd be sent to the minor leagues.

"I think he was [feeling] the pressures of not having shown enough power yet . . . and the thought that he needed to show more power," Zeile said.

It also didn't help Matsui that Suzuki never encountered a slump during his fabulous rookie season in 2001. With such blazing speed on the basepaths, many scouts and opposing players believed Suzuki was immune to slumps because he could regularly beat out infield hits.

After Suzuki beat out three infield hits in the Mariners' 3-1 win over the Cleveland Indians in the decisive fifth game of the 2001 American League Division Series, Indians shortstop Omar Vizquel told reporters that Suzuki "flies. If he hits a ball two steps to your right or left, it's almost a sure base hit."

Speed, however, was the one baseball skill Matsui lacked. Though he was considered a smart and technically sound base runner, he'd swiped just 46 bases during his 10 seasons in Japan. "Ichiro makes up [for] a lot because he's so fast, but Hideki, he's more of a power hitter," Nelson said.

At the nadir of his slump, Matsui was having a hard time hitting the pitches he normally mashed. Nelson said the scouting report during Matsui's slump was "that you could get fastballs by" him.

"He was looking for a lot of off-speed stuff early, when he was in his slump," Nelson said. "Just throw him fastballs and make him hit [them]. He couldn't catch up to [the fastballs]."

Added former teammate Jason Anderson: "I just think the pitchers [were] starting to learn him. He was trying to learn the pitchers, and as that went on, the pitchers [were] trying to figure out what he was struggling with at that point."

There was no demotion in the offing for Matsui, but had he been sent to the Yankees' Triple-A affiliate in Columbus, Ohio, chances are the throng of reporters that faithfully chronicled his every move at the big-league level would have accompanied him.

After all, Japanese reporters followed Mets outfielder Tsuyoshi Shinjo—a Japanese outfielder with a fraction of Matsui's skills and hype—when he was demoted to Triple-A Norfolk on June 28. Despite the lack of glamour in the minor leagues—where teams often bus to games played at 5,000-seat stadiums—Shinjo was still trailed as if he were a rock star.

"There's always Japanese media [following Shinjo around]," said Anderson, who was traded to the Mets on July 16 and immediately assigned to Norfolk. "There was usually like four or five [reporters] a day, at least. But there was always a [television] camera."

Shinjo put up good numbers for Norfolk (.324 with three homers and nine RBI in 111 at-bats), but those who were covering him were more interested in his life away from the diamond. Anderson said it reminded him of "Americans with reality television shows. We're just hanging out during a rain delay, waiting to go play the game, and [the television reporters] want to know how he eats his peanut butter and jelly or [record him] playing ping pong."

Anderson said observing the coverage of Shinjo made him realize how ingrained baseball is in the Japanese culture. "You can tell [Japanese fans are] very excited about new things, and [Japanese] players are relatively new over here," Anderson said. "They're almost like rock stars or idols over there. They want to know what they're doing and how they live their life."

The idea that Matsui could go to the minor leagues appeared ludicrous. For one thing, despite his May struggles, he had still started every game but one for the Yankees and he still ranked among the team leaders in RBIs. Shinjo, on the other hand, was signed by the Mets to serve as a fourth outfielder.

Plus, Matsui was making $6 million—Shinjo was making just $600,000—which is a lot of money to pay someone riding the buses in Ohio.

Still, while demoting Matsui sounded like a crazy idea, Steinbrenner had already shuttled Jose Contreras and his $8 million salary to the minors after just five appearances during the Yankees' hot stretch in early April. Now that the Yankees were skidding—they followed up the sizzling 18-3 by losing 19 of their next 30 games, including eight in a row at home from May 16 through May 26—who knew what Steinbrenner had up his sleeve?

As it turned out, Matsui wasn't going to the minor leagues. He was going someplace worse—Steinbrenner's doghouse.

It's a place every Yankee employee eventually—and often frequently—occupies. Steinbrenner has a well-deserved reputation as the most demanding "Boss" on the planet, and he seems to take great pride in living up—or down—to the image he's created for himself since he bought the Yankees in 1973.

In his book *You Gotta Have Wa*, Robert Whiting wrote, "A two-game losing streak was cause for absolute panic" in Japan, which meant the Japanese took twice as long to panic as Steinbrenner.

A player doesn't even have to struggle on the field to earn the ire of the blusterous Steinbrenner. In 1991, first baseman Don Mattingly, regarded as one of the finest Yankees of all time on and off the field, earned a suspension and fine from Steinbrenner for keeping his hair too long. (In this way, Steinbrenner was no different than Japanese owners, who ordered their players to cut their hair above the ears and threatened to release any players who ignored the policy.) In 2001, relief pitcher Jay Witasick angered Steinbrenner by taking a day to report to the Yankees following his trade from the San Diego Padres.

Most recently, Steinbrenner had criticized star shortstop Derek Jeter—the owner of four World Series rings and the unquestioned leader of the Yankees—for his supposedly active nightlife.

Steinbrenner, who had been ornery during the Yankees' awesome April, was really on the warpath by Memorial Day. The struggling Yankees were scheduled to play the hated Red Sox in a matinee, which would normally be reason enough for Steinbrenner to be on edge. However, Roger Clemens was also going for his 300th win—against his former team—and the Yankees were expecting a capacity crowd of more than 55,000.

But the day started badly for Clemens and the Yankees. After a rain delay of nearly two hours, the Red Sox complained right before the first pitch that Clemens' glove, which pictured a logo commemorating his 300th win, was distracting, so home plate umpire Bill Miller forced Clemens to use a different glove. It only got worse for the Yankees as the Red Sox tattooed Clemens for eight runs in 5.2 innings in beating the Yankees, 8-4.

Matsui's diving catch of Millar's liner in the third inning provided one of the Yankees' few highlights. Immediately after he caught the ball, Matsui somersaulted, leaped to his feet and, for a split second, looked towards the left field stands, and appeared ready to fling the ball there. But Matsui figured out where he was and instead fired the ball into the infield and ensured that Trot Nixon and Manny Ramirez did not advance on the play.

"When I got up, I wasn't sure which way I was facing and I was going to throw the ball," Matsui told reporters. "Then I saw the foul pole."

However, Matsui's sparkling defensive play wasn't nearly enough to remove him from Steinbrenner's crosshairs. As he departed Yankee Stadium following the soggy defeat, Steinbrenner made it clear he was unhappy with Matsui's meager home run totals.

"This is not the guy we signed in terms of power," Steinbrenner told a handful of reporters. "This falls to my hitting coach figuring out a way to straighten this guy out."

In other words, hitting coach Rick Down should rent, and not buy. Steinbrenner even sounded as if he were willing to fill the job himself when he suggested Matsui was standing too far from the plate.

"I am in the crosshairs," Down told the *New York Post* on May 27.

If Down was fired, it wouldn't be for a lack of effort. He and Matsui had worked tirelessly throughout the month in hopes of snapping Matsui out of his ground ball funk.

"He's still trying to find his swing," Down told *Newsday*. "He's hitting an awful lot of ground balls. He works hard at not trying to hit ground balls. That's still in the making."

However, there was no controversy in the making between Matsui and Steinbrenner. Plenty of Steinbrenner's targets over the years had exacerbated the situation by firing back at "The Boss," who would, one way or the other, always get the last word.

But playing for a demanding employer was nothing new to Matsui, who had long ago encountered a boss so surly he made Steinbrenner look warm and cuddly. As a member of the Neagari Junior High School team in Ishikawa Prefecture in Japan, Matsui glared at the pitcher and slammed his bat on the ground after he was intentionally walked.

Matsui's manager responded by slapping Matsui across the face—on the field. According to Matsui, his manager was most upset with Matsui for slamming his bat. Equipment is sacred in Japan, as Matsui's countryman, Shinjo, indicated when he sent his glove across the country for repairs during spring training in 2003.

"[His junior high manager] used to slap me all the time," Matsui told the *Newark Star-Ledger*. "That time it was once. Certainly, from that point on, I felt the need to respect and take care of my equipment."

Ironically, Matsui took his frustrations out on his bat a few hours later. After he flew out in the third inning of the Yankees' 11-3 win, Matsui slammed his bat to the ground.

In front of reporters, however, Matsui "absorbed" Steinbrenner's criticisms stoically and without rancor. "Certainly, I'm sure there's not a player who would be happy [hearing such criticisms]," Matsui told the *New York Daily News*. "But if I'm not producing any results so far, it's bound to happen. What I have to do is make sure to absorb it and keep working on that."

Torre, meanwhile, had seen enough of Matsui to realize he could handle Steinbrenner's barbs. But as he typically does with players who are publicly criticized by Steinbrenner, Torre spoke privately to Matsui to ensure the player wasn't too upset.

"When guys haven't experienced it before, you may have to stop and talk to them about it," Torre told reporters.

Torre added that he "just want[ed] to let [Matsui] know that what he's doing out there is fine with me. The numbers will take care of themselves. I certainly don't want him to put more pressure on himself. He's done everything we've asked."

Matsui told *Newsday* he "was very appreciative of Joe to be there."

Matsui may have landed squarely in the crosshairs of The Boss, but unlike struggling Americans in Japan, he mostly avoided harsh criticism from the media and boos from the fans.

"There's a lot less expected of [Japanese players] coming here," said Florida Marlins first baseman Derrek Lee, whose dad, Leon, played 10 years in Japan with three different teams and currently manages the Orix Blue Wave. "When an American player goes over there, even if he's coming out of the [American] minor leagues, he's expected to be the star of the team."

How high are the expectations for Americans in Japan? "It's like you're not even allowed to have a bad game," Lee said. "You're supposed to get two hits every game when you go over there."

Demands aren't quite so high for the Japanese in America, where Lee believes "players like Matsui [are] just expected to be good, solid player[s], not necessarily the superstar of the team."

The reduced expectations are partially a byproduct of the long-held—and erroneous—belief that even the best players from Japan could not compete in the major leagues. In the spring of 2001, for instance, there were plenty of whispers from unnamed scouts that Seattle Mariners rookie outfielder Ichiro Suzuki—a superstar in Japan—would struggle badly in the bigs. Of course, Suzuki proved that theory hogwash by winning both the American League Most Valuable Player and Rookie of the Year awards in 2001, only the second time in the history of baseball that feat had been achieved.

"I think there's certainly a belief that major league players from the United States would have better success in Japan than vice versa, and in general, that may have proven to [have] been true," Zeile said. "But certainly, on the individual basis, there are exceptions and will be exceptions. . . . I think as the years have gone by, there have been some players, obviously, that have started to break down some of those beliefs."

Expectations were higher for Matsui, thanks to his average annual salary of $7 million and the overwhelming success his countryman Suzuki enjoyed in 2001 and 2002, but the Yankees did their best to temper expectations by telling anyone who would listen that Matsui probably wouldn't approach the 50-homer plateau.

It also helped that Matsui was joining the Yankees, who already had several superstars (Jeter, Jason Giambi, Bernie Williams, Roger

Clemens) to deflect attention away from Matsui and a grind-it-out approach that belied the club's record $180 million payroll.

It also helped to have Torre as his manager. In his attempts to defuse the controversy surrounding Matsui, Torre—who had already endured his share of battles with Steinbrenner this season—took a humorous and subtle jab at Steinbrenner.

When Torre was told that Steinbrenner had said that Matsui wasn't the same hitter he was in Japan, Torre told reporters, "Sure he is. He's the same height, same weight. And he hits left-handed."

Matsui went 1-for-5 against the Red Sox in the Yankees' 11-3 win on May 27, and the victory over their archrivals seemed to mollify Steinbrenner, at least for one night. "I don't have anything against my centerfielder [Matsui]," Steinbrenner told *Newsday* after the game. "I think he's playing great. All I said was it might be better if he steps closer to the plate. My people said that. I'm not that sharp to know. But he's played a great centerfield, and it's a pleasure to have him on the team."

The next night, Matsui went 2-for-5 with a pair of doubles and scored the winning run in the Yankees' 6-5 win. The back-to-back wins over the Red Sox marked the Yankees' first two-game winning streak since May 7 and 8.

Not coincidentally, May 7 was also the last time Matsui had collected two extra base hits in a game. However, Matsui's long-awaited breakout failed to arrive over the next five games against the Red Sox, Tigers, and Cincinnati Reds, during which he went just 3-for-23 as his average dropped all the way to .250—the numerical definition of mediocrity.

Matsui's slump was now nearly a month long, and while he wasn't headed to the minor leagues, those who had traveled halfway around the world to cover him were still consumed and concerned by the dip in his performance. In *You Gotta Have Wa*, Whiting wrote that in Japan, "Going 0-for-4 was a serious slump."

This, then, was a crisis.

The Americans in the press box, though, tried to keep the mood light. "We'd go around, just joking to the other Japanese reporters that you'd kind of gotten friendly with," Murti said. "Every time he'd ground out, you'd turn around to one of them and say, 'Boy, he stinks.' And everyone kind of got a good laugh about it."

Matsui, though, wasn't laughing. The 2003 season was barely a third over, but he was already at a crossroads. Following the Yankees' 6-2 loss to the Reds on June 4, Matsui's numbers—a .250 average with three homers, 32 RBI, a .299 on-base percentage and a .357 slugging percentage—were more befitting a fourth outfielder than a hotly hyped Rookie of the Year candidate.

He had also gone 117 plate appearances since his last home run just over the outstretched glove of his countryman, Suzuki, May 7 against the Mariners. According to the *Newark Star-Ledger*, Matsui's longest home run drought in Japan lasted 103 plate appearances back in 1994.

In retrospect, teammate John Flaherty surmised that Matsui's slump might have been magnified because his dramatic grand slam during the Yankees' home opener may have increased the public's expectations. "His Opening Day in Yankee Stadium was incredible, but on the other hand, in a way, it might have hurt him a little bit because the expectations just went through the roof," Flaherty said. "Like 'Uh oh, the bar has just been raised.'"

Despite his struggles and the impatience displayed by Steinbrenner and others who had high expectations for Matsui, the player remained outwardly calm. "I'm sure it was frustrating for him, but he didn't show that it bothered him," Anderson said. "He just went on with his business and kept working hard."

Inside, though, Matsui was angry with himself, but determined to reverse the course of his season.

"I did have a little anger, a little upset feeling during that time, wondering, 'Why doesn't this work? Why doesn't that work?'" Matsui told Davidoff in a story Davidoff wrote for the *Sporting News*. "When I started to change my mentality, be more enthusiastic towards changing the approach, that's when things started to turn."

Matsui's placid demeanor and internal determination came as no surprise to those who knew him in Japan. "One attribute that I really liked about him is the fact that whether he goes 0-for-5 or 5-for-5, you can never tell, day in and day out," said Darrell May, Matsui's former teammate with the Yomiuri Giants. "And he would come in and have the same routine, do the exact same things and make the adjustments necessary."

Throughout his slump, those who had seen Matsui overseas warned the American naysayers that Matsui would snap out of it with a fury sooner rather than later. Shigeo Nagashima, Matsui's manager with the Yomiuri Giants, told the *Newark Star-Ledger* that Matsui "was always a slow starter. In April or May, he wasn't able to get his engine going. But when the weather got warmer, he always carried the team."

In addition, *Newark Star-Ledger* baseball columnist Lawrence Rocca wrote on June 1 that "Hideki Matsui will end up hitting .320 with 35 homers and 120 RBI, but not because of George Steinbrenner. He always waited until June to heat up in Japan, and it will prove to be no different here."

Even those observing Matsui for the first time knew it wouldn't be long until he snapped out of his slump. "He's been a superstar in Japan, so obviously he's going to have some sort of idea [how to hit]," Nelson said. "He's not a guy just starting out. Guys are going to go through slumps, and good players get through them.

"And he's been a good player over there and he's a good player here, so he's going to get through them."

Did he ever.

Sayonara, Slump!

The rebirth of Hideki Matsui occurred just a few hours after he bottomed out.

Prior to the Yankees' game against the Cincinnati Reds June 5, manager Joe Torre announced he had moved Matsui from second to seventh in the lineup. The demotion to the bottom third of the lineup—the home of slap-hitting infielders and, in the National League, the pitcher—was the clearest indication yet that Matsui's rookie season was unfolding much worse than anyone could have imagined.

Torre had first hinted he'd make the lineup change a day earlier, prior to the Yankees' 6-2 loss to the Cincinnati Reds. Shuffling the lineup was about all Torre could do.

For a team with a $180 million payroll, the Yankees were frightfully lacking depth. The backup outfielders at the time were Charles Gipson and Bubba Trammell, who combined for just 65 at-bats and were each jettisoned by the All-Star break. Plus, with

Bernie Williams expected to remain on the disabled list for several weeks, Matsui was the Yankees' only option in centerfield.

Hence, the lineup shift. "He seems to be pressing very badly," Torre told reporters June 4. At the time, Matsui had just six hits in his previous 38 at-bats.

"He may need a break but I am not sure I am going to do that. As far as changing the lineup, that's likely to happen. Defensively, we need him in the lineup."

Matsui, whose average remained at .250 following a 1-for-4 performance in the Yankees' 6-2 loss to the Reds on June 4, told reporters, "It's not my call to say where I should hit. Wherever I am told to hit, I have to do my best out there."

The Yankees were so perplexed by Matsui's extended slump—he hadn't homered in 109 at-bats, by far the longest such streak of his career—that they requested and received videotapes of his at-bats from the 2002 season in hopes of detecting a flaw in his current plate approach.

In addition, the *New York Post* reported notoriously hands-on owner George Steinbrenner held a conference call with hitting coach Rick Down and three Yankees executives—Gordon Blakeley, Damon Oppenheimer, and Gene Michael—to discuss Matsui's problems.

As for Matsui, he admitted for the first time he was having trouble adapting to the new pitchers and pitches he was seeing. "The results are that I haven't been hitting well," Matsui told reporters after he was informed of the lineup shift. "Physically I am fine. I haven't faced the pitchers, but a lot of guys haven't faced the pitchers. I am not using that as an excuse."

Torre also revealed Matsui was troubled by back spasms, but Matsui's reluctance to acknowledge the condition—never mind use it as an excuse for his struggles—came as no surprise considering he'd finished his career in Japan as one of the country's all-time "Ironmen."

"It's been a little stiff for a few days, but it's not something he likes to talk about," Torre told reporters.

"Physically, I'm fine," Matsui told reporters.

Torre had no problem with Matsui's approach or attitude, but he needed to do something to try and stir an offense that had suddenly gone stagnant. The Yankees had scored three runs or fewer in 16 of the 31 games between May 1 and June 4. In those 16 games, the Yankees were just 1-15.

"Right now we're just going to rearrange the lineup with the same cast," Torre told reporters. "He's still one of the eight best players on the team. That's why he's in the lineup."

Torre said he also wanted to move Matsui to seventh in the order "to get him out of the lights a bit. He is struggling and a very proud man and he is going to work his tail off to come out of it.

"He will come out of it."

It didn't take Matsui long to make his manager look clairvoyant. Matsui snapped out of his slump in ferocious fashion by going 4-for-5 with three doubles against the Cincinnati Reds, and a long-awaited home run to centerfield—the deepest part of Cincinnati's Great American Ballpark—in the Yankees' 10-2 win. The home run by Matsui was his first since May 7 and snapped his homerless drought at 118 plate appearances.

The most notable thing about the home run, though, was that Matsui hit it on a 3-and-0 count, an indication of Matsui's impressive batting eye and the faith Torre still had in his struggling slugger. "At 3-and-0, you've got to have a little courage to swing," Matsui told reporters.

On the bench, Yankees starting pitcher Jose Contreras, another high-priced foreign import who had struggled through the season's first two months, was impressed with Matsui's aggressive approach on the 3-and-0 pitch. "I'm no hitting expert, but what I had seen prior to today, he had been a lot more passive," Contreras told reporters. "Today, he was a lot more aggressive, going after the ball and trying to drive it instead of sitting back and taking called strikes. I've seen him in Japan in years past, and he was very aggressive."

Most impressive of all, Matsui—who had endured a month in which he had suffered through countless groundouts to the right side of the infield—sprayed the ball all over the park. In addition to his homer, he doubled once apiece to right field, left center and right center.

"[Matsui] certainly looked like a different player," Torre told reporters. "Sometimes it takes just one base hit to get you started."

Or an entire team. The slumping Yankees busted out in a big way by racking up 16 hits, including a team record-tying 10 doubles.

Afterward, Matsui said he appreciated Torre's gentle handling of the lineup shuffling.

"Certainly, the fact that [Torre] was trying to create an atmosphere where I can be comfortable, that is a good thing," Matsui told reporters. "I approached the game today just the way I approach it everyday. There might be a slight difference in the lineup, batting second or batting seventh, but I don't feel the difference myself."

No manager in baseball created as comfortable an environment for his players as Torre, who had an uncanny knack for getting players "out of the lights" and into a spot in the lineup where they could produce immediately. Nearly five months later, in Game Seven of the American League Championship Series against the Boston Red Sox, Torre would drop the struggling Jason Giambi from third to seventh in the lineup. Giambi responded with two solo homers in the Yankees' 6-5 victory.

As for Matsui, when he walked into the clubhouse following his breakout game, he saw the nameplate above his locker had been replaced with one reading "OH-55"—as in all-time Japanese home run leader Sadaharu Oh. Matsui wore uniform number 55 in honor of Oh, who held the single-season record for home runs with 55.

It was the work of third baseman and noted clubhouse prankster Robin Ventura, and it was the Yankees' way of showing how pleased they were for Matsui, that his hard work and patience he had displayed—on and off the field—had finally paid off.

"Everybody realized what he was going through and how hard it was for him, not only just playing baseball but everything," WFAN Yankees beat reporter Sweeney Murti said. "Playing baseball is never easy to do anywhere, and, in this instance, going through everything he had gone through, I think [his teammates] kind of appreciated everything he was doing. And [the nameplate above his locker] was their light-hearted joking way of kind of just welcoming him into the team, finally, after having struggled for so long."

"The guys love him, and they were hurting for him while he's been fighting his way out of the slump," Torre told reporters.

"My teammates were very supportive in helping me and talking to me," Matsui told mlb.com. "I was really appreciative that they were helping me, but I felt a little bad that they were rooting just for me."

For at least one night, the Yankees got their money's worth from their international additions. In addition to the monster performance posted by Matsui, the Yankees received seven strong innings from Contreras, whom they signed to a four-year, $32 million deal in late December.

Unfortunately for Contreras, his strong showing was not a sign of things to come. Contreras went on the disabled list two days later with a sore shoulder and didn't return to the big leagues until late August.

Matsui, on the other hand, was just getting warmed up.

The night after his breakout performance, Matsui went 0-for-2 in a 5-3 win over the Chicago Cubs. Such "0-fers," so commonplace in May, would be impressively infrequent in June.

Matsui had two or more hits in 18 of the Yankees' 28 games between June 5 and July 6. In that span, he hit a blistering .432 (48-for-111) with six homers and 31 RBI. He raised his average from .250 entering play June 5 to .311 following the games of July 6. His slugging percentage, a middle infielder-esque .357 entering play June 5, was a sturdy .467 by July 6. He raised his on-base percentage from an inadequate .299 entering play June 5 to a gaudy .371 by July 6.

He also continued to display an amazing knack for delivering the clutch hit. Matsui was the Yankees' most reliable offensive player during Roger Clemens' final two attempts at his 300th victory. Against the Cubs June 7, Matsui broke up Kerry Wood's no-hit bid and snapped a scoreless tie with a fifth inning home run. The homer came on a 3-2 pitch and ended a protracted eight-pitch battle between Matsui and Wood, who mixed his nearly 100 mph heater with a knee-buckling curveball.

"He had a great at-bat," Torre told reporters afterward. "Against a guy who throws the ball 97 miles per hour, he hit a curveball after fouling off a curveball. That was an experienced at-bat."

Matsui ended the day 3-for-4, but Clemens' bid at history was momentarily derailed when Juan Acevedo allowed a three-run homer to Eric Karros in the seventh inning of the Cubs' 5-2 win.

Six nights later, Matsui snapped a 1-1 tie with a solo home run leading off the bottom of the second inning against the St. Louis Cardinals. The homer was his third in a span of 25 at-bats; prior to that stretch, he had just three homers in his first 241 at-bats of the season.

Matsui went 2-for-4, and this time the Yankees' bullpen held on to the lead for Clemens, who departed after 6.2 innings and watched three relievers nail down the 5-2 win—the 300th of Clemens' storied career.

Matsui's ability to lift his game to another level on the bigger stages impressed his teammates, even if no one could quite put a handle on why he played better whenever the stakes were higher. "Why do guys compete and perform well in big situations? Who knows? Your guess is as good as anybody else's," former Yankees infielder Todd Zeile said. "But the fact is he's a good hitter, but a smart hitter too in situations. Whether he concentrates a little bit more or [whether he's more] confident [in] those types of situations, it's hard to say what makes it happen.

"It just does."

Matsui was so hot, it took a history-making effort to slow him down. Among the five hitless games Matsui had between June 5 and July 6 was the 0-for-4 "collar" he took against the Houston Astros on June 11.

Unfortunately for the Yankees, everyone else took the "collar" too. The Astros used six pitchers to no-hit the Yankees, 6-0, and it was a historical evening in more ways than one.

Never before had six pitchers combined on a no-hitter, but the Astros had no choice but to cobble together the no-no once starter Roy Oswalt departed due to a groin injury before he recorded an out in the second inning. Peter Munro, Kirk Saarloos, Brad Lidge, Octavio Dotel, and Billy Wagner finished the gem.

The flame-throwing Dotel and Wagner, each of whom can hit 100 mph on the radar gun, combined to strike out six of the final seven batters they faced, which made Matsui's game-ending grounder to first something of a moral victory.

It was the first no-hitter thrown against the Yankees since the Baltimore Orioles' expert knuckleballer Hoyt Wilhelm did so on September 20, 1958—a span of 6,980 games, a major league record. It was also the first no-hitter thrown against the Yankees at Yankee Stadium since August 25, 1952, when the Detroit Tigers' Virgil Trucks performed the feat.

Unofficially, the no-hitter also set off the angriest tirade of Torre's eight-year career as Yankees manager. After the loss, Torre held a blistering team meeting in which he lit into the Yankees for their often-lackadaisical play over the past month-and-a-half.

"He's been upset before," Derek Jeter told reporters. "I don't think he's been more upset than this at any other point."

Torre told reporters the Yankees' performance "was terrible. That was one of the worst games I've ever been involved in. I have no explanation. I can't find a reason for what happened tonight."

Worst of all, the loss dropped the Yankees into second place in the AL East, a half-game in back of the rival Boston Red Sox. "Maybe this is rock bottom," Yankees general manager Brian Cashman told reporters.

Cashman proved to be correct. The no-hitter was just a momentary hiccup for Matsui but a turning point for the rest of the Yankees, who recovered from the no-hitter to beat the Astros the next day, 6-5, and move into first place in the AL East for good.

Between June 12 and the end of the regular season, the Yankees went a blistering 65-33.

Matsui, meanwhile, would notch two hits apiece in each of his first four games following the no-hitter, all of which the Yankees won. And against the Cardinals June 14, Matsui began displaying his remarkable knack for playing ahead of the weather.

That's right, playing ahead of the weather. With rain and a heavy wind already engulfing Yankee Stadium—and Cardinals starter Matt Morris clearly laboring due to a sore shoulder—Matsui laced a three-run double to give the Yankees a 3-0 lead. After Morris threw one pitch to the next batter, Ruben Sierra, the umpires waved the teams off the field. Play resumed after an 87-minute delay and the Yankees cruised to a 13-4 victory.

More than three months later, Matsui would save the Yankees from a rain-shortened defeat in Baltimore when he made a quick and on-target throw to home on a single to left. Upon seeing Matsui's throw whiz by him, the Orioles' Pedro Swann tried to make it back to third but was tagged out in a rundown. Yankees pitcher Mike Mussina escaped the inning, and with a hurricane rapidly moving in, the umpires called the game after five frames with the teams tied 1-1.

But by then, the Yankees had already grown accustomed to Matsui's better-than-advertised defensive abilities. Not only did he play a seamless centerfield in Williams' absence—indeed, considering the step Williams had lost to age, his weak throwing arm, and his penchant for the absent-minded play, Matsui may have actually represented an improvement over Williams—but Matsui also displayed impressive speed in catching a sinking liner off the bat of Kerry Robinson in the right-center field gap during the Yankees' 5-2 win on June 15.

"That was a heck of a catch," Torre told reporters afterward. "He ran a long way, but the thing that made that possible was his first step."

As usual, Matsui downplayed his performance. "It wasn't that difficult," he told the *Newark Star-Ledger*. "The ball flew pretty high and I was able to catch up with it. As I was running back there, I thought I'd be able to get it. I place as much emphasis on my defense as I do my offense. I take pride in my defense and my running as well."

That was obvious to his teammates. "Just the all-around game—he's a lot more than just an offensive player," Yankees backup catcher John Flaherty said.

But it was his sudden offensive upturn that had the Yankees—and fans—gushing. Unbelievably, Matsui surged into the team lead in batting average at .289 on June 15—just 11 days after he had been mired at a pedestrian .250.

It seemed no coincidence that the Yankees' offensive revival coincided with the one experienced by Matsui. After averaging just 4.48 runs per game in the 23 games between May 10 and June 4, the Yankees averaged 5.74 runs per game during Matsui's blistering 27-game stretch between June 5 and July 6.

"We have been having good at-bats, and the at-bats Matsui has had in the last 10 days or so [have] been big in our lineup," Torre told reporters following the Yankees' win over the Cardinals on June 15.

Not even the first doubleheaders of Matsui's professional life could derail his brilliant run. Due to rainouts earlier in the season, the Yankees played twin bills against the Tampa Bay Devil Rays June 17 and the crosstown Mets on June 28. Matsui had hits in all four games and went 7-for-16 overall with a homer and seven RBI.

"It was long, but no problems," Matsui told *Newsday* following the Devil Rays doubleheader, which was his first since high school. "I feel fine."

The Mets would be feeling particularly sickly after their double encounter with Matsui on June 28. Matsui was a one-man wrecking crew against the Mets as he went a sizzling 6-for-7 in the doubleheader with six RBI. He reached base in each of his last nine plate appearances on the day (six hits, two walks, one hit by pitch). His grand slam in the opener broke a scoreless tie and got the Yankees rolling in their 7-1 win, while his RBI single in the fifth inning of the nightcap proved to be the decisive run in the Yankees' 9-8 victory.

Matsui's nearly perfect day lifted his batting average to .305, 13 points higher than it was entering the day and 55 points higher than it was just 24 days earlier. It was the first time he'd been above .300 since April 20.

"I've just tried to be patient, give it my best effort and be positive," Matsui told reporters after the doubleheader. "I'm certainly not hitting as many home runs as I did before, but this is my first season. As I get used to baseball here, hopefully I'll hit more."

He'd already hit enough to convince the Mets of his ability. "I just don't know how to get that guy out," Mets catcher Jason Phillips told reporters. "I'm running out of fingers."

"He was on a roll [when] he hit against us," said Roberto Alomar, who was the Mets' second baseman until he was traded to the Chicago White Sox on July 2. "He was swinging the bat real well. It seems like he was learning more about [the] pitching here, and he has an idea [of] how they're pitching to him."

The Yankees, meanwhile, were running out of adjectives to describe a player who had been mired in a seemingly endless slump just three weeks earlier. "We've appreciated him, but the numbers that he posted [during the doubleheader against the Mets] will get a lot of other people's attention," Torre told reporters. "We know we have something special. You can't appreciate what he does by looking at the box score. Today, he was there every time we needed him."

Overall against the Mets, Matsui hit a blistering .522 with three homers and 10 RBI in just 23 at-bats in leading the Yankees to a season sweep of their Big Apple rivals. In the entire month of May, Matsui hit just one homer and collected just 11 RBI.

Matsui's dominance over the Mets certainly got him back into Steinbrenner's good graces. If there's anything "The Boss" hates more than losing, it's losing to the three teams he's identified as his main rivals: The Red Sox, the Mets, and the Devil Rays (Steinbrenner lives in Tampa). Matsui ended up hitting .297 against the Red Sox,

Mets, and Devil Rays during the regular season with three homers and 27 RBI in 175 at-bats.

Watching Matsui own the Mets had to be painful for the Yankees' beleaguered crosstown rivals, who were on their way to losing 95 games and finishing in last place in the NL East. While the Yankees went overseas to find a difference-maker such as Matsui, the Mets ended up with Tsuyoshi Shinjo, whose flair far surpassed his ability.

Ironically, though, the Japanese were more alarmed by Shinjo's defection than by Matsui's. Shinjo, the second Japanese position player to sign a Major League Baseball contract, received a fraction of the fanfare afforded Matsui and Ichiro Suzuki when he left Japan and signed with the Mets following the 2000 season. Shinjo was viewed as a defensive whiz and a colorful character (he performed a little hop after catching a fly ball, wore bright orange wristbands, and regularly dyed his hair) who was also a liability with the bat.

But Shinjo enjoyed a surprisingly solid all-around rookie season with the Mets in 2001. He made several highlight film plays in centerfield and ended the season as the Mets' cleanup hitter. Shinjo hit .268 with 10 homers and 56 RBI in 400 at-bats and won an outfield spot on the Topps baseball card company's "All-Star Rookie" team, but he was not on the same level as the Japanese superstars.

Kansas City Royals pitcher Darrell May, who spent four seasons in Japan, including two as a teammate of Matsui's with the Yomiuri Giants, said the reaction in Japan to Shinjo's success was one of "fear. He came over and people saw he had success over here, even though he wasn't a great player [in Japan]. [He] saw a lot of Japanese players thinking 'Wow, I could probably go over there and be successful' and I think that was kind of the thought process throughout Japan: Fear of losing a lot of our talent to the states."

As it turned out, another season in the states exposed Shinjo's weaknesses. He batted just .238 with nine homers and 37 RBI in 2002 for the San Francisco Giants, who acquired him from the Mets in December 2001. Shinjo re-signed with the Mets after the 2002 season, but he never won the approval of new manager Art Howe and was sent to Triple-A Norfolk after hitting .193 in 114 at-bats.

The reunion between Matsui and Shinjo wasn't nearly as anticipated as the late April meeting between Matsui and the Seattle Mariners' Suzuki, who signed with the Mariners 23 days before Shinjo inked his deal with the Mets in December 2000. But Matsui and Shinjo, who played against each other regularly in Japan—Shinjo played for the Hanshin Tigers, who were to Matsui's Yomiuri Giants what the Red Sox were to the Yankees—still met behind the batting cage prior to the first game of the Subway Series June 20 and shook hands as cameras captured the moment.

"We played against each other a lot [in Japan]," Matsui told mlb.com. "As an opponent, he's a very respectable player."

But to observe the scene from the Mets' viewpoint was to wonder what might have been.

The *Newark Star-Ledger*'s Lawrence Rocca reported June 29—the morning after Matsui's sizzling doubleheader performance—that the Mets, who have almost always been overshadowed by the Yankees, very nearly swooped in and signed Matsui during his free agent courtship the previous December.

Rocca reported there was a misunderstanding between Matsui and the Yankees regarding the language of the fourth-year club option in his contract. Matsui's father, Masao, thought the Yankees could simply decline the option at the end of Matsui's third season and send him back to the Yomiuri Giants. The Yankees explained that was not the case and that such a clause would be illegal, but with negotiations slowed to a crawl, Matsui called the Mets' top Japanese scout, Isao O'Jimi.

Matsui told O'Jimi he would think about signing with the Mets. O'Jimi in turn told Mets ownership of Matsui's interest, at which point Mets owner Fred Wilpon called his son Bruce into action. Bruce Wilpon was living in Tokyo at the time and had dinner with Matsui at the house of Wilpon's in-laws.

Matsui told Rocca the dinner "was great," and for a short time the Mets believed they might actually stun the Yankees and sign

Pregame communication between Yankees manager Joe Torre, Hideki Matsui, and interpreter Roger Kahlon (left to right) was vital, since Kahlon was not allowed in the dugout during the game.

How popular was Hideki Matsui? He was the only rookie in the bigs to have his own bobblehead doll day in 2003.

Yankee fans indicated their approval of Matsui by snapping off the shelves T-shirts and uniforms bearing his name and number.

Matsui was tracked at home and on the road by a sizable Japanese media contingent, which reported his every move.

A vocal group of Japanese fans showed up in Toronto for a September series and filled the SkyDome with the type of collegial atmosphere Matsui was accustomed to back home.

Hideki Matsui hit it off immediately with the Yankees' resident superstar, Derek Jeter (third on right), and by the World Series, the duo were regularly the first two Yankees out of the dugout to greet teammates crossing home plate.

Unlike many stars, Hideki Matsui regularly signed autographs for fans. Matsui told *Time* magazine's Asian edition that "talking to the press and signing autographs as often as I can is my way of fulfilling my obligations as a player."

Hideki Matsui's gentle demeanor in the face of unprecedented international scrutiny—not to mention his ability to remain focused on the field—continually amazed the Yankees and those who followed the team.

Knowing that the games would be televised in Japan, certain advertisers took advantage of the on-field presence of Matsui and Ichiro whenever they played in Toronto.

Little was said about Hideki Matsui's defense prior to his arrival, but he displayed uncanny instincts in both left and centerfield and helped solidify left field, which had been a problem spot for the Yankees for more than a decade.

It didn't take long for the Yankees to begin appreciating Matsui's all-around game. "He's a lot more than just an offensive player," teammate John Flaherty said. "You don't get to where he is in his career without being a consummate professional. I've enjoyed watching him day in and day out."

Hideki Matsui won over teammates and foes alike with his businesslike demeanor and refusal to "strut" following his home runs. He acted as if he'd done it before—which he had, 332 times in Japan.

Given his "Godzilla" nickname, the Yankees assumed Hideki Matsui would be swinging from his heels. But after a few days of spring training workouts, manager Joe Torre realized "he's more of a line-drive type hitter, and I like that a whole lot better because that [fits] with us a lot better."

Hideki Matsui is as calm and tranquil inside the batter's box as he is outside it.

For Hideki Matsui, pictured here settling underneath a fly ball during a spring training game, the exhibition season was an opportunity to get acquainted with left field. He had played centerfield throughout his nine-year career in Japan.

Hideki Matsui, pictured here swinging in a spring training game, provided the first proof he'd be worth the hype when he hit .324 with three homers and 10 RBI during the exhibition season.

Hideki Matsui was following a trail blazed by the likes of the Seattle Mariners' Ichiro Suzuki (upper left) and the New York Mets Tsuyoshi Shinjo (upper right), who were the first two position players from Japan to sign major league contracts, and the Los Angeles Dodgers' Hideo Nomo (pictured left) pitching for the Boston Red Sox in 2001, whose Rookie of the Year season in 1995 inspired other Japanese players to pursue careers in America.

Matsui. "We were hopeful," Mets interim general manager Jim Duquette told Rocca.

"Certainly, it was possible," Matsui told Rocca.

Eventually, though, the Yankees got rid of the fourth-year option entirely, and after that, Matsui quickly agreed to a three-year, $21 million deal. It worked out pretty well for him: While the Mets sunk into the NL East basement by mid-April, the Yankees had another successful season.

"I don't really compare the organizations," Matsui told Rocca. "I'm just glad I'm with the Yankees."

So were they.

Matsui's phenomenal performance against the Mets not only earned him AL Player of the Week honors for the week ending June 29 (he hit .500 with two homers and 14 RBI in eight games from June 23 to 29) but also thrust him into contention for a starting berth on the AL All-Star Team.

Major League Baseball announced June 30 that Matsui had moved into second place among AL outfielders. The top three vote-getters earned starting spots, and Matsui held a healthy 170,000-vote lead over fourth-place Manny Ramirez. A Yankee rookie outfielder had not started the All-Star Game since 1936, when all-time great Joe DiMaggio earned the honor.

Torre said starting the All-Star Game "would be great" for Matsui. "That would be wonderful," Torre told reporters. "A hell of a feather in his cap. The All-Star experience is great. It's not three days off, but it's fun."

Matsui had played in nine All-Star Games in Japan, but winning Player of the Week honors was a new experience. Japan's Central League did not have a Player of the Week, though it did select a Player of the Month. Matsui said he earned the latter honor seven times as a member of the Giants.

As for earning Player of the Week honors, Matsui told mlb.com, "There's nothing like being able to win something like that. It's a result of your daily work ethic.

"Maybe if I hit three home runs today, I can win Player of the Month."

Matsui actually ended the month with an 0-for-4 night against the Baltimore Orioles June 30, but he probably wouldn't have won the monthly honor anyway. Instead, teammate Jason Giambi— who, like Matsui, snapped out of an extended funk in June—took home the hardware. Giambi, who hit just .227 with 11 homers and 34 RBI the first two months of the season, hit .373 with 11 homers and 29 RBI in June, while Matsui hit .394 with six homers and 29 RBI in June.

Matsui's performance was still enough to easily earn him AL Rookie of the Month honors. Matsui, who led AL rookies in June in batting average, RBI, hits (41), doubles (11), walks (15), on-base percentage (.484), and slugging percentage (.673), was the first AL player to win the award other than Tampa Bay outfielder Rocco Baldelli, and his victory was the latest indication that Baldelli—all but anointed as the Rookie of the Year during his impressive first two months—was in for quite a race for the award.

"I'm very happy to win the [Rookie of the Month] award," Matsui told mlb.com. "It's a pleasure and an honor.

"It's funny. I have been able to play for the last 10 years, so it doesn't feel like I'm a rookie."

Matsui wasn't the only one to feel that way, as he'd learn when opposing managers and media relations executives began pounding the pavement for their Rookie of the Year candidates later in the summer.

But Matsui had one thing the rest of the potential Rookie of the Year candidates lacked: A starting spot in the All-Star Game.

Following the Yankees' 7-1 win over the Red Sox July 6—a win in which Matsui's batting average peaked at a season-high .311—the Yankees learned Matsui, second baseman Alfonso Soriano, and catcher Jorge Posada had been elected to start the All-Star Game the following week in Chicago.

And while the Yankees were miffed that AL manager Mike Scioscia declined to select any other Yankees as reserves—eventually,

Giambi made the team as an injury replacement while Major League Baseball added Roger Clemens, who said he was in the midst of his final season, to the roster as a goodwill gesture—everyone was thrilled for the Japanese import who had turned his season around over the previous month.

"To get people's attention that quickly is a great credit to him," Torre told reporters.

"It's exciting, considering how he started out," Giambi told reporters. "It's great for him. He's been on fire, and the fans recognize that. The new kid in town has done well. The Japanese vote probably didn't hurt him either."

As for Matsui, he was predictably excited, in his uniquely low-key way, to earn the honor. "To be chosen as an All-Star really ranks up there for me in my career," Matsui told mlb.com. "I'm honored to be chosen by the fans. For the fans to write my name on the ballots is a great honor."

Actually, many of the people who voted for Matsui didn't need to use a pencil to do so. The traditional voting method—in which fans would pick up a ballot at the ballpark and punch out the hole next to the name of their favorite players—had been replaced by Internet voting, which allowed fans all over the world—and particularly those in Matsui's home country—to vote for their favorite players as many as 20 times.

There was no doubting the validity of Matsui's candidacy, though. Ballot-stuffing or not, his all-around excellence, not to mention his ability to adapt on the fly at the game's highest level, made him a deserving All-Star.

And in the clearest indication yet of just how global baseball had become, Matsui wasn't even the only All-Star from the Far East. Ichiro Suzuki also won a starting spot in the American League outfield while Scioscia selected Seattle Mariners reliever Shigetoshi Hasegawa to his pitching staff.

As a result, the All-Star Game on July 15 was far more than an exhibition game for the Japanese trio and the fans watching the game half a world away. For them, it was a cultural milestone.

"I think maybe we can show the other players who are playing in Japan what their dreams can be," Matsui said during a press conference the day before the All-Star Game.

"We never thought about it—three Japanese guys on the All-Star team, that's awesome," Hasegawa told the *Newark Star-Ledger*. "I think it's good for the Japanese people, too, [and] kids watching the All-Star Game. If you watch it, [you realize] it can happen. I never thought about it. That's pretty tough to imagine. Now, I think a lot of Japanese kids are going to start thinking about it."

And while Hasegawa was popular in his own right in Japan, most of the nation's baseball fans were far more passionate about Matsui and Suzuki. So two and a half months after their first meeting on an American diamond dominated the news in Japan, Matsui and Suzuki again made headline news when they shook hands and chatted in the outfield during the AL's workout the day before the All-Star Game. The moment was captured and transmitted back to Japan's television sets and newspapers by 250 media members from Japan.

Suzuki batted first for the AL while Matsui batted seventh. Matsui ended up getting the AL's first hit, a bloop single off NL starter Jason Schmidt, on the first pitch of his first at-bat in the second inning.

"I wasn't nervous, it was just like any other game," Matsui told mlb.com. "When I stepped to the plate, I was just trying to concentrate, get a base hit."

Matsui also reached base on a fielder's choice grounder in the fourth inning and flawlessly handled his two chances in centerfield. He left the game for pinch-runner Vernon Wells following his second at-bat and watched the AL come from behind to edge the NL, 7-6, on a two-run home run by the Texas Rangers' Hank Blalock in the eighth inning.

The win gave the AL the home field advantage in the World Series, which was especially relevant to the Yankees, who expected to advance to the Fall Classic after a one-year sabbatical. "If we can get to the World Series, this will be very good for us," Matsui told mlb.com. "I'm happy we could help get home field advantage for the American League."

The entire All-Star experience was a happy one for Matsui, who spent part of the night before the game watching teammate Bernie Williams perform selections from his jazz album at the House of Blues in Chicago.

"I always respected Bernie Williams as a baseball player," Matsui told the *Newark Star-Ledger*. "I respect Bernie Williams as a musician now. I'm surprised he is so good both ways, as a baseball player and musician."

Matsui's presence at Williams' concert was just another example of how quickly and easily Matsui was becoming "one of the guys." Ventura indicated as much on June 5, when he replaced Matsui's nameplate with the one reading "OH-55" following his breakout game against the Reds.

Matsui also won an admirer in the hard-to-please Roger Clemens, who said later in the summer he'd like to visit Matsui in Japan during the off-season.

"He's a nice guy," Zeile said of Matsui. "I like him a lot. He's confident but he's humble. He's had some humility. He's a very good teammate."

When June began, the idea of Matsui making the All-Star team was incomprehensible. So what happened to the player the press jokingly dubbed "Groundzilla?" How did he go from an international bust to starting the All-Star Game in centerfield seemingly overnight?

Part of it was the natural adaptation process endured by every rookie. But a bigger factor was a subtle, seldom-reported yet vital change in Matsui's swing—which, in turn, helped him stop "rolling over" the two-seam "sinker" thrown by many major league pitchers.

"When we were in Cincinnati, he made some technical changes—partially pointed out by Jorge Posada, partially [by Yankees hitting coach] Rick Down," Zeile said. "He made a little adjustment to his 'trigger.' He wasn't getting started with his hands, and was subsequently sort of in between on a lot of things. It seemed like once that 'trigger' got rectified, then he started swinging the bat well and his confidence improved."

Matsui also helped himself out by engaging in "shop talk" with Down and players such as Posada, Giambi, Ventura, and Bernie Williams, all of whom either switch-hit or hit exclusively from the left side. The language barrier was no problem, since the topic of conversation was universal and required no translation.

"All guys talk to each other about [hitting], no matter what language you speak," Zeile said. "If somebody has a knowledge of a pitcher and knows how the ball's going to move and what he might tend to do to a left-handed hitter, guys share those types of facts. That kind of information gives you a little better game plan when you go up there."

Matsui clearly absorbed all the information he received, and his plan at the plate in June was nearly flawless. Jason Anderson, who appeared in 22 games for the Yankees before he was dealt to the Mets July 16, said he could tell that Matsui "was starting to get comfortable.

"The learning [process] was starting to [conclude], and he was just getting comfortable and letting his abilities take over," Anderson said. "The big thing about being up here, when you first get up here, [is a player has to] learn and take everything in and get used to the atmosphere. And then once you do that, you just do what you can do and let your ability take over."

Said Jeff Nelson, "He's adjusted. It's a whole different year [for Matsui]."

Those who knew Matsui weren't surprised at his ability to make such drastic adjustments in the middle of a season. "Over there [in Japan], you've got six teams in each league, so one person figures out how to pitch someone successfully, all of a sudden, everybody that's facing you is pitching you that way," May said. "He would be quick to pick up on that [and] make the adjustments."

Finally, Americans were getting a lasting glimpse of the real Matsui.

Chicago White Sox pitcher Mark Buerhle, who pitched against Matsui in the All-Star Series between the United States and Japan the previous winter, admitted he wondered what the fuss was about when Matsui hit just .161 in eight games against the Americans. "But since then," Buerhle said, "he's come over here [and] he's done pretty decent."

He certainly had. But Matsui wasn't done struggling just yet.

A Tired Matsui, A Tired Debate?

Oh and Two. Oh and Two

The American reporter smiled at his Japanese counter-
part as they stood among the more than two dozen
reporters waiting to file into the Yankees' clubhouse
following the Yankees' 11-2 loss to the Chicago White Sox
August 27. "That's your lead story for tomorrow," the American
reporter said. "The Yankees are oh-and-two without Matsui in the
starting lineup. They can't win without him."

Matsui had nothing to do, literally, with the Yankees' lopsided
defeat: For the second straight night, he wasn't in the starting
lineup.

Matsui entered the series against the White Sox in the midst of
an extended slump. He'd followed up his breakthrough June with
an impressive July in which he hit .299 with two homers and
15 RBI. He hit his first-ever "sayonara" home run—a walk-off

homer—to lift the Yankees past the Cleveland Indians in the first game following the All-Star break July 17. Matsui had nine multi-hit games in the month and his seasonal average never dropped below .294.

And in the clearest indication yet of his burgeoning popularity, he was the subject of Hideki Matsui Bobblehead Doll Day on July 22. He was the only rookie in Major League Baseball to be honored with a Bobblehead Doll Day in 2003.

The game against the Blue Jays was rained out and rescheduled for September 9, when the Yankees again would hand out Matsui's bobbleheaded likeness. "I'm honored to have them make a bobblehead of me," Matsui told reporters after the July 22 game was rained out. "The backside of it looks just like me. I don't know about the face. That's for everybody else to decide."

Matsui's batting average was right at .300 after going 0-for-2 in the Yankees' 2-1 win over the Anaheim Angels July 31. It would be his last day at .300.

While Matsui's slump wasn't quite as drastic as the one that enveloped him for 23 games in May and early June, his August swoon was still pronounced and cause for concern among the Yankees and the Japanese reporters following the team. Matsui displayed impressive patience at the plate in August, when he had 14 walks and 14 strikeouts, but he had just two multi-hit games in the month and hit just .233 with 4 homers and 15 RBI.

Even his most productive stretch of the month was wobbly: Matsui had a nine-game hitting streak from August 8 to 16, during which he only racked up 11 hits.

Finally, with Matsui deep in a 3-for-22 slump entering play August 26, manager Joe Torre decided to hold him out of the starting lineup for two consecutive days in hopes it would help Matsui snap out of his funk.

"It looks like his bat is a little slower," Torre told reporters. "He's in a slump and it could be caused by fatigue."

Torre was one of many people who thought Matsui might be struggling because he wasn't used to playing so many regular season games or traveling so much during the season. In Japan, Matsui was used to a 140-game regular season—in 2002, five games were added to the regular season schedule—and taking a train to and from most destinations.

Late-season struggles were nothing new for Japanese imports. During his rookie season in 2001, the New York Mets' Tsuyoshi Shinjo hit .281 before the All-Star break but just .255 after it.

The Seattle Mariners' Ichiro Suzuki had no slumps at all on his way to winning the American League Rookie of the Year and Most Valuable Player awards in 2001, but he slumped badly in the second half of the 2002 and 2003 seasons: Suzuki hit .352 before the All-Star break in 2003 but just .259 after it. In 2002, his pre– and post–All-Star break splits were .357 and .280.

"It's a huge adjustment process, I think the length of the season is definitely something that wears them out," said *Newsday* Mets beat writer David Lennon, who covered Matsui during the All-Star Series between the United States and Japan the previous winter. "When it shows up in those numbers, I think it's undeniable, especially when you can compare it to the [differing lengths of the] seasons between the two places. And the travel [in Japan] is much closer. There are places they do fly to, but [on] a number of [road trips], they can take a bullet train."

Said WFAN Yankees beat reporter Sweeney Murti: "He admitted he was run down a little bit, [that he had] run into a wall. It's only natural. You see it [in] other sports—you see rookies in the NBA who never played more than 30 games in a season [in college]. They get to the 50, 60 game mark and they're dragging. So it was only natural for something like that to happen, but he managed to make his way through it."

Interestingly, two Americans who had played in Japan—Dan Gladden and Joe Vitiello—disagreed that Matsui was tired from either the extended schedule or travel itinerary. "If they were playing in Triple-A, yeah, I would believe [they were tired because of the travel], but in the big leagues, the travel's still travel," said Montreal Expos utility man Vitiello, who played for the Orix Blue

Wave in 2001. "But over [in Japan], they practice all the time when they have off-days.

"I'm not saying they're not tired, but I don't think it's because of the travel," Vitiello said. "They play less games over there. It might be a little more taxing on you [in America], but I don't think it's really that big of a deal."

Torre, though, still wanted to do whatever he could to try and keep Matsui fresh down the stretch and into the postseason. So he "rested" Matsui August 26 and 27 against the White Sox but planned to get Matsui into each game as either a pinch-hitter or late-inning defensive replacement so that Matsui could maintain a consecutive games streak that had spanned two continents.

Matsui had played in 1,379 straight games—1,250 in Japan from 1994 to 2002 and all 129 games as a Yankee. He would become one of just six big leaguers to attain "perfect attendance" in 2003 as he ran his consecutive games streak to 1,413 games overall.

No Yankee had ever before played in every game of a single season under Torre, but it didn't take long for Torre to grow fond of Matsui nor understand how much his "Ironman" streak meant to him.

"I have no problem trying to continue his streak, because he's such a good defensive player," Torre told reporters August 27. "We're going out of our way to do it, but it's not disrupting anything. He had this streak before he got here. If you're going to let him bite off one at-bat or one inning, I don't think that's a detriment to anybody."

Matsui appeared as a defensive replacement in the top of the ninth August 26 with the Yankees trailing 11-2. The following evening, with the Yankees down 7-2 in the top of the fifth, he entered the game to a warm ovation in place of the injured David Dellucci.

Matsui went 0-for-2 at the plate. After such an inconsequential performance in a lopsided defeat, most players would be able to shower and escape the locker room unnoticed within 20 minutes of the final out.

But, as was the case on a daily basis for Matsui, there was plenty to talk about. So as the rest of his teammates made a quick exit, Matsui walked a few hundred feet to an auxiliary locker room, where more than three dozen Japanese reporters—about half the total number of Japanese media at the game—from the country's newspapers, news agencies, and television and radio stations were gathered.

The conversation in the room stopped as Matsui walked through the door with Yankees media relations assistant Isao Hirooka and headed for the podium at the front of the room.

Matsui, dressed in a Yankees t-shirt and his uniform pants, turned around and folded his hands in front of him. In cautious, almost reverential fashion, the reporters formed a comfortable circle around Matsui. The usual mosh pit-like pushing and grumbling that normally accompanied the rush to engulf an American athlete was nowhere to be found, seen, or heard.

The group of reporters around Matsui asked 11 questions, many of which were asked or answered with a smile and/or a laugh. Hirooka said Matsui was asked about, among other things, his two plate appearances, Dellucci's injury, and how he felt knowing he'd likely be back in the starting lineup for the next afternoon's game.

The give-and-take was noticeably more quiet and polite than most interviews between American players and reporters. Matsui and his inquisitors spoke in tones so low that they were often drowned out by the simplest of noises: the clubhouse kids slapping cleats in the hallway outside or someone in the room zipping a duffel bag. And instead of several reporters shouting a question at the same time, a pause of a few seconds followed each of Matsui's answers as the reporters made sure he was completely finished responding to the previous question.

Six minutes after he walked in, with no more questions from the group, Hirooka announced the interview session was complete. But two more reporters approached Matsui, who patiently answered their questions before he conducted a television interview.

On his way back to the Yankees locker room, Matsui was again approached by another reporter; again he patiently answered his question. Inside the clubhouse, Matsui made small talk with yet another reporter and shared a joke with him before he walked into the off-limits shower area.

It was almost 11 P.M.—45 minutes since the last pitch of the game—by the time Matsui finally took his shower. And he had to be back at the Stadium by 11:30 A.M. for the series finale against the White Sox.

Just as he did in Japan, Matsui wore uniform number 55 in honor of Japanese baseball icon Sadaharu Oh, who holds the all-time single season record there with 55 home runs. The fact he got to wear number 55 with the Yankees was another sign of just how fond the Yankees already were of Matsui, considering that number could have been taken by beloved coach Don Zimmer.

The Yankees' bench coach and baseball lifer usually chooses the uniform number corresponding with the number of years he's been in the game. The 2003 season was Zimmer's 55th season in pro ball, but he deferred to Matsui and wore uniform number 53 throughout the season.

However, the sight of Matsui wearing number 55 evoked images of Joe DiMaggio, who exuded so much class and accomplished so much as a Yankee that his number 5 was retired in 1952, less than a year after his retirement. Like DiMaggio, Matsui almost made things look easy with his smooth, seemingly effortless motions both at the plate and in the field.

Like DiMaggio, Matsui took pride in remaining dignified and stoic even as he lived the most public of lives. DiMaggio almost never expressed emotion on the diamond, which is why the image of DiMaggio kicking the dirt in frustration after Al Gionfriddo made a running catch of his line drive during Game Six of the 1947 World Series remains one of the most played clips in baseball history.

Matsui made national headlines in Japan when he took a few steps toward then-Hanshin Tigers pitcher Darrell May after May plunked Matsui in the left shoulder in 1999. In America, the closest thing to an "outburst" may have occurred against the White Sox on August 27, when, with Matsui in the midst of a 6-for-27 slump, he popped out to centerfield with two men on base to end a sixth inning rally in a game the Yankees eventually lost 11-2.

As he jogged to first base, Matsui held the bat in his right hand for a few seconds, as if he was contemplating whether or not to throw it down in anger. Eventually, he calmly tossed it into foul territory and continued to run towards first. He then ran right into the dugout, retrieved his hat and glove, and sprinted on to the field ahead of a handful of teammates.

Those who observed Matsui on a daily basis were just as impressed with Matsui's ability to maintain his composure during slumps as they were with how he swung the bat during June.

In good times and bad, baseball players spout clichés about how they've got to take things one day at a time and how they can't get too high or too low or get too excited or despondent because baseball is a humbling game and everything eventually evens out.

Alas, most of those players fail to practice what they preach and let slumps consume them to the point of obsession. "I think some guys are lying and some guys aren't [when they talk about not getting too high or low]," *Newsday* Yankees beat writer Ken Davidoff said. "I think Derek Jeter doesn't let a slump get him down, whereas Jason Giambi does."

Matsui was certainly more Jeter than Giambi. Throughout his two extended slumps, Matsui never indicated any outward signs of frustration.

Asked if he's ever seen any changes in Matsui's demeanor, Tyler Kepner, the Yankees beat writer for the *New York Times*, said, he's "exactly the same. He's *exactly* the same. You hear a lot of 'Oh, [a player is] the same when he's going well or when he's going badly, but in his case, I think it's really true. I can't think of any change in his demeanor at all. I don't think it's an act. I get the feeling that he's very genuine."

When Matsui slumped, it actually magnified how solid he was in all other facets of the game and how he could help the Yankees even when his bat was on ice.

"All we ever heard about before we saw him play was [that he hit] 50 home runs [and he was a] power hitter in Japan—all these offensive accolades," Yankees backup catcher John Flaherty said. "And he's an all-around player. Defensively, he's an excellent outfielder. He might not have the arm strength of some other guys out there, but he gets rid of the ball very quickly, [he] always hits the cutoff man."

He also made one of the greatest defensive plays of the Yankees' season against the Orioles in Baltimore on August 14. With runners on first and second, two outs in the seventh inning and the Yankees nursing a 6-5 lead, the Orioles' Larry Bigbie hit a shot to deep left. Matsui raced over, made the catch, and held on to the ball even though he slammed into the wall. The Yankees went on to win, 8-5.

The play went unnoticed by many in the Northeast, which was in the midst of a blackout when Matsui made the catch. But those who saw it marveled at Matsui's ability to not only catch up to the ball but also hold on to it.

"I didn't think he'd catch up to it, and if he did, you knew he was going to have to go into the wall," Torre told reporters afterward. "It was unbelievable. You talk about a play that can start a winning streak, that was one of them."

Sure enough, that win started a seven-game winning streak for the Yankees—their second-longest spurt of the season.

"[He's] just [got] the all-around game," Flaherty said. "He's a lot more than just an offensive player. You don't get to where he is in his career without being a consummate professional."

For most Yankees, road trips are an escape from the unrelenting attention the team receives during home stands, when the team is usually covered by at least two reporters from each of the area's eight newspapers and all of the local television and radio networks.

Still, as much attention as the Yankees receive from the press, it's nothing compared to what Matsui and the Yomiuri Giants received overseas. Darrell May, a teammate of Matsui's with the Giants in 2000 and 2001, estimated that "20 [or] 25" reporters followed the Giants both at home and on the road.

Dozens of reporters attended Yankee games home and away, but their American traveling contingent consisted of only the beat reporters from the area newspapers (*The Daily News, New York Post* and *New York Times* in New York City, *Newsday* on Long Island, *The Journal News* in Westchester County, *The Record* and *Star-Ledger* from New Jersey and *The Hartford Courant* from Connecticut) and the team's official website, yankees.com.

Flaherty said Matsui told him during spring training that the coverage he received in Japan dwarfed what he received in America. "So in an odd way," Flaherty said, "this might be a break for him."

Said May with a grin: "Oh, this is a cakewalk compared to what he had to deal with in Japan [for] him and Ichiro. You've got to realize, over there, they couldn't step foot out in public without being seen, without being noticed. Here, I'm sure he can walk around Manhattan, and a few people might recognize him, but it's not going to be like what it was in Japan. The pressures of that are not as bad."

The pressures for the Yankees tend to abate on the road, when the only New York media accompanying the team are the newspaper daily beat writers. As a result, the clubhouse is sparser and the atmosphere more relaxed than at home.

"At home, there's more local [television and radio] channels [and] video cameras, but not on the road," Yankees catcher Jorge Posada said. "[It's] a little bit [of a relief]. A lot of the same guys [from the] newspapers [are on the road], but when it comes to cameras, it's always a little less."

Except for Matsui.

Whether the Yankees were at palatial Yankee Stadium or inside the Toronto Blue Jays' antiseptic home stadium, the SkyDome, for a series in the first week of September, Matsui was always covered like a blanket by a bevy of Japanese writers and television crews.

Before the Yankees left the visitors locker room at SkyDome for stretching and batting practice, Matsui chatted with several reporters. On the field, several cameramen and photographers stood in the brown area in between the dugouts and captured his every motion, whether he was stretching, playing catch with teammate Ruben Sierra, signing autographs for fans, or merely running into the dugout to get his bat, batting helmet, and batting gloves.

During batting practice, Torre called over Matsui's interpreter, Roger Kahlon, and Matsui. A Japanese cameraman located near the Blue Jays dugout nearly tripped over himself as he raced over to capture the summit between the three men.

It was, as ex-teammate Jason Anderson observed, as if Matsui was the subject of Japan's version of American "reality television." And at first glance, the scene in Toronto was about what everyone expected when it became clear Matsui was going to come to America with his media entourage in tow.

But those who regularly traveled with the Yankees marveled at how calm things actually were around Matsui, as well as the professionalism and kindness exhibited by those who covered him. "There was this concern before [the season] that [the Yankees'] clubhouse is going to see double or triple the media," Kepner said. "But they are as respectful as he is. They do their job, and they all work hard, but they don't get in the way at all of the beat writers."

The Japanese beat writers were allowed in the clubhouse, but usually received their Matsui briefings outside the locker room. As a result, the human traffic jam many expected to find inside the Yankees clubhouse never materialized.

"You can see it on the road, when other media from other cities would talk about the Japanese invasion or 'reporters descending'— words that made it look like these hordes of just paparazzi [would be covering Matsui]," Kepner said. "But when you're around them everyday, you realize [that's not the case]."

Fortunately for all writers, though, teams in visiting cities planned for an overflow crowd of media, which allowed things to run smoother in the press box and in the press dining room. With a laugh, Kepner recalled that "very rarely do you see [a] press box run out of food . . . visiting teams were much better prepared for the New York media than ever before, because there are so many Japanese reporters. They have to be told in advance [who is covering the game, which] makes them prepare for everybody. Whereas before, we would go into a city and there wouldn't be enough seats, there would be a hassle and everybody would be surprised [at the crowd], even though you should know what you're getting into."

It didn't take long for the Japanese and American writers to hit it off, socially and professionally. In fact, on a rare night off in Toronto September 2, the Japanese and American writers went out to dinner at a local restaurant.

"They seem very respectful, and they seem to respect what you do," Kepner said. "And I think that makes it easy for us to give them respect."

Matsui's teammates also came to respect and appreciate the politeness displayed by the Japanese press. Flaherty said the conversation between him and the Japanese reporters was a matter of "just exchanging pleasantries—[a] 'hi, how are you?' type of thing."

Flaherty said he was most interested in learning why Japanese reporters and Matsui always bowed at one another at the beginning and conclusion of an interview. "I kind of wanted to find out what that tradition is all about in Japan," Flaherty said. "And it was explained to me [that] it's like a handshake, it's almost a sign of respect.

"They've been very pleasant to deal with on an everyday basis—very friendly and a pleasure to have around, as is Hideki," Flaherty said. "Their culture is very friendly, very polite [and] appreciative—just fun to be around."

The American writers were also respectful of—and moved by— what brought the Japanese reporters here. "You realize that they're, in many cases, a long way from home, and they're covering one guy," Kepner said. "In some ways, it's easier, I would think, but in some ways it's harder than covering an entire organization."

"I think, in general, there is great respect among the American reporters for how hard the Japanese reporters work, how well they cope with such strange circumstances and how difficult it is to try and cover just one person every day, day after day," *New York Post* baseball columnist Joel Sherman said.

The media attention in Toronto wasn't the only thing to make Matsui feel right at home. Though there were only 21,770 in attendance at SkyDome for the Yankees' 4-3 loss to the Blue Jays on September 3, the boisterous groups of college kids that chanted, whistled and stomped in the left- and right-field stands filled the stadium with the type of energy Matsui experienced on a daily basis in Japan.

And in the sixth inning, Torre pulled a page out of the Japanese managerial stylebook when he had Posada lay down a bunt leading off the inning. Posada had homered in his previous at-bat.

Power hitters regularly bunted in Japan. May said the bunt sign went on if "the first guy gets on [in an inning]—it doesn't matter if the next guy coming is a .300 hitter or a .250 hitter."

The only exception? If Matsui happened to be the second batter up in an inning.

The mini-vacation Torre gave Matsui from August 26 to 27— when Matsui came off the bench in back-to-back games against the White Sox—didn't do much to snap him out of his slump. Matsui went just 5-for-31 with no homers and only two RBI in 10 games between August 26 and September 5. His average after the Yankees' 9-3 loss to the Red Sox September 5 was .283, down from .291 on August 26 and .300 on July 31.

But with the Yankees in the midst of a heated pennant race with the dogged Boston Red Sox, Torre had no plans to give his left fielder any more rest. "He's going to have to beg me for a day off now," Torre told reporters August 29.

Actually, a lack of days off might have been the best thing for Matsui. Playing everyday allowed Matsui to bury the memories of the struggles he'd endured the previous game, whereas starting pitchers who got torched had to sit and stew for at least four days before their next turn on the hill.

"I'm not a pitcher, so I don't really know what they go through," Vitiello said with a laugh. "It's easier to forget a bad game when you play everyday."

Vitiello also believed it was easier for an American hitter to snap out of a funk than a Japanese hitter "because in Japan, each pitcher probably has five or six pitches. Over here, pitchers probably have three [pitches]."

American pitchers threw harder than their Japanese counterparts, but Japanese hurlers were more challenging in that they rarely threw the same pitch more than once in an at-bat and rarely attacked a hitter with a fastball.

"I think in a way the mentality over there is, 'Why would you throw a guy a fastball? That's an easy pitch to hit,'" May said. "Which I don't quite get. I don't understand that. But if you threw a fastball and got a home run hit off you, you come back in the dugout [and] your pitching coach or manager [would be] screaming at you."

Just as he did during his May slump, Matsui seemed to be "rolling over" the ball and pulling it to the right side of the infield in late August and early September. He grounded out to first or second base nine times in his 31 at-bats between August 26 and September 5, and he'd finish the season first in the AL in groundouts (223) and second in double plays (25).

And once again, Torre was spending a lot of time reassuring Japanese reporters that Matsui would be fine. Matsui was one of just two Yankee starters without a hit in the Yankees' 4-3 loss to the Blue Jays September 3, but afterwards, Torre, with a hint of defiance in his voice, reminded a reporter that the Yankees were in the midst of a team-wide slump. The Yankees scored just 13 runs in six games from September 1 to 7.

"We've had a lot of guys [who] didn't get a lot of hits [recently]," Torre said.

Torre had seen his left fielder snap out of a slump before, and he was sure he'd do it again. "He's going to come out of it," Torre said. "One thing he's not going to do is quit.

"I don't think he's tired," Torre said. "I think he's pressing."

Torre could be a stern man, and once you lost his trust, it was gone forever. Just ask former Yankees outfielder Raul Mondesi, who got mad at Torre when the skipper pinch-hit for Mondesi in the eighth inning of a 6-3 loss to the Boston Red Sox on July 27. Mondesi expressed his disgust by leaving the clubhouse before the end of the game. Two days later, he was traded to the Arizona Diamondbacks.

However, Torre was more patient than most managers when it came to dealing with slumping players, largely because he'd traveled in their shoes plenty of times during his own often-stellar playing career (he won the National League Most Valuable Player award in 1971 and hit .297 overall with six 20-homer seasons and five 100-RBI seasons) and understood that no one puts more pressure on a player than the player himself.

Torre had separate conversations with Matsui, first baseman Giambi, centerfielder Bernie Williams, and second baseman Alfonso Soriano when the four were in the midst of deep slumps in late August and early September.

"It's probably more magnified for them than it is to us," Torre said. "I know as a player, I always [felt] that my slumps were bigger than they actually [appeared] on the outside. I just try to let them know that it's no big deal, that something's going to happen, and show you're confident in them."

Torre even went so far as to hold impromptu midgame meetings with his hitters. In 1998, after the Yankees won an American League–record tying 114 regular season games, Torre sensed his players were pressing during their first-round playoff series against the Texas Rangers.

"[It seemed] we won every game [during the season] and everyone was putting so much pressure on themselves that we had trouble spitting," Torre said. "[Players had] cotton mouth."

The meeting worked: The Yankees swept the Rangers, three games to none, in the American League Division Series and went on to win the World Series.

Such interaction between a player and manager was rare in Japan. In Robert Whiting's book *You Gotta Have Wa*, Leon Lee, who starred in Japan for 10 years and managed the Orix Blue Wave in 2003, recalled that Chibe Lotte Marines manager Michiyo Aritoh "hasn't talked to me my entire career. I've been on the same team with this man for eleven years [prior to managing the Marines, Aritoh was their first baseman and captain]. I batted next to him in the lineup, but I've never spent a social evening with him. After all these years, I still don't know who he is."

Matsui's teammates, however, knew who he was: A clutch hitter, an outstanding defensive outfielder, and a great guy to have around the clubhouse.

He was also, no matter what he had accomplished overseas, still a rookie in America. So that meant he had to partake in the most American of rookie hazing rituals: Dress-up day.

Veterans "initiate" rookies by making them wear hideous outfits on a late-season road trip. Ideally, the team will be heading to Canada, which means the rookies have to look like buffoons as they go through customs.

The Yankees weren't that cruel: They chose to initiate the rookies—Matsui, catcher Michel Hernandez, and pitchers Jose Contreras and Jorge DePaula—as the team prepared to depart for its final road trip of the season, which began with a brief flight to Baltimore.

And so following Yankees' 5-2 loss to the Tampa Bay Devil Rays on September 14, the quartet of rookies returned to the clubhouse to find their suits replaced by outfits better suited for a Halloween party.

Contreras (who started the game and took the loss for the Yankees) and Matsui were forced to dress as pimps. Contreras wore a wig, a white fur hat, a white fur coat, and a blue dress shirt, the latter of which was unbuttoned to the middle of his chest. He also had a gold medallion hanging from his neck, carried a cane in his left hand, and wore between his forefinger and index finger a gold ring with the word "GANGSTA."

Matsui, meanwhile, was even more outrageous in a leopard-skin hat and suit with plunging neckline. He also sported a fake gold tooth.

There have been plenty of rookies who have chafed at the ritual in the past, and it can be a source of contention with foreign-born players who may not understand the reasoning behind the act. But Matsui and Contreras were tremendous sports as they laughed and posed for pictures both inside the locker room and outside the Stadium where, as part of their hazing, the rookies were forced to sign autographs in full garb.

"I think the rookie hazing and thousands of other items large and small during the season said Matsui was never going to put his status as an icon in Japan above his belief that he was part of this team," Sherman said. "He wanted to fit in. He did fit in."

"I was surprised everybody took it so well," Murti said. "But I think everybody kind of came to expect it, so they weren't too taken aback by it. It was kind of like Halloween—they almost enjoyed wearing those things."

Added Murti with a chuckle: "I'm not really sure they got the full effect of it, because they almost seemed too happy to wear that stuff."

That day, though, Matsui was happy to be wearing anything other than a hospital ID bracelet.

A day before he played dress-up, Matsui had the biggest injury scare of his rookie season when he collided with Devil Rays pitcher Joe Kennedy as Matsui tried to beat out a bases-loaded grounder up the first base line in the bottom of the seventh inning. Kennedy tagged out Matsui, but he ran into Matsui's left knee.

Matsui went to the ground clutching his knee. He got up and limped away, but Juan Rivera replaced him.

"You see collisions all the time," Kennedy told reporters. "I was going for the ball. The ball just forced me right into him. It was all adrenaline. I needed to make a play. I didn't know where he was."

Not surprisingly, Matsui's injury had the potential to be front-page news in Japan. Fortunately for Matsui, he was fine: In between games of the doubleheader, Matsui was driven to an area hospital, where x-rays were negative.

And to the surprise of nobody, he managed to make it into the starting lineup for the nightcap—his 1,398th consecutive game, going back to his days in Japan. Matsui went 0-for-4 with two strikeouts in the game but was proud he played at all.

"I've never missed a game because of an injury," Matsui told the *New York Daily News* the next day.

Matsui also went 0-for-4 the day after his brush with disaster and failed to score from first base on a double with the game still scoreless in the fourth. Matsui, who stopped at third on the play, told reporters that his failure to score "might have been somewhat related [to his sore knee], but there's no guarantee that even if it was 100 percent that I would have been able to score."

But in a sign of the burgeoning respect Matsui was earning from the New York press, nary a negative word was written about his streak being detrimental to the team. On the other hand, the American "Ironman," Cal Ripken Jr., heard plenty of criticism from those who thought he was being selfish during his 2,632-game streak.

"I have a lot of pride because I've been playing for so long," Matsui told the *New York Daily News* the day following the scare. "The team comes before that, though. This was not the kind of injury that would have kept me out of a game."

"You don't see guys like that too often anymore," Williams told the *Daily News*. "Some guys are looking for ways to get a day off. If you want to win, you better have guys like that who are willing to play hurt."

Another valued statistical mark would have been endangered had Matsui's injury been more serious. He notched his 99th RBI of the season with a solo homer against the Detroit Tigers in the fourth inning of the Yankees' 15-5 win on September 10, but he remained stuck there as he failed to drive in a run in his next 26 at-bats.

Finally, Matsui reached the century mark with a single to left to score Posada in the sixth inning of the Yankees' 13-1 win over the Baltimore Orioles on September 15. Matsui was the second Yankee to reach 100 RBI; Giambi hit the milestone mark with a solo homer two innings earlier.

"I'm pretty happy about it," Matsui told the *Newark Star-Ledger.* "I didn't have any numbers in mind when I first came here, but since I was close to 100, I'm happy I reached it."

Matsui joined some pretty good company by collecting his 100th RBI. The only other Yankee rookies to do so were Hall-of-Famers Tony Lazzeri (114 RBI in 1926) and Joe DiMaggio (125 RBI in 1936).

"It's a great honor to be a part of a historical team like this one," Matsui told mlb.com. "To be part of a group like that, it's special."

Aside from his nearly week-long RBI drought, Matsui performed considerably better at the plate in September than he did in August. He had seven multi-hit games in September along with 14 RBI and an on-base percentage of .369, the latter of which was his second-highest single-month total of the season.

Matsui finished the season with 106 RBI, tied for 10th in the American League. His ratio of 6.63 RBI per home run was outstanding and an indicator that his clutch hitting ability went far beyond hitting the ball out of the park. Among the 37 players with 100 or more RBI, only one, St. Louis' Edgar Renteria, had a better RBI per homer ratio (7.69 RBI per homer).

Even more remarkable was that Matsui reached the magic number despite the struggles of those hitting in front of him. Leadoff hitter Soriano hit just .253 between May and August. Jeter and Williams missed six weeks apiece due to shoulder and knee injuries, respectively, and Williams wasn't the same following his return. Giambi won Player of the Month honors in June but was terrible the rest of the season: Outside of June, Giambi hit .223 with 30 homers, 78 RBI, and 120 strikeouts in 452 at-bats.

Murti had said prior to the season he thought Matsui would "knock in 100 runs by accident." Once Matsui reached the number, though, Murti realized Matsui didn't do it by accident.

"And the reason I say it wasn't by accident is what I mentioned—that the guys that were hitting in front of him, well, look at the types of years that those guys had . . . none of those guys in front of him had the types of year that you expect, yet he still did drive in 100 runs," Murti said.

Matsui's performance was more than enough to keep him among the leading contenders for the American League Rookie of the Year Award—and, by extension, keep alive a debate that had raged all season long:

Should Matsui, with nine years in the Japanese major leagues and three MVPs under his belt, be eligible for the Rookie of the Year award?

Even Matsui said he didn't consider himself a rookie, and he was certainly far more experienced than other AL Rookie of the Year candidates such as Tampa Bay Devil Rays outfielder Rocco Baldelli, Kansas City Royals shortstop Angel Berroa, and Cleveland Indians outfielder Jody Gerut.

However, according to Major League Baseball rules—which defined a rookie as someone who had accrued less than 130 at-bats, 50 innings pitched or 45 days on the 25-man roster in a previous season or seasons—Matsui was clearly a rookie. And as many people pointed out, the Rookie of the Year Award was named after Jackie Robinson, who was a Negro League star long before he broke Major League Baseball's color barrier and won the inaugural Rookie of the Year award in 1947.

Still, as the season wound down, the argument against Matsui's candidacy grew. In many cases, the anti-Matsui bent was nothing more than provincialism: Of course Berroa's teammates and those who covered him in Kansas City thought he should be Rookie of the Year. And of course the Devil Rays' media relations department sent emails touting Baldelli's credentials to BBWAA members on a weekly basis.

However, there was also a sentiment that Matsui's age and/or his experience in Japan somehow negated his rookie status. According to the *New York Daily News*, when Matsui stepped to the plate during a September series at Tampa Bay's Tropicana Field, a message reading, "Played nine years of pro ball in Japan, was MVP three times" was displayed on the scoreboard.

And ESPN announcer—and 1979 NL Rookie of the Year Award winner—Rick Sutcliffe said Matsui, who turned 29 in June, was "simply too old" to win the award.

Of course, as many people pointed out, Robinson was 28 years old when he won the award.

Davidoff said that among the Baseball Writers Association of America—the voting body that determines Major League Baseball's award winners—"there's definitely a sizable contingent that feels" Matsui shouldn't be considered a rookie.

"I don't do polling, but I hope he's not disqualified by certain writers because of this idea that he should [not be] a rookie," Davidoff said. "He should be treated as fairly [as any other rookie]."

The debate over the merit of Japanese players in the Rookie of the Year race was nothing new: Similar questions had been pondered in 1995, 2000, and 2001, when Japan's Hideo Nomo, Kazuhiro Sasaki, and Ichiro Suzuki—all decorated veterans of the Japanese leagues—won the Rookie of the Year award.

"[Matsui is] not the prototype rookie—neither was Ichiro [Suzuki] and [Kaz] Sasaki," Torre told reporters September 11. "They've all had experience. But the rule states that you're a rookie if it's your first year in this league. To say he's raw, like some minor leaguers—no. But I don't know how you get around that."

In 2001, Suzuki came within one first-place vote of unanimously winning the Rookie of the Year. Instead, that first-place vote went to Cleveland pitcher C. C. Sabathia, and it was filed by Cleveland writer Chris Assenheimer.

"I took a lot of heat for it, but there were also a lot of people who agreed with it," Assenheimer told SI.com in 2003. "Even before Ichiro was having a great season, people were saying 'This guy's not a rookie.'"

Ironically, one of the loudest voices against Matsui's candidacy was Tampa Bay Devil Rays manager Lou Piniella, who just happened to be Suzuki's manager with the Mariners in 2001. "When I was in Seattle, I liked the idea of Ichiro winning the Rookie of the Year," Piniella told reporters in New York with a smile. "I'm here in Tampa Bay and I like the idea of Baldelli winning the Rookie of the Year.

"Whoever is on my team is who I'm going to campaign for."

Piniella said to vote for Matsui as Rookie of the Year was "almost a little bit of a slap to Japanese baseball. It's a good league, they play good baseball. We're getting the elite players from there. I would equate it almost like Derek Jeter going to Japan and winning the Rookie of the Year."

ESPN.com baseball columnist Jayson Stark agreed it was insulting to the Japanese leagues to consider Matsui a rookie and suggested it was "time we start treating Japanese baseball for what it is—a third 'major' league," to the point where the Japanese statistics of American major leaguers are included among their official career stats.

"It would be a farce to adopt that stance just to keep foreign players from being the Rookie of the Year," wrote Stark. "We should adopt it to respect and honor the accomplishments of the Ichiros, the Matsuis, and the Nomos in Japan—in *every* way.

"Those accomplishments, those stats belong in their listings in the baseball encyclopedias and registers. Those feats should be part of those players' credentials when we consider their Hall of Fame worthiness. And all we ask, as we lend them that respect, is that it means they *shouldn't* be eligible for Rookie of the Year awards."

Warren Cromartie, the former big-leaguer and Yomiuri Giants star, also disagreed with the notion Matsui was a rookie.

"To be quite frank with you, I don't consider him a rookie," Cromartie said. "I wasn't a rookie when I went over there. I think they should change that rule. He shouldn't be considered a rookie.

Sometimes, I think the Americans make it too easy for [the Japanese]. It's extremely difficult for the American to go and play over there. They don't make it any easier [for the Americans]. It's just the opposite over here."

"When I went to play in Japan my first year in '84, I wasn't expected to be a rookie," Cromartie said. "I had eight years in the big leagues already. So they've got to change that rule. What's fair is fair."

Making the arguments even juicier was the fact Matsui, Baldelli, Berroa, and Gerut were all legitimate candidates for the Rookie of the Year. All four players ranked among the top five rookies in the bigs in RBI and among the top six in batting average.

Baldelli, just three years removed from high school, hit .289 with 11 homers, 78 RBI, and 27 stolen bases for the last-place Devil Rays. Berroa had an outstanding second half for the Royals and finished with a .287 average, 17 homers, 73 RBI, and 21 stolen bases. He also had a 49-game errorless streak on defense. Gerut, meanwhile, hit .279 with 22 homers and 75 RBI for the Indians.

"Matsui had a terrific season and should have been considered for the Rookie of the Year," said Sherman, who did not have a vote but said he would have voted for Berroa. "The fact that Berroa, Rocco Baldelli, Jody Gerut and others were serious considerations for the award should speak to the fact that a foreign star is not going to simply win it every year."

The debate over who should be named Rookie of the Year would continue until the winner was announced November 10. As for Matsui, he, not surprisingly, remained unfazed over the merits of his candidacy.

"I don't focus on getting it," he told reporters on September 11. "I focus on winning a championship."

And that pursuit began in earnest September 23, when the Yankees clinched the American League East crown with a 7-0 win over the Chicago White Sox. Later in the week, the Yankees clinched the best record in the AL, which gave them home field advantage throughout the playoffs and allowed the team to relax just a bit during the final weekend of the regular season.

Matsui continued his consecutive games streak, but Torre gave him some rest by limiting him to just one at-bat in three of the Yankees' final four games. By playing in every game though, Matsui made two bits of history: He was not only the first Yankee to play in every game in the Torre Era, he was also the first Yankee ever to play in 163 games. The Yankees ended up with an extra game because the statistics counted from a rain-shortened 1-1 tie against the Baltimore Orioles on September 18.

The Yankees concluded the season with a jovial 3-1 win over the Orioles on September 28 in which they were managed by Roger Clemens. Torre always hands the reins to a player on the final day of the season, and choosing Clemens, a 300-game winner who insisted he planned to retire after the playoffs, was a no-brainer.

Clemens did everything a manager would do, from writing out the lineup card, walking out to the mound in the eighth inning and removing David Wells (who earned his 200th career win in the game) to holding court with the media in Torre's office afterward.

"I can't ever see myself doing this," Clemens told the reporters. "But it was fun."

The real work, however, was just about to begin.

Matsui Torments the Twins—Again

With the light-hearted regular season finale behind them, it was time for Matsui and the Yankees to get down to the only business that matters at the corner of 161st Street and River Avenue in the Bronx: the postseason, where every move is parsed to the finest detail, as if it is some valuable bit of information at a crime scene, by a bevy of newspaper reporters, rabid talk show hosts, and obsessive fans.

In other words, it was business as usual for Matsui.

The increased media attention—hundreds of writers, cameramen, and television reporters were credentialed to each game— sometimes bothered players, even if they actually had to deal with a lot less demands on their time than they would during the regular season. Due to the swarm of media covering the playoff games, locker rooms were closed beforehand. Typically, the only people made available for comment during mass interview sessions prior to games were the managers and the next day's starting pitchers.

Matsui, of course, was comfortable with all the attention and with the mass press conferences journalists often dubbed "cattle calls." But while he had played for a demanding and impatient owner in Japan in Tsuneo Watanabe, he hadn't quite experienced anything like playing in the postseason for the Yankees and their quick-triggered owner, George Steinbrenner.

The Yankees' stunning and embarrassing first-round playoff defeat at the hands of the Anaheim Angels a year earlier had "inspired" the win-at-all-costs Steinbrenner to sign the big-name likes of Matsui and legendary Cuban starting pitcher Jose Contreras, moves that helped push the Yankees' payroll to nearly $200 million, which was far and away the highest payroll in the history of organized sports.

Steinbrenner had acted irrationally all season—even by his own well-known standards—and a baseball source told *Newsday* September 30 that Steinbrenner could "blow this whole thing up" if the Yankees fell short of the ultimate prize.

Many area sportswriters and talk show hosts believed the key to the Yankees' postseason hopes rested on the shoulders of those who had yet to win a World Series ring in pinstripes—particularly Matsui, first baseman Jason Giambi, second baseman and star lead-off hitter Alfonso Soriano, and starting pitcher Mike Mussina.

Matsui, not surprisingly, appeared unfazed by the high expectations surrounding the Yankees nor the heated atmosphere sure to fill Yankee Stadium, which gets so crazed during playoff games that *Bergen Record* baseball columnist Bob Klapisch often calls it an "open air asylum."

"This is what he did in Japan, because like the Yankees, the Yomiuri Giants are built for the postseason," Yankees assistant general manager Jean Afterman told mlb.com. "Being with the biggest club over there made a difference."

Matsui thrived in the postseason with the Giants, who won the Japan Series title three times during his nine-year career. He was named the MVP of the 2000 Japan Series and batted .333 with 4 RBI in leading the Giants to a four-game sweep of the 2003

Japan Series. Overall, Matsui had 4 homers and 14 RBI in 21 Japan Series games.

During a brief news conference during the off day in between the regular season finale and the start of the playoffs, Matsui said he was "really looking forward to [the postseason]. These are going to be pretty special games."

"I'm pretty sure the atmosphere is going to be different than what it was during the season," Matsui said. "But my approach is to just take the same approach I've been taking all year."

After observing Matsui for a season, Joe Torre was confident nothing would intimidate Matsui, not even the glare of the mid-to-late afternoon sun at Yankee Stadium, which had given left fielders fits for more than 80 years. Yankee legend Yogi Berra, in fact, once said he and his teammates used to pray for cloudiness so that it would be easier to pick up the ball.

A handful of Matsui's eight errors during the season occurred on balls he lost in the sun, but Torre wasn't worried.

"We played at 1:00 [P.M.] all year," Torre said. "I'm not saying you're not going to have a problem, but Yogi and I were talking about it earlier, and I think [it may have been] more of a problem [in] the old stadium. Since they renovated here [in 1976], it's a little bit different. You never get used to trying to keep the ball out of the sun, but I don't think it's anything different than what we've had to deal with on a regular basis."

Matsui wasn't the only Yankee to remain calm as the stakes—and tensions—grew around Yankee Stadium in the hours leading up to Game One of the American League Division Series against the Minnesota Twins September 30. During the early innings of the ESPN's broadcast of the Twins-Yankees game, announcer Joe Morgan observed that Torre looked as calm as he'd seen him in years.

Torre exuded that same calmness a few hours earlier at his pregame press conference. There was a lull in the questioning early in the press conference, at which point Torre smiled and said, "I get tired of this thing after eight years."

Later, Torre elicited a laugh from the assembled press corps as he recalled his youth, when playoff games were always played during the day. "At school, they used to let us [pay attention to playoff games]. We did have TV in those days.

"Still had the rabbit ears, though."

The Twins, meanwhile, appeared almost as relaxed as the Yankees. Manager Ron Gardenhire laughed as he imagined the verbal abuse Yankee fans would heap upon his players.

"My right fielder, Jacque Jones, I can't believe how many names he'll have by the end of the day," Gardenhire said. "That's very entertaining."

Twins pitcher Brad Radke, who was scheduled to start Game Two of the series, exhibited a laconic nature bordering on the comatose. Asked if he remembered his first start at Yankee Stadium back in 1995, Radke said, "No."

The Twins' good nature disappeared, though, when they had to answer questions about how the Yankees had dominated them over the past two seasons. Since the start of the 2002 season, the Yankees were 13-0 against the Twins and had outscored Minnesota 90-36.

Included in that span, of course, were a pair of moments etched in Yankee lore: Jason Giambi's walk-off grand slam against the Twins on May 17, 2002, and Matsui's grand slam in the Yankees' home opener on April 8, 2003.

Gardenhire called the Twins' lack of success against the Yankees in 2002 and 2003 "a two-year setup, folks. That's all it is—we've been setting them up for two years now to get them in the playoffs."

Twins centerfielder Torii Hunter was a little less jovial. "We don't care what they did in the past," the normally bubbly Hunter said. "They have dominated in the past, I give them that. But I don't care what happened in the past. This postseason, this is a different feeling."

In defense of the Twins, the six losses they suffered at the hands of the Yankees all occurred during the Yankees' blistering 18-3 stretch in April. "I don't think anyone had a lot of success against them in April," Gardenhire said.

In addition, the Twins had undergone a facelift since their April struggles against the Yankees. The Twins were just 44-49 and 7.5 games out of first place in the AL Central at the All-Star break, but they acquired leadoff hitter Shannon Stewart from Toronto during the break and went on to post the best record in baseball (46-23) during the second half.

The most symbolic indicator of how the Twins had evolved over the past five months took the mound for the Division Series opener. Johan Santana, a lefthander who threw 95 mph but used a nasty changeup as his "out pitch," opened the season in the bullpen but moved into the rotation in June in place of Joe Mays, the soft-tossing hurler who surrendered Matsui's grand slam in the home opener April 8. Santana finished the regular season by going 8-0 in his final 11 starts.

"Santana has great stuff," Gardenhire told reporters. "He's not a location guy, really. He's got a great change-up and a breaking ball and we are not going to worry about him trying to hit his location. He's going to give them everything he has."

Steinbrenner, meanwhile, gave Yankee fans everything they expected from a marquee game at Yankee Stadium. The bald eagle Challenger flew to the pitcher's mound shortly before the ceremonial first pitch, which was delivered by Rudy Giuliani, the lifelong Yankee fan and former mayor of New York City, and caught by Berra.

Everything went off without a hitch. If only the Yankees and Matsui could have said the same about the game itself, which the Twins won, 3-1.

Matsui placed a single between second and short on the second playoff pitch he ever saw in the bottom of the second inning. The capacity crowd of 56,292 gave an appreciative cheer as Matsui smiled and spoke to first base coach Lee Mazzilli.

In the top of the third, Twins shortstop Cristian Guzman raced from first to third on Stewart's single to left field and just barely beat

Matsui's throw to third baseman Aaron Boone. Luis Rivas then gave the Twins a 1-0 lead by hitting a sacrifice fly to centerfield.

"Matsui is a very good outfielder, solid in all respects," Gardenhire said. "He gets to the ball, he made an accurate throw. We have to play like that. That's the only way we can . . . win baseball games is [to] run around the bases hard, take extra bases, try to do those things."

Matsui stepped to the plate with Bernie Williams on first in the bottom of the fourth, but he hit into a 4-6-3 double play—his 26th double play of the season and the 17th time he had hit a double play grounder to the right side of the infield.

Matsui made Torre look clairvoyant in the top of the fifth, when he had no trouble catching Doug Mientkewicz's fly ball for the final out of the inning. In the top of the sixth, Matsui almost perfectly played Matt LeCroy's base hit, which ricocheted off a railing in foul territory into short left field, and limited LeCroy to a single.

But Matsui's effort went for naught when Torii Hunter's base hit skipped under the glove of Bernie Williams and rolled all the way to the wall for an RBI triple. Hunter scored when Soriano's relay throw to third sailed over the head of Boone and the Twins took a 3-0 lead.

Matsui did his best to earn a measure of redemption in the bottom of the seventh, when he fought back from a 1-2 count to draw a walk off lefthander J. C. Romero. But he was stranded at third as Twins reliever LaTroy Hawkins escaped the jam by striking out potential tying runs Soriano and Nick Johnson.

Matsui would get one more dramatic chance at late-inning heroics with the Yankees down 3-1 in the bottom of the ninth. Following Bernie Williams' leadoff single, Matsui stepped to the plate as the potential tying run. He pulled the first pitch he saw from Twins closer Eddie Guardado and smoked a long fly ball to left field.

It looked like nothing less than a double. But Twins left fielder Shannon Stewart—who, like Matsui, has often been labeled a mediocre defensive player—backpedaled to the warning track and, even though he was staring straight into the bright late afternoon sun, leaped and snared the ball a split second ahead of the glove-toting fan leaning over the fence.

"I hit the ball pretty well, and I hoped it would be over his head," Matsui told Japanese reporters.

Stewart held on to the ball even as he crashed into the Kodak sign in left field. Later, in the Twins' locker room, Stewart, who hadn't yet seen a replay of the catch, asked, "Did it look good?"

It looked so good it elicited "oohs" and "ahhs" from the Japanese and American reporters watching it on television inside the press work room at Yankee Stadium. It looked so good it would become a staple on highlight shows the rest of the year.

Stewart said he had "no idea what was going on. [He was] going back on the ball and I tried to make the catch, I could hardly see the ball."

Stewart's Kodak moment sent Williams scurrying back towards first, ended the Yankees' best chance at a game-winning rally and proved Torre right:

The sun wouldn't be a problem today.

Now that the loss was complete, the Yankees' real work began: Ignoring two days worth of doomsday scenarios presented by newspaper writers and panicked talk radio callers.

Thanks to Major League Baseball's typically quirky scheduling methods, the Yankees and Twins, who were the first teams to play in the postseason, would be the last teams to play the second game of their opening round series. Game Two between the Yankees and Twins was not scheduled until October 2 at 8 P.M., or roughly 52 hours after the final pitch of Game One.

Fifty-two hours to hear just how bad they were.

"We know there are a lot of distractions in New York," Torre said later in the playoffs. "But when you get to the postseason, you have to multiply it."

Of course, the Yankees didn't get this far by letting the pulse of the city infiltrate the clubhouse. And this wasn't the first time the

Yankees had faced an early deficit in a best-of-five series: The Yankees also lost Game One of the ALDS in 1996, 2000, and 2001 and won the series each time.

The day off may have helped relax a Yankee team that was atypically tight in Game One. "I sensed we were just pumped up, maybe had a little bit too much energy and didn't, you know, channel it properly," Torre said before Game Two. "It is just something that human beings are subject to or vulnerable to when you play games that are important. I think I sensed that we may have tried a little bit too hard the other day. . . . I just think that we probably were wound a little too tight."

With the Yankees' season in danger of completely unwinding, Torre put the ball in the hand of the pitcher he trusts the most, Andy Pettitte. The lefthander had won Torre's eternal devotion during Game Five of the 1996 World Series, when Pettitte out dueled the Atlanta Braves' John Smoltz—one of the best big-game pitchers of all-time—in a 1-0 Yankees win that gave the Yankees a 3-2 series lead. The Yankees won the championship in Game Six, and Pettitte's gem is often viewed as the jumping-off point for the Yankees' dynasty.

And Pettitte was in fine form again against the Twins. Armed with a crackling fastball, Pettitte struck out 10 and allowed just four hits and one run in seven innings, but he was on the verge of departing without a chance at the victory when the Yankees came to bat with the score tied at one in the bottom of the seventh.

Johnson led off by getting hit by a pitch from Minnesota's Brad Radke. After Juan Rivera sacrificed Johnson to second, Radke was replaced by LaTroy Hawkins, who had struck out four batters in two innings and earned the win in Game One.

But Hawkins didn't have his best stuff in Game Two, and Alfonso Soriano laced his fifth pitch into left field to bring Johnson home with the tie-breaking run. Derek Jeter then reached on a throwing error by Hawkins, and Jason Giambi—sharply criticized following Game One for both his 0-for-4 performance and his contention that he was just one of many struggling Yankees—hit a single up the middle to score Soriano and Jeter, chase Hawkins and finally bring Yankee Stadium to life.

The Stadium, known as a bubbling cauldron of emotion during the playoffs, had been strangely muted for the first 16 innings of this postseason. A 1 P.M. start had a lot to do with the low-key atmosphere in Game One, and the tautness of Game Two kept the fans quiet until Giambi's hit, which finally allowed the crowd of 56,479 to stand and roar so loud the Stadium actually swayed.

Mariano Rivera came on in the eighth and retired all six Twins he faced to lock up the Yankees' 4-1 win to tie the series heading into Games Three and Four at Minnesota's Metrodome.

With Giambi untracked, the Yankees were receiving contributions from three of their big guns. Soriano was 5-for-9 in the two games while Jeter had reached base in six of his seven plate appearances.

Jorge Posada was off to a slow start in the ALDS (1-for-8 with three strikeouts), but his track record as the starting catcher on three World Series champions indicated he'd bounce back sooner rather than later.

Matsui, however, had no such shared history with the Yankees. His performances in the postseason in Japan only enhanced his superstar legacy—Matsui led the Yomiuri Giants to three Japan Series championships, won the Japan Series MVP in 2000 and hit .333 with four RBI in the Giants' four-game sweep of the Seibu Lions in 2003—but he'd been pretty quiet during his first two playoff games with the Yankees.

He was 1-for-6 with two walks through two games, including an 0-for-3 performance in Game Two in which he stranded five runners. Matsui struck out with two runners on in the first, grounded out with a runner on second in the fourth, walked in the sixth, and grounded out with runners on second and third in the seventh.

Torre, though, had no worries about his left fielder. "He's getting the feel," Torre said during a press conference between Games Two and Three. "I sense that he was probably a little anxious the first game, like we all were. I think everybody was probably over pumped. [In Game Two] I felt a little bit better.

"He didn't swing the bat like he did toward the end of the year, but I think a lot of that was just the adjustment period, and hopefully that improves tomorrow," Torre said. "I trust him. He knows what he's doing and it's just something he deals with and finds a way to get through it. Hopefully he'll be hot for us tomorrow."

Entering Game Three, much of the talk centered on the Twins' quirky ear-splitting home, the Metrodome, and how it would affect the Yankees. The Metrodome is one of the few stadiums left with artificial turf, which makes ground balls bounce a little quicker. That was of special concern to the Yankees, who had seen second baseman Alfonso Soriano and centerfielder Bernie Williams misplay grounders on the grass at Yankee Stadium.

"The ball goes up a little bit different than outdoors," Torre said. "You have to just make sure you don't take your eye off it, because finding it again could be a problem. The turf, it's a different game. It's a lot faster game."

Visitors to the Metrodome also had to contend with the bright white ceiling, which made catching fly balls an adventure, and the stadium's odd ground rules. For instance, any ball hit off the giant speakers attached to the roof was in play.

Most of all, the Metrodome was loud, especially when filled to capacity with towel-waving Twins fans. Because of the noise, Torre said the Yankees were "not going to get a lot of help on 'I've got it' and 'You take it' and that stuff because it's very noisy.

"There's no place for the noise to go but to bounce on the turf and go back up to the ceiling and all that stuff. It's going to be exciting."

But the noise would not be a factor in Game Three, thanks in large part to Matsui, who might have been the only Yankee with considerable experience in a Metrodome-like setting. He played his home games for the Yomiuri Giants at the Tokyo Dome, which was filled to capacity every night with unyieldingly loud and frenzied fans who waved signs, sang team songs, and exerted as much effort cheering for the home team as the Giants did playing the game.

Ex-Giants star and former big leaguer Warren Cromartie said the Giants "took everything from the Metrodome" in building the Tokyo Dome. "They really got their influence from the Metrodome—same feeling, they got everything but the plastic bags out there."

In his book *You Gotta Have Wa*, Robert Whiting recalls how a New York television producer marveled at the enthusiasm displayed by Giants fans. "These people are lunatics!" the producer said. "There is more noise here than the World Series and the Army-Navy game combined. How do they keep it up?"

Matsui made sure no such question would have to be asked about the Twins' faithful.

One hundred seventy-nine days after his grand slam in the Yankees' home opener vanquished the Twins, Matsui once again broke the hearts of Minnesota when he hit a two-run homer in the second inning off Twins starter Kyle Lohse. The blast snapped Matsui out of his slump and sucked the life out of the Metrodome, which never had a chance to get into the game thanks to Matsui and Roger Clemens, the latter of whom dominated the Twins for seven innings in carrying the Yankees to a 3-1 win and a 2-1 series lead.

"It was huge for us to get that two-run homer there," Torre said.

"Matsui's home run got the crowd quiet and then it was my job from that point on to keep the noise down and keep the momentum on our side," Clemens said.

Matsui's homer was especially impressive for two reasons. First, it came on a 94-mph fastball above his chest. Lohse came out in the first inning throwing harder and higher than the Yankees had expected, and Torre advised his players to wait out Lohse and try to take advantage of him when he finally began delivering the ball lower in the strike zone.

"He did mention to be careful of the high fastballs that are out of the strike zone," Matsui said.

"But in Matsui's case, he didn't understand me when I said that anyway," Torre said.

Torre laughed as he said it, but his admiration for Matsui's ability to adapt on the fly was clear. "I think when you watch him day in and day out like we have this year, you understand that he's watching himself and he really doesn't require anybody to remind him about something," Torre said. "He certainly was looking for something up. The way he got above, for a left-hand hitter, that's not easy to get above a fastball. That's a ball.

"He's such a student of the game, and when you watch every aspect of the game and how he plays it, it makes me relaxed not having to say a lot of things to him."

Secondly, Matsui wasn't trying to hit a home run on the pitch but was merely trying to lift a sacrifice fly to score Williams from third. It was yet another example of the rare blend of natural power and knack for situational hitting displayed by Matsui.

"The situation was one out and a runner on third, and what I was intending was at least to try to get a sacrifice fly," Matsui said. "So I swung at that pitch."

Typically, Matsui displayed little emotion following his first-ever postseason home run as a Yankee. Asked if it was the biggest home run of his professional career, Matsui said, "I'm not sure about that, but I think it was a very important home run for today's game."

It was a whole lot more important to the most important Yankee of all. George Steinbrenner was so emboldened by Matsui's home run that he invited *Minneapolis Star Tribune* columnist Sid Hartman into his private box at the Metrodome and said of Matsui: "I predict next year you're going to see a Matsui that you won't believe. He'll hit 35 home runs like nobody's business. He's a tremendous Yankee."

The Yankees, whose offense had been stuck in neutral for most of the first three games of the ALDS, finally exploded in the fourth inning of Game Four.

The Yankees batted around and scored six runs in the fourth to chase Twins starter Johan Santana, and David Wells was never threatened by the Twins as the Yankees clinched the ALDS with an 8-1 victory.

As usual, Matsui was at the center of the key rally. With one out and the Yankees ahead 1-0, Matsui smoked a ground rule double to center to score Bernie Williams. Matsui, who finished the day 1-for-5 with the RBI, scored on a two-out double by Nick Johnson, and from that point on the only worry the Yankees had was escaping Minnesota injury-free.

But disaster almost struck in the bottom of the seventh. With the Yankees leading 6-1, Matsui and Williams nearly collided as they each converged on a fly ball by Corey Koskie. Matsui darted in front of Williams to make the catch, but ESPN announcer David Justice—a former Yankee—knew the two had dodged potentially serious injuries.

Justice figured it was a combination of the Metrodome's famously white ceiling and the noise of the crowd. "It looks as if he's having a tough time picking up the ball, period," Justice said of Matsui. "Matsui went at it like he was the only guy in the outfield . . . he knew Bernie was there but probably couldn't hear him."

No one was hurt, and with two outs in the bottom of the ninth, the cameras captured Jeter smiling ever so slightly at shortstop. Following Cristian Guzman's game-ending fly out to Williams, the Yankees exchanged high-fives on the field before filing into the locker room, where they celebrated in less restrained fashion.

Even though the ALDS was only the first of three rounds of playoffs the Yankees expected to win, the champagne flew in the clubhouse. At one point, Clemens used Matsui's interpreter to shield himself from the champagne heading his way.

"It feels great," Torre told reporters. "Since I've been here, we've been knocked out twice in the first round, which is such an empty feeling. It's nice to get past the first step, but we know there's a whole lot of work ahead of us."

The best thing the Yankees did against the Twins might have been beating them in four games. Clinching the series on Sunday allowed the Yankees two extra days of rest and provided manager Joe Torre the opportunity to set up his American League Championship Series rotation just the way he wanted it: Mike Mussina in Game One, followed by Andy Pettitte in Game Two, Roger Clemens in Game Three, and David Wells in Game Four.

While the Yankees were resting and reloading, the travel-weary Red Sox and Athletics were playing a tension-packed Game Five of their ALDS. The Athletics won the first two games at home, but the Red Sox came back from late deficits in both games at Boston to send the series back across the country for a winner-take-all finale.

Red Sox ace Pedro Martinez departed with a three-run lead in the eighth inning, but manager Grady Little had to empty the bullpen in order to preserve what turned out to be a 4-3 win. Derek Lowe, who had started Game Three two nights earlier, came on and, with the winning run on second base, struck out Adam Melhuse and Terrence Long to clinch the series for the Red Sox and set up a storyline-rich ALCS with the Yankees.

Yanks Haunt Sox Again

The greatest rivalry in sports was born out of equal parts geography and fate. The two cities, separated by a little more than 200 miles, harbored a mutual dislike for one another long before Boston and New York began play in the American League in 1903.

The one thing the cities have in common is a love for baseball, and the passion surrounding the coverage of the Red Sox and Yankees is unmatched anywhere else.

"There still is a rivalry and a lot of it has to do with you guys in the media, and a lot of it has to do with the closeness in the region of the United States," Red Sox starting pitcher Tim Wakefield said. "We are both up in the northeast. It's been rivalries for a long time between New York and Boston."

But the Red Sox and Yankees weren't really intertwined until January 3, 1920, when the Red Sox, who had won all five World Series they participated in from 1903 to 1918—a stretch that inspired the *New York Times* to write, "Boston is the luckiest baseball spot on Earth, for it has never lost a world's series"—sold star pitcher/outfielder Babe Ruth to the Yankees.

The Yankees, who had never appeared in a World Series prior to Ruth's arrival, lost the 1921 and 1922 World Series before they finally won it all in 1923 behind Ruth, who anchored a lineup that was dubbed "Murderer's Row" and is often considered the greatest lineup of all-time.

It was the first of the Yankees' 26 World Championships.

Meanwhile, Red Sox owner Harry Frazee used the money he got from trading Ruth to produce a play called *No, No Nanette*. It tanked. And for the next 85 years, so did the Red Sox, who have failed to win a single World Series since Ruth's departure, thanks to what is commonly called "The Curse of the Bambino."

Oh, the Red Sox have come close to earning baseball's ultimate prize: They advanced to the World Series four times following Ruth's trade—in 1946, 1967, 1975, and 1986—and lost in Game Seven every single time. In Game Six of the 1986 World Series against the Mets, the Red Sox took a 5-3 lead in the top of the 10th inning and, in the bottom of the frame, were one strike away from clinching the crown 11 times.

Yet the Mets came back and won the game when Mookie Wilson's grounder skipped underneath the legs of Bill Buckner, otherwise known as the most reviled man in New England.

But the near-miss that most haunts Red Sox fans occurred in 1978, when the Red Sox raced out to a double-digit lead in the American League East only to see the Yankees—buried 14 games back as late as July 18—come all the way back and tie the Red Sox for the division crown.

The two teams played a one-game playoff to determine the AL East victor on October 2, and Yankees shortstop Bucky Dent, who hit just 40 homers in his 11-year career, hit a three-run shot into the netting behind the 37-foot high Green Monster in left field to plate the winning runs in the Yankees' 5-4 win. A quarter century later, fans in Boston still refer to Dent as "Bucky F**king Dent."

The Yankees have continued to dominate the Red Sox on and off the field in recent years. The Yankees and Red Sox have finished 1-2 in the AL East in each of the past six seasons. In 1999, the Yankees beat the Red Sox in the ALCS, four games to one, and, for good effect, won the clinching game at Fenway Park.

On Christmas Eve 2002, the Yankees outbid the Red Sox for Cuban pitcher Jose Contreras, whom the Red Sox wanted so badly they reportedly snapped up every available room in the Nicaraguan hotel where Contreras—who had defected to Nicaragua—was staying in an attempt to convince him to sign with Boston. Losing Contreras to the Yankees, who already had seven starting pitchers under contract, so angered Red Sox president Larry Lucchino that he called the Yankees "the evil empire," which has now "extend[ed] its tentacles even into Latin America."

Most agonizing of all for Sox fans, though, has been the sight of Roger Clemens in pinstripes. Clemens won 192 games and three Cy Young Awards for the Red Sox from 1984 to 1996 but left for the Toronto Blue Jays following the 1996 season. Before the 1999 season, Clemens demanded a trade and ended up with the Yankees. Clemens ended up winning the first two World Series rings of his career with the Yankees in 1999 and 2000 and won his 300th career game, as a Yankee, in 2003.

"The Curse of the Bambino" is worn like a badge of honor in New England, where the state of the Sox is a constant source of debate and agony and where Sox fans obsess over the "Evil Empire" on a yearly basis. The headline of the *Newark Star-Ledger*'s special ALCS preview section October 8—"It's more than a rivalry, it's an obsession"—referred less to Yankee fans than it did to the Sox fans who saved most of their venom for Yankee fans.

Alas, the hatred was not reciprocated. Yankee fans, with one notable exception, viewed Sox fans as pesky gnats unworthy of contempt.

The notable exception being George Steinbrenner.

Many things send "The Boss" into an irrational frenzy, nothing more so than the Red Sox. The idea of losing to the Red Sox—

at any time, but especially during the playoffs—appears to be the one great fear for Steinbrenner.

After the Yankees beat the Red Sox on July 7, Steinbrenner broke down in tears as he extolled the virtues of his players. And a few hours before the Red Sox took on the Athletics in Game Five of the ALDS, Steinbrenner issued a statement that read, in part, "For us, winning isn't the only thing. It's second to breathing. As [General Douglas] Macarthur said, 'Victory is essential.' "

Failing to win the World Series ranks as a catastrophic failure in Steinbrenner's mind. But to lose in the postseason to the Red Sox, and to potentially go down in history as the team the Red Sox beat on their way to breaking "The Curse of the Bambino" . . . well, such a fate would be unthinkable.

No wonder, then, that the Sox appeared considerably looser than the Yankees entering the ALCS. The Sox, who were about as blue-collar as a team with a $100 million payroll could be, adopted the "Cowboy Up!" rallying cry—the phrase had been coined by Red Sox first baseman Kevin Millar following a loss to the Athletics in August—while manager Grady Little, general manager Theo Epstein, and most players on the team shaved their heads in a show of camaraderie.

"I don't think we're battling the 'Curse of the Bambino' here," Little said before Game One. "We're battling the New York Yankees, and this group of renegades that I'm putting out on the field, they don't care. They care about their Harley Davidsons running good enough [so] that they won't run off the Tobin Bridge over there in Boston.

"We don't put a whole lot of efforts [into] concerning ourselves with the 'Bambino.' "

Neither did the Yankees, who sounded more amused than frightened by Steinbrenner's contention that winning is more important than breathing. "I think winning is important to all of us," Mussina said the day before Game One. "We go out here and try to work as hard as we can, and to achieve important things.

"Whether winning is second to breathing, I don't know," Mussina said, a hint of a smile on his face. "But we're going out there and we are going to try to keep breathing as long as we can and win a few games while we're out there."

For Hideki Matsui, meanwhile, the Yankees' ALCS match up against the Red Sox provided his rookie season with another circuitously symbolic flourish.

Matsui made a grand entrance into the American baseball world by hitting a grand slam against the Twins in the Yankees' home opener, so it seemed appropriate when he made his postseason debut against the Twins.

And since the first game Matsui ever saw in the United States was a 1999 ALCS game between the Red Sox and Yankees, it seemed especially fitting that an ALCS rematch between the Yankees and Red Sox occurred during Matsui's inaugural postseason.

One player Matsui didn't see during the 1999 ALCS was Wakefield. The Red Sox knuckleball pitcher was left off the ALCS roster by then-manager Jimy Williams despite serving as the team's jack of all trades: In addition to racking up a team-high 15 saves, he also started 17 games.

Wakefield not only made the postseason roster in 2003, he also earned the Game One start against the Yankees. "It's exciting," Wakefield said the day before Game One. "[In] 1999, I was taken off the playoff roster when we came here, and it was just a very disappointing feeling that I helped us get to this level back then. And now it's a totally different story.

"I'm just really blessed and honored to be able to do this."

For Matsui, the presence of Wakefield on the mound presented a unique set of challenges. Matsui had never before faced a knuckleballer such as Wakefield, who keeps hitters off-balance with tantalizing pitches that flutter to the plate at less than 70 mph before they dip out of the strike zone.

It's a tough pitch to catch—so tough that Wakefield had his own personal catcher, Doug Mirabelli, who caught Wakefield for all but two of Wakefield's 202.1 innings in 2003—and an even tougher pitch to hit. Late Pittsburgh Pirates slugger Willie Stargell once said, "Hitting the knuckleball is like eating Jello with chopsticks."

Asked how he'd approach Wakefield, Matsui told the *New York Daily News* he'd do so with "patience. Wait for a good pitch to hit."

The flip side for hitters facing a knuckleballer is this: when a knuckleball fails to knuckle, it's a simple batting practice fastball liable to be tattooed all over the field.

Unfortunately for Matsui and the Yankees, Wakefield was in complete command during Game One.

Through six innings, Wakefield allowed just back-to-back singles in the second by Jorge Posada and Matsui, who hit Wakefield better than any of his teammates. During his second inning at-bat, Matsui worked a 3-1 count out of Wakefield before he fouled off a pair of pitches. Matsui appeared to be hanging back on the pitches an extra split second, but he was just a hair behind on each of the foul balls.

But on the seventh pitch of the at-bat, Matsui figured Wakefield out as he lashed a clean single into left field. Wakefield then retired the next 14 batters in a row, during which time the Red Sox hit three homers to take a 4-0 lead. But Matsui had one of the few hard-hit balls off him during that stretch when he led off the fifth by smoking a ground ball to second. Red Sox second baseman Todd Walker fell over as he fielded the ball but got up in time to throw Matsui out at first.

The Yankees chased Wakefield in the bottom of the seventh, when Jason Giambi and Bernie Williams drew consecutive walks. Alan Embree, a lefthander who throws mid-90s heat, came into the game for the Red Sox, which former Yankee and current MSG Network analyst Jim Leyritz believed was a blessing for the Yankees.

"I think you actually enjoy it [when a knuckleballer gets relieved by a flame-thrower]," Leyritz said. "I guarantee you a lot of these guys said it, and I've heard it before: 'Let's get him out of there and get the real pitchers in here,' because you're familiar with that. I think it's actually an advantage to the other team when the reliever comes in."

The Yankees wasted no time in getting to Embree as Posada brought Giambi home with a double and Matsui lofted a sacrifice fly to left field to score Williams. But Embree settled down and escaped the inning, and the Yankees didn't put another runner on base in a 5-2 loss.

Afterward, the Yankees offered a proverbial tip of the hat to Wakefield. Yankees third baseman Aaron Boone, who went 0-for-2 against Wakefield, said facing a knuckleball pitcher is "different. [It's] just so different. It's something you've got to deal with."

Unfortunately for the Yankees, only Matsui dealt with it well. And now the Yankees were three losses away from saddling their beloved "Boss" with the ultimate indignity. Steinbrenner took an atypically long time—50 minutes—to bolt Yankee Stadium afterward, and he had little time or desire to field questions from reporters searching for the back page headline.

Asked what he thought of the game, Steinbrenner growled, "I wasn't very comfortable."

Which meant no one else at Yankee Stadium was, either.

The sight of cameramen, print reporters, and television announcers forming a ring between the dugouts at Yankee Stadium was nothing new to Matsui. For once, though, all these media types were there to capture Matsui's teammates.

The locker room remained their sanctuary, but everywhere else they went, the Yankees and Red Sox were surrounded by media. Players had to navigate crowded dugouts just to get on to the field, which felt more like a zoo:

Look, but do not touch, speak to or feed the ballplayers.

But with the practiced obliviousness common to major league players, the Yankees went about their business. Matsui played catch with Karim Garcia just in front of the line separating the media and players.

One errant throw and someone in the media scrum would have a sore noggin, but the only person in danger as Matsui and Garcia fired the ball back and forth was Yankees Hall-of-Famer Reggie Jackson, who unknowingly walked in between Matsui and Garcia a split second after a throw whizzed past him. Upon realizing what he had just done, Jackson grinned, as did Matsui and Garcia.

Much of New York was worried about the Yankees, who were faced with a near must-win scenario in Game Two. The next three games would be played at Fenway Park, and Pedro Martinez—generally considered the best pitcher on the planet—was scheduled to start Game Three for the Red Sox.

Of course, when a team has won fifteen postseason series, five American League pennants and four World Series crowns since 1996, it doesn't rattle easily, either, which explains why the Yankees put on a relaxed face before Game Two.

"It's a must-[win] game tonight," Torre said. "But if we lose, I'll find a reason why it wasn't a must-[win] game."

Through two innings, it appeared as if Torre would have to spend his postgame press conference practicing spin and panic control. Seven of the Red Sox's first nine batters reached base via six hits and a walk against Yankees starter Andy Pettitte, who needed 39 pitches to get through the second.

However, Pettitte—a soft-spoken Texan with a big-game resume a mile long—allowed just one run in the two innings. He escaped a bases-loaded jam in the first and, with runners on first and second, none out and a run already across in the second, he coaxed Gabe Kapler into a double play and retired Bill Mueller on a groundout.

The Yankees, energized by Pettitte's tightwire act, took the lead for good in the bottom of the second, thanks in part to Matsui. Against sinkerballer Derek Lowe—the type of pitcher who gave Matsui so many fits during his slump in May—Matsui pulled a grounder to second baseman Damian Jackson, who could only force Jorge Posada at second base.

Two pitches later, the slumping Nick Johnson, who had just one hit in his previous 33 at-bats dating back to the regular season, crushed a Lowe offering into the second deck in right field to give the Yankees a 2-1 lead.

An inning later, Matsui had another chance to deliver. This time he stepped to the plate with the bases loaded and pulled another Lowe sinker to the right side. But first baseman Kevin Millar fired home to force Jason Giambi, and Johnson followed with an inning-ending groundout.

Matsui again came to the plate with a runner in scoring position in the fifth inning, and this time he came through, just when the Yankees and their fans needed it most. Right before his at-bat, the Fox network flashed a graphic stating the Yankees had been 1-for-8 with runners in scoring position.

And after Lowe delivered ball one to Matsui, announcer Joe Buck said the Yankee Stadium crowd was "about as subdued . . . as we've heard in quite a while."

But Seattle Mariners second baseman Bret Boone, a guest announcer for the playoffs, had a hunch Matsui would soon energize the sellout crowd of 56,295. "I bet he gets a base hit here," Boone said.

Sure enough, Matsui pulled Lowe's third pitch in between first and second for a base hit. Williams careened around third and headed for home, and as right fielder Trot Nixon wound up to throw home, Matsui rounded first and went for second. Millar cut off the ball and fired to shortstop Nomar Garciaparra, who began chasing Matsui back to first base before he finally threw to Millar, who tagged Matsui for the final out of the inning.

However, Williams had already scored to extend the Yankees' lead to 4-1, and Matsui's ability to get caught in a rundown played a big part in Williams' ability to score the key run. Due to knee problems, Williams hasn't run nearly as well as he once did, and a good throw from Nixon could have nailed him at the plate. However, there was no play at the plate because the sight of Matsui racing for second forced Millar to field the throw from Nixon and begin the rundown.

Fox announcer Tim McCarver—a former big league catcher regarded as the smartest analyst in the game—lauded the base running instincts displayed by Matsui and Williams. "Everyone did everything right on that play," McCarver said.

Matsui once again won approval from McCarver in the top of the sixth, when he made a nifty catch of David Ortiz's deep fly to left. Matsui had backpedaled all the way to the warning track before realizing the ball had begun tailing toward the foul pole. In one motion, Matsui arced back in, reached to his right, and made the catch.

"That was a terrific play," McCarver said.

Pettitte, meanwhile, was terrific after his rocky first two innings. He allowed just four base runners between the third and seventh and left to a standing ovation with two outs in the top of the seventh. Jose Contreras retired Nomar Garciaparra on just one pitch, and the Yankees salted the game away with two runs in the bottom of the seventh. Mariano Rivera allowed a token base runner in the ninth and completed the Yankees' 6-2 win to tie the series at a game apiece.

The Yankees' victory symbolized Matsui's improvement in dealing with sinkerballers and the overall evolution of his game. Sure, he pulled the ball to the right side in all three of his at-bats against Lowe, but he managed to reach base on each of those grounders.

More importantly, he contributed to the victory with contributions in the other areas of the game—defense and base running.

"Matsui just overall has been a terrific player," Torre said during a press conference the next day. "He knocked in a big run [and] did a great job base running yesterday by having the ball cut off in case Bernie was going to be close at the plate. He knows how to play the game. It doesn't surprise me.

"And defensively, I think he surprised everybody by how well he has played in left field," Torre said. "That play he made on Ortiz last night was not easy, especially on the corner where it starts coming in. He went out to the wall and sort of across the wall and caught the ball in front of him."

With a split salvaged at home, the Yankees boarded a short flight to Boston for the marquee showdown of the entire postseason: Red Sox ace Martinez against Yankees ace—and former Red Sox ace—Roger Clemens in Game Three at storied Fenway Park.

"The best you can do each [game] is go out and prepare the best you can," Matsui said about facing Martinez.

Clemens, meanwhile, waved away the notion that Game Three was all about him and Martinez. "We are not in a boxing ring," he said.

Turns out he was dead wrong about that.

There was a time, a few years ago, when a 2-0 lead in the hands of Pedro Martinez may as well have been a 100-run lead. But chronic shoulder problems and age had robbed Martinez of several miles per hour on his fastball, and he looked like a shell of his former dominating self as the Yankees gradually broke Martinez down between the second and fourth innings of Game Three, despite the two runs his teammates had posted in the first inning.

Karim Garcia's single in the second brought home Jorge Posada, who had led the inning off with a double, and halved the Red Sox's lead to 2-1. In the third, Derek Jeter tied it with a one-out homer.

Posada worked out a walk to lead off the fourth. Nick Johnson followed with a single to send Posada to third before Matsui, who had popped up on the first pitch he saw from Martinez in the second inning, smoked a ground rule double to right on the first pitch of the at-bat to bring home Posada and give the Yankees a 3-2 lead.

Later, numerous analysts and writers would theorize that Matsui and the Yankees had figured out Martinez and knew exactly what was coming. "I thought we were aggressive against him," Torre said. "Normally we like to take a lot of pitches, but he threw a lot of strikes early, and Matsui, especially, hit that first pitch for a double. I just think the velocity wasn't there like when he throws his best."

And in retrospect, not many people were surprised by what came next from Martinez.

Martinez's first pitch following Matsui's double sailed up and in on Garcia and plunked the Yankees' right fielder in the back as he ducked out of the way. A troublesome buzz immediately began to fill the air at Fenway Park as Garcia glared at Martinez and cursed at him.

The Red Sox and Yankees began edging forward in their dugouts as home plate umpire Alfonso Marquez issued warnings to both teams. Torre, meanwhile, bolted out of the dugout and began arguing loudly and pointing his forefinger in the face of crew chief Tim McClelland.

"I don't think there was any question—I know there's no question—in my mind that Pedro hit him on purpose," Torre said afterward. "Second and third, nobody out, left-hand hitter [at the plate], right-hand hitter on deck, [Martinez] can thread a needle at any time he wants. He was probably frustrated with the fact that we hit some balls hard."

Said Red Sox manager Grady Little: "Pedro never takes a shot at someone's head like that, or up in that area. But in their opinion, it was [intentional], so there you go."

Alfonso Soriano then hit into a 4-6-3 double play to score Johnson, but tempers flared again as Garcia, still steaming over getting hit by Martinez, slid out of the basepath and into Red Sox second baseman Todd Walker as Walker fired the ball to first baseman Kevin Millar. Garcia and Walker started screaming at each other and the dugouts emptied.

Afterward, Walker said he understood why Garcia took his aggressions out on the slide into second. "If I was in his shoes, and had a pitch come at my head like that, I'd do the same thing," Walker told reporters. "I'm not mad at Garcia."

In the middle of it all, Jorge Posada, still standing at the edge of the Yankees dugout, hollered something at Martinez, who yelled back and pointed at his head, as if to say, "You're next."

The field was finally cleared and Martinez retired Enrique Wilson on a pop out to escape the jam. But with Roger Clemens—who, depending on your viewpoint, was either a throwback to the days of old school, eye for an eye hardball or the biggest headhunter in the game—trotting out to the mound for the Yankees for the bottom half of the inning, it was clear the feud between the teams was still percolating.

As he walked out to the mound, Clemens received a warning from Marquez, which meant Clemens or any other pitcher could be ejected if the home plate umpire determined he intended to hit an opposing batter.

Clemens said later he told Marquez he "can't believe that" he was giving him a warning. "Obviously," Clemens told Marquez, "it won't deter me from pitching inside like I've been trying to do all night.

"He said, 'No problem.'" Clemens said. "I said that when this thing needs to get cleaned up, you'll know it. And he said, you'll understand the consequences.

"And I said the consequences of what you have to do are far greater than what I have to go through dressing and showering [with his teammates]."

It took just four pitches by Clemens for the fury between the Yankees and Red Sox to reach its crescendo in frightening fashion. Red Sox cleanup hitter Manny Ramirez was the first person to face Clemens, and judging by his body language on the first two pitches—Ramirez leaned back towards third base even though both pitches were nowhere near him—he expected Clemens to exact Garcia's revenge upon him.

Ramirez fouled the next pitch off to fall behind in the count 1-2, after which Clemens fired a fastball high but nowhere near Ramirez's head.

But it was enough to set off Ramirez, who hollered at Clemens and charged toward the mound with his bat still in his hand. Clemens cursed back at Ramirez and the dugouts once again emptied, but this time in faster and more purposeful fashion.

"[The ball] wasn't even over his head, it was over the plate," Torre said, "It was just high. And Manny—I think everybody's nerves were a little frazzled by that time—he overreacted. I can understand the overreaction because of the tensions and everything."

"I went in there and I was trying to strike Manny out, and bottom line is he started mouthing me and the ball wasn't near him," Clemens said. "If I wanted it near him, he'd know it."

There was a lot of pushing and shoving near home plate, but the tussle didn't turn violent until Don Zimmer—the Yankees' 72-year-old bench coach who had a plate in his head from a beaning he took as a minor leaguer—ran around the crowd and made a beeline towards Martinez, who was the last Red Sox player out of the dugout.

Torre would say later in the series that "the fact that [Zimmer] got hit in the head a couple of times has probably set him off a little bit easier than someone else [would]."

Martinez looked mystified as Zimmer approached him, and as Zimmer reached his arms out, as if ready to push or punch the pitcher, Martinez grabbed Zimmer's head with both hands and threw him to the ground.

Boston police and the Yankees immediately surrounded the prone Zimmer while Red Sox designated hitter David Ortiz and manager Grady Little steered Martinez away. A surreal silence filled Fenway Park as both teams turned their attention to Zimmer, who got up after a few minutes on the ground with the assistance of trainer Gene Monahan, Andy Pettitte, and Clemens and made it back to the dugout, where he watched the rest of the game.

"We were glad that he was healthy, a man of his age," Clemens said. "But that's Zim. He's got more fire than half those guys in the dugout, and that's why I love him."

With order finally restored after a 10-minute "break," Clemens promptly struck out Ramirez, and from that point Clemens and Martinez were almost unhittable. Martinez retired the final 11 batters he faced following his plunking of Garcia while Clemens allowed just one hit in his final three innings of work.

The Red Sox closed to within 4-3 off Felix Heredia and Jose Contreras in the seventh, but Mariano Rivera came on to open the eighth and retired all six Red Sox he faced on just 19 pitches to save the victory for the Yankees and give them a 2-1 series lead.

Afterward, though, the only topics of discussion were the skirmishes on the field and in the Fenway Park bullpen, where a groundskeeper got into a fight with several Yankees prior to the bottom of the ninth inning. Yankees reliever Jeff Nelson said the groundskeeper, Paul Williams, was cheering for the Red Sox and threw a punch at Nelson when Nelson asked him to root for the home team somewhere else. Williams said he was the victim of an unprovoked attack by Nelson and Garcia, the latter of whom said he raced over to the bullpen because he thought Nelson and fans from the bleachers had attacked other relievers.

Garcia ended up with a bloodied left hand and had to leave the game. He and Nelson would be the subject of a Boston police investigation that lasted beyond the ALCS.

Game Three of the ALCS, meanwhile, would forever be a hotly contested topic in Boston and New York. And after one emotion-packed day, the rivalry between the two teams—long dismissed by players, managers, and coaches as a media- and fan-driven creation—was suddenly very real, very bitter, and very relevant to everyone in uniform.

"I know it's the playoffs and a greater setting, but gosh, when I told y'all the other day it was going to be festive, I didn't know it was going to be this festive," Clemens said.

"I think when this series began, everyone knew it was going to be quite a battle, it was going to be very emotional—a lot of intensity," Little said. "But I think we've upgraded it from a battle to a war."

Not surprisingly, Matsui was nowhere near the epicenter of the brawls. The sight of the benches clearing in the postseason was an unusual one in America, but not nearly as an unusual a sight as the benches clearing at anytime in Japan. The Japanese were peaceful people, and baseball managers believed it was a sign of courage for a player to simply take his base after he was hit by a pitch.

It was extremely rare and shocking for someone to merely express displeasure after being hit by a pitch, which is why the

Yomiuri Giants' Warren Cromartie set off a national firestorm when he charged the mound after he was hit by a pitch during a game against the Junichi Dragons in 1987.

A full-scale brawl ensued, during which Dragons manager Seiichi Hoshino almost punched out Giants manager and all-time Japanese home run king Sadaharu Oh. When the dust settled, Cromartie, who had been hit by a pitch a Central League-high seven times in 1986 and spent a night in a hospital following one of the beanings, was fined 300,000 yen and suspended seven days.

As he recalled in his autobiography, he also issued an "apology," which received front-page news in the Yomiuri-owned *Hochi Shimbun* newspaper (the apology was actually written by the Giants without Cromartie's knowledge). Publicly, his teammates and managers did not offer any support for Cromartie, though most told him they believed he'd done the right thing.

As shocked as fans were by the sight of Cromartie charging the mound and setting off a near-riot, Japanese baseball observers were even more stunned in 1999, when Matsui took a few steps towards the mound after he was hit by a pitch from the Hanshin Tigers' Darrell May.

Matsui was the third player to be hit in the game by May, and Matsui's actions indicated he believed he had been plunked on purpose. However, before any skirmish could break out, the Tigers' catcher and the home plate umpire grabbed Matsui from behind and steered him towards first base.

"Yeah, I was trying to throw up and in on him and I hit him. No big deal," May said. "I guess he was frustrated because I'd been pitching him in the entire game and backed him off a few times. And it was just the way I was pitching him.

"[Matsui] kind of took a couple steps at me and then the catcher and the umpire jumped in front of him," May said. "He wasn't coming out there [to fight], I think he was just letting off some steam."

When asked about the long-ago incident during the Yankees' series in Kansas City August 11, Matsui said it was "just as well" he didn't fight with May. "That's when I started really feeling the pain in my arm from where I was hit."

A week later, during the Royals' visit to New York, May grinned when asked about the infamous plunking. "I didn't know that was such a big deal until this year," May said. "In Japan, I guess it was."

May was signed by the Giants following the 1999 season and soon became friends with Matsui. "We became teammates and actually got along very well," Matsui told reporters. "We were teammates for two years and he's actually a really good guy and a good pitcher."

Upon joining the Giants, May said, "nothing was ever said about [hitting Matsui with the pitch]. I went over and played for the Giants and nobody even asked me about it until I came here this year."

Rest assured he would have been asked about it, ad nauseum, and that the incident would have had longer legs had it occurred in America.

In 1998, Armando Benitez, then pitching for the Baltimore Orioles, set off a frightening brawl at Yankee Stadium when he first hit Tino Martinez in the back immediately after he surrendered a tie-breaking home run to Bernie Williams and then made a waving motion at the Yankees' dugout, as if to say, "Bring it on."

Afterwards, Yankees general manager Brian Cashman called Benitez's act "the most chickenshit thing" he'd ever seen while owner George Steinbrenner was nearly in tears as he described how angry he was.

Five seasons later, the Yankees, in desperate need of bullpen help in front of closer Mariano Rivera, acquired Benitez from the crosstown Mets. And on his first day in pinstripes, Benitez and his new teammates had to answer numerous questions about whether or not they could bury the bad feelings from five years earlier, even though the only people left from the '98 team were manager Joe Torre, pitching coach Mel Stottlemyre, bench coach Don Zimmer, and six players (Derek Jeter, Bernie Williams, Jorge Posada, David Wells, Mariano Rivera, and Andy Pettitte).

And the fallout and media frenzy surrounding the Roger Clemens–Mike Piazza skirmishes in 2000—when Clemens first beaned Piazza in a regular season game and then chucked a broken bat at him during the World Series—lasted for nearly two years, until Clemens finally pitched at Shea Stadium and had a pitch thrown behind him by Mets starter Shawn Estes.

Those diamond dust-ups were minor league material, though, compared to the Red Sox–Yankees fracas that got the mayors of the two cities sniping at one another and inspired the very best rabble-rousing headlines out of New York's tabloids. One story in the *New York Daily News* featured the headline: "Red Sox Stupidity Ignites Yank Fire"; while the front page of the *New York Post* had the words "FENWAY PUNK" over a photo of Martinez knocking Zimmer to the ground.

Little was right: If this was only a battle before, it was a war now.

The long-awaited follow-up to the Game Three fracas would have to wait another night. Day-long rains drenched Boston and Fenway Park, and though the skies were clear by the scheduled 8:18 P.M. start October 12, Major League Baseball elected to postpone the game.

The postponement meant there would be no more days off during the ALCS. Game Four was rescheduled for Monday night, to be followed by Game Five and, if necessary, Games Six and Seven on the subsequent three nights.

At this point in the season, everyone could use a day off. Conversely, a day off wouldn't be nearly enough time to heal the nicks and bruises incurred over the previous seven-plus months, so players and managers alike were relying on adrenaline to get them through the next couple weeks.

There wasn't a game played at Fenway, but there were still plenty of surreal goings-on. Before Torre's pregame press conference, Zimmer, still sporting a small band-aid on the bridge of his nose from his battle the previous day with Martinez, stepped to the podium and, quivering with emotion, delivered an apology for his part in "The Battle of Beantown."

"I'm embarrassed of what happened yesterday," Zimmer said. "I'm embarrassed for the Yankees, the Red Sox, the fans, the umpires and my family."

Zimmer, whose daughter and grandchildren live in the Boston area, completely broke down. "That's all I have to say, I'm sorry," he sobbed before he was escorted off the podium by Yankees media relations director Rick Cerrone.

"I'm sure he wishes it didn't happen," Torre said. "But again, you get emotions, you get caught up in it, and as we all know, Don Zimmer is a very emotional, shoot-from-the-hip guy. I think we've all reacted to things and wish[ed] the next day or the next hour that we never did say it. I think he basically feels badly about all of the attention this has gotten."

Torre said he couldn't answer any questions about Saturday's various rumbles because Major League Baseball Commissioner Bud Selig had issued a "gag order" to all parties. But that didn't stop the Red Sox ownership group from stepping into the interview room an hour or so later and conducting a bizarre 30-minute press conference in which all they did was talk about Saturday's various rumbles.

Outside Fenway, meanwhile, simmering Red Sox fans gathered along Yawkey Way. There's nothing as beloved in Boston as seeing a ballgame in Fenway Park, which might go a long way towards explaining the venom Bostonians have for Yankees starter David Wells, who said he'd like to be the person who presses the button that detonates Fenway Park.

Such words were blasphemous to those who love their quirky, outdated bandbox. Fenway Park is the oldest ballpark in the majors (it opened April 20, 1912, but news of the opening was overshadowed by the sinking of the *Titanic*; the fact the two events occurred on the same day has not gone unnoticed) and also the smallest with a capacity of 33,871.

And while it certainly lacks anything resembling modern amenities—ask players who dress in the cramped clubhouses or the fans who try to navigate the narrow walkways and attempt to sit in the tiny chairs—it also has the charm lacking from all the "retro" ballparks that have sprung up over the past decade or so.

And boy is it quirky. The dimensions down the left and right field lines are just 310 feet and 302 feet, respectively, but opposing batters must clear the 37-foot "Green Monster" in left field. The Green Monster also gives opposing left fielders fits, because a player never knows where the ball is going to go once it bounces off the wall.

However, the fences get progressively smaller moving from left to right, and the fence in right field is between three and five feet tall. Thanks to the short fence and short distance from home plate, the rightfield foul pole is the friendliest home run target for left-handed hitters in the league.

It looks and feels lived in. Most of Fenway is painted in a fading green, and the paint is chipping on the seats and inside the wooden benches in the dugouts.

It also serves as a reminder of just how haunted the Red Sox have been for the past 85 years. Painted along the awning outside the press box are pennants commemorating the Red Sox's five World Championships, the last of which, of course, occurred in 1918.

The Red Sox are so haunted that playoff games at Fenway Park are rained out when it's not even raining out. It seemed like another cruel trick administered to Red Sox Nation by the unyieldingly cruel gods, and the atmosphere in Boston following the postponement was equally mournful and simmering. As tortured as they were by the game, Bostonians still loved their baseball, as they indicated the next night.

The atmosphere prior to the rescheduled Game Four was as electric as the previous night's was damp. Half an hour before the first pitch, the streets surrounding Fenway Park were emptied. Everyone was inside the cramped, cozy park, which was jammed beyond capacity with standing, screaming fans, most of whom were dressed in something red and waving a white Dunkin' Donuts giveaway towel emblazoned with the word "Believe."

The frenzied scene was reminiscent of the home crowds that greeted Matsui back inside the Tokyo Dome, but this crowd was decidedly less friendly towards Matsui and his teammates. Red Sox fans, already conditioned to despise the Yankees in the best of conditions, were especially fired up following Game Three. The most venomous reception was reserved for Nelson. When he began warming up in the eighth inning, numerous policemen surrounded the Yankees bullpen in right field, but they couldn't shield Nelson from the boos and various profane chants filling the air.

Unfortunately for Matsui, Wakefield was considerably tougher on him than the fans were in the Red Sox's 3-2 victory. Matsui endured his worst game of the postseason in going 0-for-4 with three strikeouts—his first three-strikeout game since June 29 against the Mets, a span of 88 games, and only his fourth three-strikeout game overall.

Matsui's struggles were even more noticeable since he had been the only Yankee to hit the ball hard off Wakefield five days earlier, when Wakefield limited the Yankees to two hits in six-plus innings. But Matsui was badly overmatched this time around. He led off the second by getting ahead of Wakefield 2-0, but he eventually struck out on six pitches. In the fourth, Matsui popped out to third on the first pitch he saw. In the sixth, Matsui took the first two pitches he saw from Wakefield for strikes before he swung far ahead of strike three.

The Red Sox, meanwhile, received solo homers from Todd Walker and Trot Nixon and a fielder's choice RBI grounder from Jason Varitek and carried a 3-1 lead into the eighth, when Matsui nearly halved the deficit. With Jorge Posada on first, Matsui lofted a fly ball down the left-field line that landed just foul. Matsui ended up striking out three pitches later, and while the Yankees would draw within one on a Ruben Sierra solo homer in the ninth, Red Sox closer Scott Williamson recovered to strike out the side and preserve the Boston victory.

"[Wakefield] was tough today, tougher than he was in New York," Jorge Posada told mlb.com. "His knuckleball was really down in the zone. It was very unpredictable. You didn't know what it was going to do. He didn't even know what it was going to do. Whenever he keeps it down like that, it's tough."

It wasn't an entirely lost day for Matsui, though. He made what was considered the defensive play of the game in the bottom of the seventh inning, when he "deked" Kevin Millar into thinking he was going to catch Nixon's one-out fly ball to deep left field.

Matsui stopped a few feet in front of the warning track and motioned as if he was going to catch the ball. Millar, running towards second, slowed up.

But the ball actually hit off the Green Monster. Matsui fielded it perfectly and fired the ball back into the infield, and even though Nixon ended up at second with a double, Millar had to stop at third. Millar would eventually score on a groundout by Doug Mirabelli, but the play was another indication of Matsui's remarkable natural ability and baseball intelligence.

"[The play] really surprised me—when it first happened, I'm like 'Does he really do that?'" said former Yankee Jim Leyritz, who provided postgame analysis during the playoffs on the MSG Network in New York. "You're not used to seeing him play there. But you've got to tip your hat to [Yankees outfield coach] Lee Mazzilli, because he obviously went out there and worked with him and said, 'Here's what you can do. If you're comfortable with it, you can deke him' And Matsui did a great job of that."

Said Seattle Mariners second baseman Bret Boone, who was analyzing the game for Fox: "I've been impressed with his outfield play. I mean, he's good . . . he doesn't play too many games in Boston. That's a tough outfield, and he acted like it was his home field."

The Yankees had noted postseason horse Wells scheduled to go in Game Five, but the momentum in what was now a best-of-three series appeared to have once again shifted to the Red Sox, who had Derek Lowe fully rested and ready to go to the mound. Lowe was considerably better at home (11-2 with a 3.21 ERA in 17 starts in 2003) than on the road (6-5 with a 6.11 ERA in 16 starts).

"I don't have anything I can pinpoint [on why Lowe pitches so much better at home]," Little said. "But each year, some pitchers have some idiosyncrasies that you can't figure out."

Whatever it was, the Red Sox hoped it worked one more time.

Alas, logic, statistics, and the so-called momentum once again went out the window in Game Five.

The Yankees scored three runs off Lowe in the third inning and held off a late Red Sox mini-rally off the almost-unhittable Rivera to edge the Red Sox, 4-2, and take a three games to two lead in the series heading back home to the Bronx.

Matsui was at the center of the Yankees' big inning. After a one-out walk to Jorge Posada, Matsui pulled a Lowe sinker—the type of pitch he'd continually grounded to second base throughout the regular season—to shortstop on a hit-and-run play. Nomar Garciaparra had no chance to turn an inning-ending double play and could only retire Matsui at first.

An intentional walk to Nick Johnson and a single by Aaron Boone loaded the bases for Garcia, who delivered a two-run single. Alfonso Soriano followed with a single to score Boone and extend the Yankees' lead to 3-0.

The Red Sox closed to within 3-1 on Manny Ramirez's leadoff home run in the top of the fourth, but they stranded two runners in scoring position in the third and left the bases loaded in the fifth.

Matsui drove home an insurance run when his grounder to third scored Williams with two outs in the eighth. Rivera surrendered a leadoff triple in the bottom of the eighth to Todd Walker, who scored on Garciaparra's groundout, and David Ortiz added a two-out single before Rivera settled down and retired the last four batters he faced to close out the Yankees' 4-2 win.

"I can't tell you how huge it was for us to win this," Torre said.

Now, this series of constantly shifting momentum once again appeared to favor the Yankees, who would throw 21-game winner and noted postseason giant Andy Pettitte in Game Six against the aging John Burkett, a 38-year-old who had averaged less than six innings per start in 2003.

But once again, the only thing predictable about the ALCS was its unpredictability.

For six innings, the script went according to form. The Yankees fell behind 4-1 in the third but took advantage of a costly miscue by the Red Sox to take a 5-4 lead and chase Burkett in the fourth. Williams and Matsui opened the fourth with singles and scored on a double by Johnson and a groundout by Boone, respectively. Garciaparra then misplayed a grounder by Garcia, which allowed Johnson to score the tying run. Alfonso Soriano followed with a two-run double to give the Yankees the lead and complete Burkett's day.

Pettitte lacked his best stuff but lasted five innings, after which Jose Contreras—the Cuban right-hander pursued by the Red Sox but landed by the Yankees the previous winter—came in and, Joe Torre hoped, would nurse the 6-4 lead (Posada homered in the fifth) and serve as the bridge to Rivera in the ninth.

Contreras was filthy in the sixth as he mixed diving split-fingered fastballs with a mid-90s heater in striking out the side. At the end of the inning, cameramen from New York television networks began wrapping their equipment in plastic and started lining up outside the Yankees clubhouse in anticipation of the champagne celebration.

But there would be no celebration.

The Yankees, nine outs away from the American League championship, began to fall apart in the top of the seventh. Garciaparra led off with a seemingly routine fly ball to center field, but it got caught up in the wind, sailed over the head of centerfielder Bernie Williams and bounced off the fence. The ball caromed past Williams and towards Matsui, who fielded it on the run and fired to third base.

But the ball sailed over Aaron Boone's head and into the third row of the stands. Garciaparra was awarded home on Matsui's throwing error, and all of a sudden the Red Sox were within 6-5.

As he watched Garciaparra cross home plate, the Fox cameras caught a rare display of emotion by Matsui. His face etched in disbelief, Matsui arched his head back, closed his eyes, and stuck out his tongue.

Typically, Matsui refused to make excuses about his gaffe, even if he said the winds at Yankee Stadium—measured at 30 mph at first pitch—were the worst he'd seen this season. "The wind wasn't a factor," he told reporters afterward. "When I threw it, it was already off to the right. It was a bad throw."

Torre said the wind "was unpredictable . . . it was swirling and doing a lot of different things. The one that Nomar hit, it looked like it was just a fly ball. He didn't hit it real well."

It didn't take long for the Yankees' lead to completely unravel. Manny Ramirez followed with a double on the first pitch he saw from Contreras, went to third on a wild pitch, and scored on David Ortiz's single. Ortiz went to second on Bill Mueller's single, which chased Contreras. Ortiz then went to third on a wild pitch by Felix Heredia, who struck out Nixon and then intentionally walked Jason Varitek to load the bases.

But Heredia had completely lost the strike zone. He unintentionally walked the next batter, Johnny Damon, on four pitches to bring home Ortiz with the tie-breaking run.

Matsui singled in the bottom of the inning but was forced at second on Nick Johnson's double play grounder. Alfonso Soriano was stranded at second in the eighth, and Trot Nixon's two-run homer in the top of the ninth salted away the Red Sox' 9-6 win and set up what most of New York and Boston had believed to be inevitable for most of this ALCS:

A Game Seven for all the marbles.

A winner-take-all elimination game between the two teams seemed appropriate, given their shared history and how closely matched they had been throughout the season. The Yankees won the regular season series, 10-9, and through six games of the ALCS, each club had scored 24 runs.

"I guess it was supposed to come down to seven games, as much as you hate to think about it, coming [in] here with a one-game advantage today," Torre said. "But they battled like we've battled all year. We battled back, they battled back, and [there] just was no quitting on either ball club.

"At least we know tomorrow will be the last day."

And what a day it would be.

The Yankees and Red Sox had played 1,926 times over the years. None had been as big as game number 1,927, Game Seven of the American League Championship Series.

Ex-Red Sox ace Roger Clemens squaring off against current Red Sox ace Pedro Martinez, the man who replaced Clemens in Boston, in a rematch of the Battle in Beantown that had occurred just five days earlier. A trip to the World Series on the line between two teams that had played each other as close as humanly possible during their 25 previous meetings this season, 19 of which occurred during the regular season.

"It's been incredible, all right," Little said. "Probably the feeling for fans in the New York area and the Boston area, all of the Red Sox fans [and] all of the Yankee fans all over the country, they are getting a big thrill out of this and they are anxious for this game to get started tonight just as we are."

For the Red Sox, it was an opportunity to erase 85 years of heartache. For the Yankees, it was an opportunity to avoid the eternal hell of being known as the team that reversed the curse that it had supposedly started.

Torre indicated just how big a game it was when he announced he'd dropped the slumping Jason Giambi, who was hitting just .216 with a homer, three RBI, and 11 strikeouts in 37 postseason at-bats, from third to seventh in the lineup.

"He just feels a great deal of responsibility," Torre said. "I just sense that he's taken on more than any one person needs to take on."

The Yankees were carrying plenty of weight on their shoulders, so it wasn't surprising that the Sox seemed considerably looser than the Yankees prior to the game. Upon seeing Red Sox first baseman Kevin Millar trot out of the dugout, a Boston fan seated behind the Red Sox dugout shouted, "You gonna 'Cowboy Up' tonight so I can go to Florida?' for the World Series against the Marlins."

Millar grinned and nodded.

Inside the interview room, Little cracked reporters up when he was asked what his wife thought of the buzzcut he received following the Red Sox's ALDS win over the Athletics. "She doesn't care," Little said. "She cares about me on the 1st and 15th [of each month]. She doesn't care what I look like."

A series for the ages was going to conclude tonight, and the only question among those in attendance was this: could it possibly match the hype?

"All the years [the Yankees and Red Sox have played] leads to a lot of great moments between the teams," Red Sox general manager Theo Epstein said following Game Six. "It all comes to a collision course [in Game Seven]."

Right from the beginning, it didn't appear as if this would be the Yankees' day.

First, a water main break in nearby Washington Heights forced the closure of the George Washington Bridge and several streets near Yankee Stadium. As a result, many Yankees arrived at the park late, including Giambi, who didn't get to the Stadium until his teammates had already begun stretching.

In the bottom of the first inning, Matsui stepped to the plate with runners on first and second and two outs. He worked the count to 3-and-2, then dropped his bat and began trotting to first base, as if he had already earned a walk.

It took Matsui several steps to realize he had made a rare mental mistake. The Fox cameras caught the Yankees' Luis Sojo laughing on the bench, but fans groaned when Matsui flew out to center on the next pitch.

The Red Sox scored three runs in the top of the second off Clemens, and by the fourth, it was clear: either the Red Sox were finally going to vanquish the Yankees, or this was going to be the most painful near-miss in their tortured history.

After surrendering a homer to Kevin Millar, a single to Trot Nixon and a walk to Bill Mueller to start the fourth inning, Joe Torre made the long walk to the mound, and removed Clemens, who trudged off the field for what looked to be the last time in his career.

The Yankees were down 4-0, but history suggested the deficit was much larger than that. Only one team in history—the 1925 Pittsburgh Pirates—had ever come back from a four-run deficit to win a winner-take-all postseason game.

And those Pirates didn't have Pedro Martinez, three-time Cy Young Award winner and future Hall-of-Famer, on the mound. Martinez wasn't the Martinez of old against the Yankees, but he appeared more than good enough. The fly out by Matsui in the first began a stretch in which Martinez retired nine consecutive batters. Matsui hit a two-out double in the fourth, but Martinez got Posada to ground out to end the inning.

Giambi brought the Yankees within 4-1 with a leadoff homer in the fifth, but Martinez retired eight in a row before Giambi hit another solo homer with two outs in the seventh. Enrique Wilson and Karim Garcia followed with singles, but Martinez struck out Alfonso Soriano for the fourth consecutive time to get out of the inning and bring the Red Sox within six outs of the World Series.

Martinez looked skyward as he walked off the mound, as if to thank God, and in the dugout, teammate Nomar Garciaparra came up to him, whispered something in his ear and hugged him. With Martinez having thrown exactly 100 pitches—and with opposing batters having hit .364 against him once he hit the 105-pitch mark, as opposed to just .207 before his 105th pitch—and the recently dominant Mike Timlin and Alan Embree warming up in the bullpen, it looked as if Martinez's night was done.

But he wasn't, and as a result, the Red Sox were about to author their most horrifying collapse yet.

In retrospect, the Red Sox had given the Yankees plenty of opportunity to stay in the game long before Grady Little made the most criticized managerial call of the century. After chasing Clemens in the fourth, the Red Sox failed to pad their lead when Mike Mussina—making what he said was his first relief appearance since high school—struck out Jason Varitek and got the speedy Johnny Damon to hit into a double play.

The Red Sox also put runners on first and second with one out in the fifth against Mussina, who struck out David Ortiz and retired Millar on a groundout to escape the jam.

Ortiz hit a homer off David Wells in the top of the eighth to extend the Red Sox' lead to 5-2, yet Martinez trotted out with the rest of his teammates for the bottom of the eighth. He retired Nick Johnson on a pop out to short to start the inning to put the Red Sox within five outs of the promised land.

Inside the Yankees luxury box adjacent to the press box, general manager Brian Cashman began imagining the unimaginable. "You get those thoughts where you don't give up, but you also think that 'are you going to have to congratulate another club after this thing is all said and done?,'" Cashman said later.

Historians will forever note that two nights earlier, another supposedly cursed team, the Chicago Cubs, were also within five outs of the World Series and also had their ace (Mark Prior) on the hill nursing a three-run lead. Then a poor guy named Steve Bartman grabbed a foul ball a moment before the Cubs' Moises Alou was going to leap for it. The Marlins went on to score eight runs in the eighth, and Game Seven was a mere formality. The Cubs were toast.

And just like the Cubs, the Red Sox's fortunes took a historical turn south with five outs left. But unlike the Cubs, the Red Sox and their tortured fans couldn't blame this on an overzealous fan.

Watching the eighth inning unfold was like observing a car wreck in super slow motion. No matter how loud you yelled at Little, no matter how many times you screamed for him to take out Martinez and put in one of his reliable relievers, no matter how much you could not believe what was going on in front of your eyes, there was Little, wrapping his proverbial car around the mother of all trees.

Martinez, one of the great strikeout pitchers of this generation, suddenly could not finish batters off. Derek Jeter laced a two-strike pitch into right field for a double and ran into second base clapping his hands.

Little remained seated.

Bernie Williams singled with two strikes to bring home Jeter and cut the deficit to 5-3. Little jogged out of the dugout. Surely, with the left-handed hitting Matsui coming to the plate, Little would call on Embree, right?

Still Martinez remained out there.

"Pedro wanted to stay out there," Little said later. "He wanted to get the job done just as he has many times for us all season long, and he's the man we wanted on the mound."

Matsui took the first two pitches for strikes before he laced a fastball down the first-base line for a ground-rule double. "The key hit was Matsui's," Jeter told reporters. "He really got a hold of that one and that's when I believed we could come back. He's a complete pro."

Surely now, with the Yankee Stadium crowd now back into the game and with the switch-hitting Posada due up, one of the relievers would get the call, right?

But Martinez remained out there.

And once again, he got two strikes on Posada. But with the count at 2-2, Posada got jammed on an inside fastball and lofted a pop fly just beyond second base.

But it was headed for no man's land. The crowd roared with anticipation as Garciaparra and second baseman Todd Walker ran out and center fielder Damon ran in. The ball landed in between all of them and Damon picked it up and began throwing to second, except there was no one covering.

Posada slid in and Matsui raced around third and slid across home plate. Stunningly, shockingly, inexplicably, the comeback against the impenetrable Martinez was complete and the game was tied 5-5.

Only then did Little muster the wherewithal to signal to the bullpen.

"It's tough to come back on Pedro [down] three runs, but these guys just kept fighting," Mussina said later. "And I don't know what it is about this team or this place or whatever it is. I've seen it on other teams I've been on and I've seen it happen on this team while I've been here.

"It's gotta be for real, because we all believe in it."

The emotion and shock of the moment engulfed everyone inside Yankee Stadium, which had been the site of so many postseason heroics over the past eight decades yet had never before shook and roared so loudly and passionately. Beer and confetti rained down from the upper deck, where one fan shouted, "I'm covered in beer and I don't care!"

The most surprising display of emotion, though, came from Matsui. He had spent eight months and more than 200 games crafting a reputation as the most unflappable player in the game and establishing himself as one of the few people in baseball who actually believed in and lived by the cliché "never get too high or too low." But now, in the instant after he scored one of the most emotional runs in Yankee history, Matsui went wild.

As he bounced back up from his slide, Matsui leaped and stomped his feet. He started screaming as he violently slapped hands with teammates. He continued screaming and slapping hands all the way into the dugout. The photo of his exuberant reaction appeared on the back page of *Newsday* the next morning.

Little finally walked out of the dugout to remove Martinez after 123 pitches, but the damage was done, as were the Red Sox.

It was no longer a matter of if the Yankees would win, but when.

The Red Sox left runners in scoring position against the great Mariano Rivera in the ninth and 10th while Embree, Timlin and Tim Wakefield kept the Yankees at bay through the 10th inning. The numerologists in the audience perked up when Matsui, wearing uniform number 55, stepped to the plate with the game still tied 5-5 in the 10th, but he grounded out to Millar.

The game, already clearly one of the best ever played, grew even more legendary in the top of the 11th, when Rivera came out for his third inning of work. He hadn't worked more than two innings since 2000 and hadn't worked three full innings since 1996, back when he was a set-up man for John Wetteland.

Rivera set the Red Sox down in order. The struggling Aaron Boone, hitting just .161 in the postseason and demoted to the bench for Game Seven in favor of career sub Enrique Wilson, was scheduled to lead off the bottom of the 11th for the Yankees.

"I actually considered taking a strike, leading off the inning and everything," Boone said later. "But then I said you know what? Just take a ball.

"Get a good pitch to hit."

Wakefield, the knuckleballer who had stymied the Yankees in Games One and Four, floated his patented pitch towards Boone. But this was one of those knucklers that didn't knuckle.

One of those batting practice fastballs.

Boone swung and lofted the ball deep into the New York night. Left fielder Manny Ramirez looked up in desperation but didn't even move.

"For three innings, I was waiting for Manny to turn his back and see a ball go into the stands," Torre said. "It finally happened."

The 56,279 fans at Yankee Stadium leaped out of their seats and roared in unison and hoped the ball would stay fair. It stayed fair, by plenty, and landed deep in the left-field seats.

Once again, the Yankees were headed for the World Series. And once again, Yankee Stadium erupted in joy.

Boone chucked his bat, grinned widely, and looked towards the Yankees dugout, which was already emptying in celebration.

The celebratory sounds of Frank Sinatra's "New York, New York" were already filling the air as first base coach Lee Mazzilli threw his hat off and pointed down to first base and slapped Boone as he rounded the base.

Boone completed the trot of a lifetime, his right arm pointed skyward, as the Yankees gathered around home plate. One noticeable absentee was Rivera, who, upon seeing Boone's blast leave the yard, raced out to the pitcher's mound and fell to his knees.

In one of the most moving scenes ever captured on the diamond, Rivera began praying and weeping. Consumed by equal parts exhilaration and exhaustion, he could not get to his feet. Mazzilli finally arrived at the mound and picked up the limp Rivera as a father would lift a sleeping child.

The Yankees, led by Jeter and Matsui, cleared a path for Boone at home plate. New York's newest sporting hero leaped the final step on to the plate and was immediately swallowed up in a mosh pit of leaping, back-slapping, crying teammates.

"New York, New York" played on and on, as if on a continuous loop.

The Yankees, some already sporting "American League Champion" t-shirts and hats, began racing around the field, pointing to the frenzied fans, most of whom basked in the scene for more than 30 minutes after Boone's home run. Boone jumped into the arms of Bernie Williams, who held him aloft. Boone gave a wonderfully rambling interview to Fox as his brother, Bret, watched proudly from the broadcast booth.

Rivera, still crying, was lifted on to his teammates' shoulders and carried off the field. Torre cried as he hugged Matsui, Boone, Jeter, and anyone else in sight. Mussina, usually as demonstrative as a mime, jumped around the field before he grabbed Boone and held aloft a bottle of champagne. No one wanted to leave.

Finally, the Yankees made their way into the locker room, where the scent of champagne filled the air and the carpet was filled with corks and the tags from the Yankees' American League Champion hats.

Millions of wiffle-bat swinging boys in the backyards of America had imagined a moment just like the one Boone experienced. But Boone, now assuredly known as "Aaron F**king Boone" in Boston, was still almost speechless as he tried to explain how it felt to turn backyard dream into Yankee Stadium reality.

His hat and hair drenched by champagne and his face covered by shaving cream, Boone stood in the middle of a huge throng of cameras and tape recorders. "It's a blessing," said Boone, who began his season with woebegone Cincinnati and was traded to the Yankees shortly after the Reds fired his father, Bob, as their manager. "This game humbles you all the time, in good ways and bad ways. [This is] just another one of those moments."

It was a moment Matsui had traveled halfway around the world to experience—and a moment most of Japan experienced with him. Game Seven was almost as big in Japan as it was in New York and Boston (in Boston, 77 percent of television sets were tuned in to Game Seven). Coverage of the deciding contest led newscasts in Japan—ahead of the historic meeting between President Bush and Japanese Prime Minister Junichiro Koizumi.

Like most of his teammates, Matsui was just a touch more restrained in the locker room than he was during the euphoric on-field celebration. He hobbled out of the shower area, a giant wrap on his left knee, a soaked hat covering his soaked head, and a tired yet satisfied grin plastered on his face.

Not surprisingly, reporters were curious to know: Just where did that display of emotion come from in the eighth inning?

"By becoming the tying run, that led to what happened today," Matsui told the *Yomiuri Shimbun*. "I was so happy, I guess I showed my true emotions."

As someone long accustomed to the idea that a season without a championship is a failure, and someone who thrived on the biggest stages, Matsui had already earned his "Yankee stripes" prior to the postseason. But the Yankees' thrilling win over the Red Sox in the ALCS validated his decision to leave his homeland in order to play in America.

"I've wanted to be in the World Series," Matsui told reporters. "It's the reason I wanted to play for this team. I am very excited."

He wasn't the only one. Those who had observed previous Yankee championship celebrations were stunned at how joyous and emotional this one was.

There's little room for elation within an organization whose boss applies unyielding pressure to all his employees. The Yankees are robotic, stoic, and emotionless on and off the field, and winning titles is cause not for celebration but relief. By winning, the Yankees satisfy, at least briefly, Steinbrenner's ravenous appetite, and avoid the unspeakable consequences of defeat.

"Bottom line: In October, you either go to bed happy or you go to bed mad," Cashman said. "And we're going to bed happy."

But to win the biggest game in the history of the Red Sox–Yankees rivalry, to win the one game they absolutely positively could not lose, to do it by piecing together eight innings of stellar relief following Clemens's departure, and to do it by coming back to beat the supposedly unbeatable Martinez . . . well, the Yankees were going to enjoy this one.

"This is the best," Torre said. "To come here and play against the Red Sox, and play them 26 times and beat our rival like we did, it couldn't be more satisfying. This has to be the sweetest taste of all for me. They never quit."

Asked where this victory ranked, Rivera—who had been on the mound for the last three World Series–clinching victories—didn't hesitate. "Oh, my God," he said. "Number one. I believe it's number one."

And after all that, there was still one more series to play.

Fish Squish Matsui's Dream

Joe Torre had to pull out all the stops in order to lock down a victory over the hated Red Sox in Game Seven of the ALCS, so the Yankees had to scramble in order to piece together a rotation for the World Series against the Florida Marlins.

Mike Mussina would have been on schedule to start Game One, but he threw three innings of relief in the first bullpen outing of his career in Game Seven. Roger Clemens threw too many pitches in Game Seven to come back for the Series opener, and Andy Pettitte, the Game Six starter, couldn't start Game One on two days of rest.

That left either David Wells, the Game Five winner who also pitched an inning in Game Seven, going on three days rest, or the forgotten Jeff Weaver, who had imploded numerous times during the regular season.

"I think we should send Roger back out for three and we'll do it the same way all over again," Mussina said with a grin in the Yankees' celebratory clubhouse following the ALCS victory. "I don't know what else to do right now. We'll figure it out tomorrow."

Tomorrow seemed a long way off for the Yankees, who cele-brated deep into the night following Game Seven. Matsui ended up at a Korean restaurant with about 10 friends and didn't go to sleep until 5 A.M., but he still got to bed a lot earlier than most of his teammates, including Rivera, who went home after the game but stayed up all night reliving it with his wife.

But Game One of the World Series was scheduled for Saturday night at 8 P.M., which meant the Yankees had to not only settle on their rotation—it would be the rubber-armed Wells in Game One, followed in Game Two by Pettitte—but also had to drag their tired bodies into Yankee Stadium for a scouting meeting Friday afternoon.

The hero of the moment was probably dragging more than any-one else. Boone was awoken early Friday morning by Torre, who wanted Boone to join him at a Yankees pep rally in Manhattan.

"I got his number this morning, called him [and gave] him a wakeup call," Torre said. "I said, 'I know you're tired, but so am I. Get up, put on a pair of jeans and come on down.' He did. He was terrific."

Unfortunately for Boone, he wouldn't be nearly so popular fol-lowing Game One.

Yankee Stadium seemed as if it were still hung over during Game One of the World Series. The fans, who had spent so much energy during the later innings of Game Seven, were positively sedated for most of Game One. Dave Buscema, a columnist for the *Times-Herald Record* of Middletown, New York, wrote that Game One "stirred no more excitement than a June interleague game."

The Yankees, meanwhile, seemed a bit off as well, right from the moment the Marlins' leadoff hitter, Juan Pierre, laid down a per-fect bunt that trickled past Wells and landed between first and sec-ond base. Pierre's bunt came as no surprise—the 6-foot, 180-pound dynamo had racked up 45 infield hits, including 29 via the bunt—but the Yankees were still caught flat-footed.

Pierre went to third on a single and scored on a sacrifice fly by Ivan Rodriguez. Four innings later, Pierre's two-run single scored the deciding runs in the Marlins' 3-2 victory and made Boone the target of incessant postgame second-guessing.

Pierre's single to left field easily scored Jeff Conine from second. But Matsui fielded the ball cleanly and fired home, where he appeared to have a play on Juan Encarnacion, who was coming home from second and still several strides away from home as Boone fielded the ball.

However, Boone fired back to first in hopes of nabbing Pierre, who had made a wide turn. Pierre made it back to the bag, Encarnacion scored easily, and Boone's 15 minutes of fame expired as soon as Nick Johnson flew out to center for the last out of the game.

As a third-generation big leaguer—and as a player who, in the span of a week in late July, endured the firing of his dad, Bob, as manager of the Reds and his subsequent trade to the Yankees—Boone had a better understanding of baseball's quirky ebb and flow than most of his brethren. And so he stood at his locker for several minutes afterward, explaining again and again his decision to cut the ball off.

"[Matsui] had to throw across his body and the ball was actually tailing off a little bit," Boone said. "But it was a good throw, even if it took Jorge a couple steps to his left, which I kind of thought it might. Looking at the replay and talking to Posada, now I think we would have had a chance."

Finally, though, Boone had enough of the repeated questioning. At 12:19 A.M.—exactly 48 hours after his home run heard around the world—yet another reporter asked Boone about the play.

Boone sighed disgustedly and rolled his head toward the ceiling before he resumed eye contact with the questioner. "I've been talking about it for 10 minutes," he said.

"I'm sorry but I just got here," the reporter said.

Boone inhaled deeply and acidly stared at the reporter. For a split second, it appeared as if he'd say something he might regret, before he calmly, if disgustedly, told the story yet again.

His teammates and manager had no problem with Boone's decision. "We tell our infielders in situations when you have 50,000 people in the stands, that you pretty much can't rely on hearing somebody say 'Cut it off' or 'Relay,'" Torre said. "You have to use your own judgment.

"He knows how to play third base."

As for Matsui, he told mlb.com that he "couldn't tell about the throw. Could we have gotten him at the plate? I don't know. It's hard for me to say. Those plays are just part of what happens in baseball."

At the plate, however, Matsui performed as if he'd been playing in the World Series all his life. And in a way, he had.

"He played in so many Japan Series, this is almost his comfort zone," Yankees assistant general manager Jean Afterman told mlb.com.

Matsui went 3-for-4 in his American World Series debut with a single in the fourth, a single in the sixth, and a single in the eighth. "As far as my offense, what I did tonight was focus and I had some success," Matsui told mlb.com. "I hope to continue to take the same approach."

The eighth inning at-bat perfectly summarized Matsui's flawless approach at the plate. In a matchup of the two potential Rookie of the Year winners, Matsui stepped into the batter's box against Marlins lefthander Dontrelle Willis, whose funky delivery had befuddled opposing hitters—especially lefthanders, who hit just .216 against him—all season. Willis winds up by kicking his right leg high above his body, parallel with his head, before he fires the ball, across his body, towards home plate.

Then, of course, his fastball arrives at around 94 mph. It's a handful for anyone, but Matsui not only handled Willis but also changed philosophies in the middle of the at-bat.

With Jason Giambi at first and Matsui the potential go-ahead run—and Mariano Rivera warming up in the bullpen—Matsui swung from the heels on a 2-1 pitch. He fouled it off, but two pitches later, he delivered a more compact swing and delivered a crisp single through the middle of the infield to send Giambi to third.

Giambi and Matsui never came home, as Ugueth Urbina came on and struck out Jorge Posada, but Matsui's ability to adapt on the fly impressed everyone, said Marlins starter Brad Penny, who had faced Matsui during the All-Star Series in Japan in November 2002: "He's a great contact hitter."

He'd make more resounding contact a night later.

The most shocking thing about Matsui's game-altering three-run home run in Game Two wasn't that he hit it but that he hit it on a 3-0 pitch.

Among the few sure things in baseball is this: The hitter takes a 3-0 pitch. The pitcher quite obviously hasn't thrown a strike yet in the at-bat, so the batter should make him do it once, sometimes twice, without even taking the bat off his shoulders.

In fact, hacking away at 3-0 is the type of thing that can earn a player a tongue-lashing or a trip to the bench.

So with runners at first and second and Marlins pitcher Mark Redman laboring—13 of his first 21 pitches were balls—what does Matsui do?

Swing away.

With Torre's blessing.

"He's pretty good at being able to detect a strike, as opposed to 'I'm gonna look for a fastball and swing at it no matter where it is,'" Torre said afterward. "I think that's an indication of a real good hitter that knows his ability."

Torre recalled how he'd change his approach when told to swing away at 3-0 and try to pull the ball. "I was never a pull hitter," he said. "I pulled some balls, but I was never a pull hitter. When I got to 3-0, I tried to pull a ball and normally hit a ground ball or popped up.

"But he knows where his strength is. He stayed within himself and didn't try to pull the ball. He wanted to hit the ball hard and he did what he did."

What he did was even the World Series.

Matsui crushed the fastball from Redman to the deepest part of Yankee Stadium. Pierre raced back, all the way to the 408-foot sign in center field, but the ball cleared the fence easily.

"If I lay a fastball down the middle on 3-0," a grumpy Marlins manager Jack McKeon said afterward, "I think you could be a pretty good hitter."

Matsui's home run put the Yankees ahead 3-0 and once again proved he had an impeccable sense of timing. The Yankees, who had struggled offensively for much of the ALCS before looking lethargic throughout Game One, needed a quick boost in a must-win Game Two, especially after Pettitte struggled during his first inning of work.

But armed with the three-run lead, Pettitte suddenly found his form and dominated the Marlins with his usual assortment of 92-to-94 mph fastballs and bat-breaking cutters. The Yankees went on to win, 6-1, and the only suspense after Matsui's home run was whether or not Pettitte, pitching on three days rest, would get a complete game shutout (he fell one out short).

"I was struggling with my command in the first inning," said Pettitte, who threw 21 pitches in the first inning but just 90 over the next 7.2 innings. "I was trying to throw a lot of two-seamers. [It was] kind of tough early just to get a feel and get in a good rhythm. I was missing, falling behind everybody.

"When he hits a home run right there, I'm able to really start concentrating a little bit more with some four-seamers [regular fast-balls] in the zone," Pettitte said. "I found out that I had a pretty good fastball."

Matsui's home run was remarkably similar to the one he hit in Game Three of the ALDS against the Twins. With the series tied at a game apiece and the momentum of the series at stake, Matsui's two-run homer in the second inning took the fabled Metrodome crowd out of the game and gave the Yankees a 2-0 lead in a game they would win 3-1. The next day, the Yankees finished off the Twins, 8-1.

This homer both buried the Marlins and brought the Yankee Stadium crowd back into the Series. Asked if the two postseason homers were similar, Torre said, "No question. We had been strug-gling for runs through that whole Boston series. To jump up there and get three runs, it really helped our personality. There's no question."

There was also no question the Yankees were beyond being surprised by Matsui's performance under pressure. "I didn't know how good he was going to be," Pettitte said. "I heard he was great and a great power hitter. But just from spring training, watching him, you realized he was going to be a good hitter. He's got too good of a swing and he knows what he's doing. His approach is very good.

"He's been awesome for us, no doubt about it. He's stepping up right now in the postseason and that's great to see."

Matsui's homer also bolstered his star status in New York and introduced the rest of the nation to the player who had captivated the Yankees and their fans the previous six months.

As he rounded the bases, the Yankee Stadium Jumbotron showed a clip of Godzilla wreaking havoc in an old monster movie. Upon completing another emotionless home run trot, the sellout crowd of 55,750 continued to stand and roar until Matsui jogged up the dugout steps and doffed his cap.

It was his second curtain call of the year—but his first on the national stage. And throughout the numerous press seating areas inside Yankee Stadium, columnists and writers from all over the country began filing stories on this wunderkind from Japan.

The front page of Monday's *New York Daily News* featured a full-color photo of Matsui connecting for his home run and a "tease" for a column by the city's most powerful sports columnist, Mike Lupica.

How powerful is Lupica? So much so that Lupica was pictured next to the words: "MIKE LUPICA SAYS: 'The guy from Japan turns out to have as much Yankee in him as anybody.'"

Inside, Lupica bestowed some high praise on Matsui: "He showed from the start that he was the kind of professional ballplayer who fit right in with [Derek] Jeter and [Jorge] Posada and [Bernie] Williams, the old-school Yankees who have been here the longest. He would have gotten along just fine with Tino [Martinez] and [Scott] Brosius and [Paul] O'Neill."

After the Yankees' victory, Matsui, not surprisingly, was one of the Yankees selected to appear in the interview room. For most in attendance, it was their first up-close glimpse of this unfailingly modest player who had single-handedly attempted to rewrite the book on relations between superstar and media, and some appeared a tad disappointed by the tepidity of Matsui's answers.

Asked why he performed better in big games both here and abroad, Matsui said, "I just take the same approach. Even going into this postseason and this World Series, I just took the same approach."

Asked if he understood how important his home run proved to be, Matsui said, "The three-run [homer] was really big for the team and it also was very important for today's win. Hopefully, it was also a help to Andy with his pitching today."

On the transition from Japan to America, Matsui simply said: "I think this season, I think I was able to give it my best throughout the season."

The next day, *Washington Post* columnist Thomas Boswell wrote: "Unfortunately, according to Japanese journalists here, Matsui's interviews tend to 'get lost in the translation.' Sunday night, he gave long, animated answers that are translated as short clichés, worthy of *Bull Durham*."

Of course, Matsui was anything but the second coming of Nuke LaLoosh, the dimwit pitcher who took cliché lessons from hardened pro Crash Davis in the classic baseball movie *Bull Durham*. No one ever had to give Matsui a proverbial slap in the face in order to remind him to maximize his talent, and those who covered Matsui regularly had long ago grown accustomed to interpreter Roger Kahlon breaking Matsui's elongated responses into something comfortably vanilla.

After all, anyone who would take the time to learn the names of the reporters regularly covering the team was certainly thoughtful enough to provide sincere and intelligent answers to their questions.

"I've had guys that I've walked up to and introduced myself to 50 times [that] still don't know my name," WFAN Yankees beat reporter Sweeney Murti said. "And here this guy is, going through everything he's going through, and he still finds the time to be polite every day, walking past me and saying 'Hi Sweeney, how are you?' I thought that part was pretty amazing."

With a day off Monday, there was plenty of opportunity for America's columnists to bring a glimpse of that fascinating person into Tuesday's newspapers. Ian O'Connor, a columnist for the Gannett newspaper chain, wrote a column for the USA Today in which he theorized the Japanese import had infused America's bruised national pastime with a much-needed dose of fresh-faced earnestness:

"But Matsui has pumped fresh blood into our most endearing baseball notions. He plays hard, hits line drives and never misses a game. He cuts a bullish, country-boy figure in his uniform, and his hair blows gracefully with the chase of a fly ball.

"The point? Sometimes myths don't have to be myths. Sometimes it only takes a trip to Tokyo to find a real all-American boy."

Alas, nobody ever waxed poetic about the Florida Marlins.

The shift to Florida for Games Three, Four, and Five of the World Series provided yet another reminder of the stark differences between the two teams vying for baseball's top prize.

It was Team Tradition vs. Team Teal.

The Yankees were celebrating their 100th anniversary and played in Yankee Stadium, a hallowed, 80-year-old icon that oozed with royal blue and white tradition. The Marlins were founded in 1993 and were tenants of Pro Player Stadium, which was named after an underwear company, built to house a football team (the Miami Dolphins had played there since 1987) and bathed in teal, the "it" color for early-1990s expansion teams.

The Yankees were 26-time World Champions but despised by many people who believed their deep pockets allowed them to buy the bulk of those championships. Ironically, though, no team had ever bought a championship as brazenly as the 1997 Marlins, who, under former owner Wayne Huizenga, loaded up on big-name free agents in 1995 and 1996 and won it all in 1997 before Huizenga, a billionaire who griped that Miami-area taxpayers would not fund him a new stadium, sold off the Marlins piece by piece in what is considered the most disgusting fire sale in the history of sports.

But that fire sale begat the core of the '03 Marlins, who had a payroll one-third the size of the Yankees and were in last place in late May before they took off under new manager Jack McKeon. No one really believed in the Marlins until new owner Jeffrey Loria, viewed with a suspicious eye by most after he ran the Montreal Expos into the ground before he bought the Marlins in one of Major League Baseball's typically convoluted backroom dealings, surprised all of baseball by resisting the urge to conduct another fire sale, and the Marlins outlasted the Philadelphia Phillies to win the wild card before they upset the San Francisco Giants and Chicago Cubs in the NLDS and NLCS, respectively.

The Marlins came back from a three games to one deficit to win the final three games of the NLCS, against the Cubs including Games Six and Seven at Wrigley Field against Cubs aces Mark Prior and Kerry Wood. Florida's comeback disappointed the baseball romantics, who wanted to see storied Wrigley Field host a World Series game for the first time in 58 years.

But instead, it was Team Tradition vs. Team Teal, and 60,000 mostly neophyte Marlins fans would fill Pro Player Stadium for the middle three games of the Series. The Marlins' fire sale in 1997, coupled with the ownership shift to Loria, turned off most of the South Florida fans who grew to love the Marlins during their World Championship season. Florida ranked next-to-last in the majors in attendance in 2002 and 28th in 2003.

Marlins third baseman Mike Lowell recalled "hear[ing] the radio guys doing their broadcast while we were hitting" during one sparsely attended game. "It felt like A-ball, where you have to hope the radio guy shuts up in between pitches so he doesn't distract you," Lowell said.

There'd be no such worries in Game Three. Instead, the Marlins had to deal with a quartet of obstacles much more imposing than an empty stadium: The weather, Derek Jeter, Mike Mussina, and Hideki Matsui.

With the teams tied 1-1 in the fifth, a driving rain storm inter-rupted the game for 39 minutes. When it resumed, Mussina, who allowed his only run in the first inning, battled out of a sixth-inning jam by fielding Derrek Lee's comebacker and firing home to nail Ivan Rodriguez.

Jeter, meanwhile, got the Yankees' only three hits off filthy Marlins starter Josh Beckett. Jeter doubled with one out in the sec-ond, went to third when Matsui was hit by a pitch, and scored the tying run when Jorge Posada drew a bases-loaded walk.

Jeter doubled again with one out in the eighth to chase Beckett. Rookie Willis came in to face the lefthanders in the heart of the Yankees' order, but he walked the first batter he faced, Jason Giambi. Bernie Williams followed with a fly out that sent Jeter to third.

Up to the plate stepped Matsui, who had already delivered a hard single off the hard-to-hit Willis in the first game of the Series three nights earlier. "It's always a key situation when a left-handed pitcher comes in and tries to strike out left-handed hitters," Matsui told mlb.com.

But Matsui wasted no time in jumping on Willis again. With the count 1-0, Matsui pulled a single into left field to score Jeter with the go-ahead run.

"That's the hit of the night," Boone told mlb.com.

"He did a good job of staying with the ball and hitting it where it was pitched," Willis told mlb.com. "Bottom line, he did exactly what he wanted to do. He hit the ball the other way and you've got to tip your hat to the guy."

It was the first hit for a Yankee other than Jeter. "I wasn't look-ing to hit it the other way," Matsui told the *Times Herald-Record* of Middletown. "I just reacted to the pitch."

With Mariano Rivera coming in for another one of his patented two-inning saves, the Marlins were as good as done, but the Yankees added four runs in the top of the ninth anyway to win, 6-1, and take a 2-1 series lead.

Two World Series wins for the Yankees, two game-winning RBI for Matsui.

"Matsui," Torre said admiringly during the postgame press conference. "This guy's incredible."

"He's been that way all year," Boone told mlb.com. "In a key situation, tough spot, he's a great guy to have up there. I don't care if they have a righty or a lefty up there. He seems to always put a good bat on it and the same was true tonight."

"He's been doing that all year for us," Jeter said. "You hear [the nickname] 'Godzilla' and you automatically assume he's going to be up there swinging for the fences. The thing about him is he understands the game and he'll take a hit the other way. That was huge for us."

It was so huge, Matsui earned comparisons to Mr. Clutch himself, Jeter. His statistics pale next to those of the other big-name shortstops in the game (Alex Rodriguez, Nomar Garciaparra, Miguel Tejada), but few players ever elevated their game in the postseason like Jeter, whose arrival in 1996 coincided with the start of the Yankees' dynasty.

And now, in his first postseason, people were beginning to mention Matsui in the same breath as Jeter. *Newsday*'s Johnette Howard wrote a column October 23 titled "Matsui Showing Hints Of Jeter."

Like Jeter, Matsui had a knack for delivering the type of key hit that not only jump-starts the Yankees but also ensures an opponent never gets a chance to maintain momentum. After the Mets won Game Three of the 2000 World Series to close within 2-1, Jeter hit a home run on the very first pitch of Game Four. The Yankees won the Series in five games.

Like Jeter, Matsui lived by and actually believed in clichés such as "one game at a time" and "never get too high or too low."

"He's always on an even keel," Jeter told mlb.com. "He has no problem playing on a big stage, because he can have a bad game or a bad at-bat and not let it carry over."

And like Jeter, Matsui appeared to have been born with some kind of sixth baseball sense. How else to explain how Matsui "deked" Kevin Millar into thinking he had caught a deep fly ball at Fenway Park 10 days earlier? And how else to explain the tremendous play Jeter made against the Oakland Athletics in the 2001 ALDS, when he streaked across the diamond, cut off Paul O'Neill's throw to the plate, and made a backhanded relay to Jorge Posada, who tagged out Jeremy Giambi?

Maybe it was cosmic: Matsui and Jeter were born two weeks apart in June 1974.

Whatever it was, the two kindred baseball souls seemed to get along and understand each other off the field, as well. Jeter, by far the best-known Yankee and the only player on the team who might have an idea of what it's like for Matsui to be under a microscope 24-7, was one of the first players Matsui introduced himself to back in February.

In addition, as the postseason wore on, it appeared as if Matsui was easing into a Jeter-like team leader role. Jeter is always the first Yankee off the bench after a teammate gets a big hit, but throughout the playoffs, Matsui closely followed him.

"I did notice Matsui being more animated during the playoffs," *New York Post* baseball columnist Joel Sherman said. "His joy at key moments was interesting. I don't think it was leadership as much as him enjoying the moment. He obviously was brought here to help win a championship and he seemed to be reveling in these games."

And after their combined efforts lifted the Yankees to the Series lead in Game Three, Jeter made it clear how much he appreciated Matsui in a loud yet subtle way. As he walked into the shower, Jeter saw Matsui conducting interviews.

According to the *Times Herald-Record* of Middletown, Jeter shouted, "Hey hey HEY!" Mot-soooooooooooo! Whataswing! WHATASWING!"

Matsui smiled back, the respect and affection evident between the two Yankees most suited for the spotlight of the postseason. And with the Yankees ahead in the Series 2-1, and Roger Clemens making what would likely be his final career start in Game Four against the Marlins' Carl Pavano, the only question left seemed to be this:

Who'd win the World Series MVP—Matsui or Jeter?

Not so fast.

lemens, who had been making what might have been "the last start of his career" for weeks now, nearly made a second straight premature exit. He was torched for four runs in three-plus innings by the Red Sox in Game Seven of the ALCS, and only the ineptitude of Red Sox manager Grady Little saved Clemens, the former Red Sox ace, the ignobility of losing to the Red Sox in the last start of his career.

And Clemens was struggling so badly against the Marlins in the first inning of Game Four that Joe Torre got forgotten man Jeff Weaver up in the bullpen. Clemens retired the first two batters he faced before he allowed five straight hits—including a two-run homer by Miguel Cabrera and an RBI single by Derrek Lee—and put the Yankees in a 3-0 hole.

But Clemens finally got out of the inning by retiring Alex Gonzalez on a fly out, and Clemens settled down enough to last seven innings and retire 18 of the last 21 batters he faced, including the last eight in a row.

Pavano, though, was even better. The Yankees nicked him for a run in the second, when Williams, Matsui, and Posada all singled. Williams came home on a sacrifice fly by Aaron Boone to cut the gap to 3-1, but Clemens grounded out to end the frame.

The Yankees threatened again in the third, when Giambi and Williams hit back-to-back two-out singles, but Matsui flied out to left on the first pitch of his at-bat to end the inning. Pavano faced the minimum 15 batters over the next five innings and, with the Marlins still nursing a 3-1 lead, handed the ball over to closer Ugueth Urbina, who promptly raised blood pressures throughout South Florida.

With one out, Urbina allowed a single to Williams. He got ahead of Matsui 1-2, but Matsui managed to coax a walk—the first walk issued by either team—to bring up Posada as the tying run.

"I think everyone has the impression of the 50 home runs I hit last year, but what I always have tried to accomplish was to be an all-around baseball player," Matsui told the *Newark Star-Ledger*.

Posada's grounder forced Matsui, and Ruben Sierra, who had batted just seven times in the postseason, stepped to the plate as the Yankees' last hope. With the count full, Sierra fouled off a pair of nasty changeups before Urbina floated a fastball right in Sierra's wheelhouse. Sierra turned on it and roped it down the right field line for a two-run, game-tying triple.

The comeback was remarkably familiar to anyone who had watched the Yankees break hearts in the late innings on their way to four World Series crowns between 1996 and 2000, but the end result here would be shockingly different. With the go-ahead run 90 feet from home, and Rivera ready to come on and save the victory, which would have given the Yankees a commanding 3-1 Series lead, Urbina got out of the inning by retiring Boone on a grounder to short.

The game went into extra innings and the Yankees atypically left runners on base in the 10th, 11th, and 12th. They loaded the bases in the 11th on a double by Williams and walks to Matsui—his first two-walk game since September 22 against the Chicago White Sox—and Juan Rivera, but Braden Looper struck out Boone and got John Flaherty on a pop-up to end the inning.

Weaver finally made it into the game in the bottom of the 11th and was surprisingly effective in retiring the Marlins in order. But Marlins shortstop Alex Gonzalez, mired in a postseason-long slump, worked the count full leading off the bottom of the 12th before he hit a liner down the left field line. It landed just fair over the fence and below the "330" sign to give the Marlins a shocking 4-3 victory that tied the World Series at two games apiece.

Gonzalez exulted as he rounded the bases and, just like Boone six nights earlier, leaped on to home plate before being swallowed up by jumping, back-slapping teammates. It wasn't quite as monumental a victory as the Yankees' ALCS-clinching win, obviously, but it was enormous nonetheless.

The resilient Marlins had taken the Yankees' best shot and survived. And for the third time in as many postseason series, the Yankees' season came down to a best of three.

Back in spring training, Torre cautioned the Japanese media not to read too much into his lineup machinations during exhibition games.

More than 200 games later, with the Yankees on the biggest stage of all, Torre knew there'd be no dodging the questioning about his decision to shake up the Yankees' lineup.

Torre benched Alfonso Soriano, who had been slumping both as the leadoff hitter and in the field at second base, and dropped Jason Giambi, who usually bats third, into the seventh spot. The new lineup featured Jeter in the leadoff spot, seldom-used infielder Enrique Wilson batting second and playing second, and Matsui batting cleanup.

Matsui had hit a meager .059 (1-for-17) in limited duty as the cleanup hitter during the regular season, but Torre's juggling was equal parts proof of his faith in Matsui—during the off-day between Games Two and Three, Torre said, "I trust [Matsui] about as much as I trust anybody"—and his impatience with Soriano and Giambi, who had combined for 79 homers in the regular season but were hitting just .220 combined with four homers, 14 RBI, and 40 strikeouts (including a playoff-record 25 by Soriano) in 123 postseason at-bats.

"It's something that, believe me, was not easy," Torre said. "It was just something I felt I needed to do with the way [Soriano's] at-bats were going. . . . I think the one thing the players are all comfortable with is the fact that I'm going to do whatever I can, and they understand that individual needs are not as important as what we hope is best for the team at this point in time."

Torre had to further tweak his lineup less than an hour before first pitch, when Giambi and Torre agreed Giambi would not start because his chronically sore left knee was bothering him. Giambi said he didn't want to be a liability on defense, but his willingness to ask out of the lineup, with the Yankees just two wins shy of a World Championship—or just two losses shy of a shocking defeat—raised plenty of eyebrows in a city still unconvinced Giambi had the championship makeup possessed by the likes of Jeter, Paul O'Neill, Scott Brosius, David Cone, and Tino Martinez.

In a column he filed before the end of Game Five, Lupica recalled how O'Neill played in Game Five of the 1996 World Series even though he was badly hobbled by a torn hamstring. O'Neill ended up making a running catch for the last out of the Yankees' 1-0 win over the Atlanta Braves, and two nights later, they won the first of their four championships in the Torre Era.

Wrote Lupica: "Giambi said he didn't want to be a defensive liability. Neither did O'Neill that night in Atlanta."

And Torre had to make even more modifications in the bottom of the first, when starter David Wells—who a day earlier had bragged about lasting 20 years in professional baseball despite exercising as much as the average couch potato—departed due to back spasms.

"I was shocked Soriano wasn't in the lineup," Marlins first baseman Derrek Lee told reporters afterward. "I was shocked Giambi wasn't in the lineup. I was shocked when David Wells came out after the first inning. We had an advantage, and we had to capitalize on it."

That they did. The Marlins exposed the Yankees' suspect relief corps, and the results of Torre's lineup changes were mixed as the Marlins held off the Yankees, 6-4, to take a 3-2 Series lead.

Matsui went 0-for-5—it was only his third hitless game of the postseason and it ended a seven-game hitting streak, the latter of which was just three games shy of his regular season high—and, as the potential tying run in the ninth, made the final out of the game by grounding sharply to first.

Wilson had an RBI double in the ninth, but he displayed less range than Soriano in the field and failed to make a diving stop on Marlins pitcher Brad Penny's two-run single in the second inning. He was also charged with an error in the fifth inning when he threw to third base even though no one was covering it as the Yankees tried to catch Ivan Rodriguez in a rundown. The Marlins went on to score twice in the inning.

Now, a team that had experienced the most euphoric of highs just a week earlier—the thrilling victory over the Red Sox in an ALCS many people considered to be the "real" World Series—the

Yankees were on the verge of a defeat that would be almost as shocking and embarrassing as a loss to the Red Sox.

The $180 million Yankees, Team Tradition, losing to the $60 million Marlins, Team Teal, in the World Series. And needless to say, George Steinbrenner was none too pleased at the thought.

Steinbrenner watched from a luxury box as the Yankees fell inches short of tying the game in the ninth. Marlins right fielder Juan Encarnacion caught Williams' long fly ball in the middle of the warning track right before Matsui scorched a grounder down the first base line, which was snatched by Lee on a nasty one-hop.

"I thought [Williams' shot] was gone," Wilson told the *Newark Star-Ledger*. "He just missed that. We had a good chance. Matsui hit the ball hard."

But Lee, a potential Gold Glove winner, deftly snared it and beat Matsui to the bag. Lee jumped in the air and pumped his fist as he crossed the bag and headed for the group of Marlins rushing from the home dugout.

"I really hit that ball well and thought it would be a hit," Matsui told the *New York Daily News*. "It was right at him. There was nothing I could do, as much as I wanted to."

Steinbrenner, meanwhile, turned to leave the luxury box, and according to the *Newark Star-Ledger*, appeared to express "consternation" at Matsui's decision to swing at the first pitch. With "The Boss" calling the shots, the Yankees lived in a "what have you done for me lately?" world, and with the Yankees a game away from elimination, Matsui's accomplishments over the previous eight months meant little.

In The Boss's universe, the entire season would be a failure unless the Yankees won the final two games of the season. And if they didn't, then Matsui would be just one of many people in the organization to feel Steinbrenner's full wraith.

The Yankees had history on their side entering Game Six. They were playing at home, where they supposedly had ghosts, aura, mystique, and rabid fans on their side. In addition, the last seven teams that headed home for Game Six of the World Series down 3-2 came back to win the championship, including the previous two World Champions—the 2002 Anaheim Angels and 2001 Arizona Diamondbacks.

The last team that failed to come back from a 3-2 World Series deficit even though it was hosting Games Six and Seven? The 1981 Yankees.

The Yankees had Andy Pettitte, their best big-game pitcher, going in Game Six with Mike Mussina, who seemed to be a new man following his relief outing in Game Seven of the ALCS, scheduled to go in Game Seven. And the Yankees had not been eliminated at home since the 1981 World Series.

Unfortunately for the Yankees, the Marlins had Josh Beckett.

Beckett was 17 months old when the Yankees lost to the Dodgers in Game Six of the 1981 World Series and 16 years old when Pettitte solidified his legacy by out-dueling the Atlanta Braves' John Smoltz in Game Five of the 1996 World Series. He was young, brash—he brushed Sammy Sosa back in the NLCS, and later said Sosa "overreacted" in glaring at Beckett—and unimpressed by history.

He also had a 95-mph fastball, a curveball he could throw to both sides of the plate, and the distinctly good fortune of pitching to a Yankees squad that swung as if it had a 9 A.M. tee time the following morning.

Beckett threw a complete game in which he surrendered just five hits and did not allow a runner past second base in leading the Marlins to a World Series–clinching 2-0 victory. The Marlins scored single runs in the fifth and sixth—the latter of which scored thanks to a rare error by Derek Jeter—and displayed the killer instinct and knack for the fundamentally brilliant play the Yankees showed in winning four World Series from 1996 to 2000.

Indeed, when Alex Gonzalez brushed the plate with a finger and avoided the tag of Jorge Posada in scoring the Marlins' second run, it evoked memories of Jeter streaking across the diamond in the 2001 ALDS and shoveling a relay to Posada, who tagged out Jeremy Giambi to preserve the Yankees' 1-0 lead.

But the story of the game was Beckett, who was throwing on three days rest for the first time in his career but needed just 107 pitches to complete the gem and earn World Series MVP honors. Of the 27 outs he recorded, 14 came on three pitches or less.

"[The Yankees] came out swinging," Beckett said. "I thought they were more patient in my last outing [in Game Three]."

Matsui was the most impatient Yankee: He went 0-for-4 in his second game as the cleanup hitter and saw a total of just nine pitches in the process, by far the lowest total among the Yankees who had four at-bats in the game.

Matsui symbolized the Yankees' impatience and inability to hit with runners in scoring position. In the first inning, the crowd buzzed as Matsui stepped to the plate with Bernie Williams on second. However, there would be no momentum-swinging home run this time: Matsui flied out to right on the second pitch he saw.

It wasn't the most egregious example of the Yankees' utter lack of situational hitting in the most important game of the season. That occurred in the seventh inning, when Jorge Posada hit a lead-off double but was stranded there because Jason Giambi followed with a grounder to third base.

Matsui made the penultimate out of the Yankees' season in the ninth inning, when he flew out to left on just two pitches. Three pitches later, at 10:54 P.M., the Yankees dynasty officially expired when Posada hit a slow roller up the first-base line.

Beckett picked the ball up and tagged Posada himself. It went down in the scorebook as "1U"—appropriate considering Beckett single-handedly dominated the Yankees in his two World Series starts, during which he struck out 19 and allowed only 13 base runners and two runs in 13.1 innings.

Beckett leaped in the air upon tagging Posada, turned and raced towards the infield, where the Marlins began a wild celebration as Frank Sinatra's "New York, New York" inexplicably began blaring out of the Yankee Stadium speakers. Fans watched in shock as the Yankees trudged off the field and into the clubhouse, where the mood was comprised of equal parts somber and dread.

As upset as the Yankees were with the World Series defeat, they knew the response from owner George Steinbrenner would be much worse. In his mind, he had just blown $180 million to finish in second place—to Team Teal, no less.

"It's a long winter," said ashen-faced general manager Brian Cashman. "We'll all just have to see how it goes."

Derek Jeter, one of the few Yankees to perform well throughout the playoffs, sat fully dressed at his locker for nearly an hour after the game. He was more curt than usual in responding to the waves of questions, but providing clipped answers sure beat the alternative, which was take off the uniform, shower and head out the door, where he could easily hear and smell the Marlins' euphoria.

"You play for one thing: You play to win," Jeter said. "If you can't win, it feels bad. You can't describe it."

Matsui exhibited less rage than Jeter, but he was just as disappointed. He sat at his locker, a wrap on his left knee and his downcast expression fixed on the floor, before he got up and patiently answered questions.

This time, Kahlon's famously brief translations really did summarize everything Matsui had to say.

"It's too bad," Matsui said. "As a member of the team, our goal was to win a World Championship. So from that standpoint, it's just tough."

Matsui wasn't much happier when he arrived at Yankee Stadium the following afternoon—mere hours before Game Seven would have taken place—to pack up his belongings. "I'm not satisfied, but I just gave it my best effort every day," Matsui told reporters. "In that sense, I don't have any regrets. But I'm certainly not satisfied with my numbers."

By most standards, Matsui had enjoyed a fabulously successful rookie season. He recovered from an extended early slump to earn a starting spot on the All-Star team and drive in more than 100 runs, which no Yankee rookie had done since 1936. He wowed the Yankees with his defensive ability and professionalism and appeared ready to evolve into a team leader.

"If the Yankees had 25 Matsuis," Sherman said, "they would have won the World Series."

He played for a larger audience—all of Japan—than anyone else in Major League Baseball, and received more media attention than any 10 players combined, yet he displayed a remarkable amount of patience with all who requested his time and still managed to seamlessly fit into the Yankee fabric. He was a much better player and person than anyone expected, and people expected a lot out of this power-hitting outfielder with the gentle demeanor.

Matsui was on pace to win World Series MVP honors after the first three games of the Series, but he struggled badly during the final three games, when he went 1-for-12, including an 0-for-9 skid as the cleanup hitter in Games Five and Six.

And he had lost his last game of the season, and that was hard to stomach for Matsui, who was so used to meeting high expectations and had come to the United States to experience one thing: Winning a World Series with the Yankees.

During the World Series, Matsui was one of several players to appear in commercials touting Fox's baseball coverage. "Only a few in the world get to wear this uniform," he said over a montage of his highlights.

Then, with the camera focused on him, Matsui smiled and said, "I live for this."

But the storybook ending never happened.

In the words of Brooklyn Dodgers fans, Matsui would have to wait 'til next year.

Epilogue

N ext year for the Yankees and Matsui started the moment Josh Beckett tagged Jorge Posada for the final out of the World Series. And it was probably of little consolation to Matsui, but at least the fans of New York wanted him back for 2004.

The week after the World Series, the *New York Daily News* asked readers to vote on the fates of manager Joe Torre, general manager Brian Cashman, pitching coach Mel Stottlemyre, and 15 of the 25 players on the Yankees' World Series roster.

Matsui was not listed, as sure a sign as any he had won over New Yorkers during his rookie season. Jerseys and t-shirts bearing his name and number flew off the shelves, and prices for Matsui-related memorabilia—from baseball cards to bobblehead dolls—soared.

Even a controversial second-place finish in the American League Rookie of the Year balloting failed to tarnish Matsui's impressive rookie campaign. Matsui, whose candidacy had been the source of controversy among media members and American League executives all season, finished just four votes behind Kansas City Royals shortstop Angel Berroa in the results announced November 10.

However, Matsui was not named at all on the ballots submitted by Jim Souhan of the *Minneapolis Star-Tribune* and Bill Ballou of the *Worcester* (Mass.) *Telegram & Gazette*.

Had Matsui placed first on one of their ballots or second on both, he would have won the award.

Instead, the Yankees were forced to cancel the press conference they had scheduled for Matsui November 10. And while Berroa was actually left off two ballots himself, the explanations offered by Souhan and Ballou regarding their refusal to vote for Matsui—both men admitted they did not believe Matsui was a rookie, despite the clearly defined rules which state a rookie is anyone who has yet to collect 130 at-bats, 50 innings pitched or 45 days on the active 25-man roster in previous seasons and despite the fact three other Japanese players with considerable overseas experience had previously won the award—left them defending their decisions in various New York newspapers.

"My regard for Japanese baseball is too high for me to consider Matsui a rookie," Souhan told the *New York Daily News*. "Even if I had considered him a rookie, I'm not sure he would have made my ballot."

"It's a controversial issue," Ballou told the *Daily News*. "I made my decision knowing there might be controversy."

Of course, no one was quite as mad as Yankees owner George Steinbrenner. The day after the results were announced, Steinbrenner issued one of his typically blusterous press releases in which he said, among other things, "I firmly believe that a great injustice has been done to Hideki Matsui. Two misguided writers . . . in voting for American League Rookie of the Year, clearly made up their own rules to determine who was and was not eligible for the award and disqualified an eligible candidate who could have won.

"This year's voting farce, where the appropriate qualifications for the award were blatantly ignored, clearly demonstrates unfairness to first-year players from Japan. And that must be stopped."

Not surprisingly, the most composed person in the entire debate was Matsui, who nonetheless subtly tweaked the notion he was too experienced to be considered a rookie.

"I guess I just looked too old for a rookie," Matsui said in a statement released by the Yankees. "First and foremost, I would like to thank the Baseball Writers' Association of America for their consideration of me for this award. It is an honor to be chosen as a candidate for this achievement. I congratulate Angel Berroa for winning the rookie of the Year award. I think he deserves to win and I am very happy for him. He was a very solid player all around, both offensively and defensively, and I believe he was one of the key players that helped Kansas City with their winning record."

Matsui was just as key to the Yankees' run to the World Series, and he should take on an even bigger role this season. He adapted on the fly to an entirely different brand of baseball and culture in 2003, which means he should be even more comfortable in 2004.

"I think he will hit for more power and a higher average over the next few years," *New York Post* baseball columnist Joel Sherman said. "I don't think he is a 50-homer guy. But I think he is a .300-hitting, 30-homer guy. His second season should be vastly easier. He knows the surroundings, customs, et cetera, better and he is more familiar with the pitchers and the style of pitching here."

"Maybe he hits more home runs next year," said Warren Cromartie, who spent seven seasons with the Yomiuri Giants. "I'm sure his game is improved. He took his game up a notch. [He'll have to] quicken his bat again next year. The pitchers know how to pitch to him, and vice versa, so it's going to be kind of interesting. It's all about making the adjustments."

Matsui didn't need the Rookie of the Year award in order to win over America's toughest sports fans. His earnest, hard-working style—not to mention his penchant for the dramatic hit and ability to thrust himself into key rallies—had long ago made him one of New York's most popular players.

And New York had won him over as well: After the season, he said he planned to spend about a month in the city before heading home to Japan.

"I think the New York fans are tough—I'm a native New Yorker, so I know better than anybody," Yankees backup catcher John Flaherty said. "But I also think that the way he's gone about his business [has won over the fans because he] keeps his nose clean, does his job, works hard, plays well when he's out there, does all the right things. And he might not get some hits on any given day, but the fans, you can tell that they appreciate what he does everyday to prepare and how he goes about his business.

"And in New York, if you play hard for [the fans], they're not going to have any problem with you," Flaherty said. "And obviously, in Hideki's case, that's been more than true."

Matsui also won over his teammates. From the first day of spring training, when he introduced himself to each player, he made an effort to be "one of the guys," despite the fact he was one of the most famous people in the world. He also managed to hurdle the language barrier, and by the end of the season, he could often communicate with teammates without the aid of an interpreter.

"Informally, I think there are times he speaks better English than most of the players brought up here," WFAN Yankees beat reporter Sweeney Murti said.

"He had a sense of who he was," Sherman said. "He obviously recognizes his star power in Japan and wanted to accommodate that. And he knew he was walking among many stars in the Yankee clubhouse. It was a tricky juggling act, and Matsui handled it marvelously."

Matsui managed to also do what was heretofore thought impossible: Accommodate everyone who wanted to talk to him without losing his patience nor his ability to focus on the on-field task. He may not have enjoyed the type of breakthrough season Ichiro Suzuki had in 2001, but Matsui certainly made more friends along the way, both inside and outside the clubhouse.

"He had a big chore to cope with so many Japanese reporters and he did it with grace and a smile," Sherman said. "He never said no to an American reporter that I saw. He was never a scintillating interview, but he was always accessible and cordial."

Murti was impressed by the effort Matsui made to know each of the beat reporters on a daily basis. "There [are] 10 of us who cover the Yankees on a regular basis [and] he knows a lot of us by name and will walk past us and address us by name," Murti said. "You can have minimal English conversations, like 'Hi, how are you? Fine,' but that's something that you hardly get with most of the English-speaking players. That part, I think is pretty amazing."

New York Times Yankees beat writer Tyler Kepner, who believed Matsui should win the Good Guy Award—given to the player who is most cooperative with the media—from the New York chapter of the Baseball Writers Association of America, said, "I think he's been wonderful. I think all of the players and the club executives could really learn some lessons from him in terms of how he manages expectations and demands most of them cannot even imagine. He's a true professional."

And while Matsui fell short of his ultimate goal, he accomplished something almost as important. As much as they hated to see Matsui leave—Ryuki Katayanagi, the manager of the Baseball Café in Tokyo, told the *Bergen Record* in August that Matsui's former team, the Giants "have a lot of star players who can replace Matsui on the field . . . but somehow they haven't replaced his heart"—Japan's baseball fans wanted to see one of their own succeed with America's preeminent franchise.

Kozo Abe, a sportswriter for the Fujisankei Communications Group, told *Time* magazine that Matsui joining the Yankees was "like a dream come true. Baseball fans in Japan had never imagined that something like this could happen."

But it did. By season's end, Matsui had clearly earned his Yankee pinstripes. He would have fit in perfectly on the 1996–2000 Yankees, the four-time World Champions whose sum was greater than their parts.

"He has been such a steady influence and leader," Yankees manager Joe Torre said.

And Matsui's success was a dream come true on both sides of the Atlantic. In a game increasingly overrun by style instead of substance and by players who wanted fame and success but none of the responsibility, Matsui proved there was still room for a gritty "grinder" who embraced the relationship between player and fan.

"While he didn't hit 40 to 50 home runs, he hit a home run of a different kind," Sherman said. "He was not a great player. But he was a winning player.

"And that is pretty darn good."

As *USA Today* columnist Ian O'Connor wrote October 21: "The more we learn about the human flaws of Yankee heroes past, the more we see that Matsui embodies the myth more than any face on any Bronx monument beyond his left-field wall."

The legend lived up to the hype. And Yankee fans can't wait to see what he does for an encore.

About the Author

Award-winning writer **Jerry Beach** has covered New York baseball for newspapers, magazines, and websites since 1977. He continues to cover the Mets for *New York Mets Inside Pitch* newspaper, game program, and EsportsNY.com website, and covers the Mets and Yankees for Long Island's largest weekly newspaper, *The Long Island Press*. Jerry is a native of Torrington, Connecticut, and began his sportswriting career at his hometown newspaper, *The Register Citizen*. A graduate of Northwestern Connecticut Community-Technical College and Hofstra University, Jerry lives in Bay Shore, New York, with his wife, Michelle, and their two cats. *Godzilla Takes the Bronx* is his first book.